Night of the
Restless Spirits

Night

of the

Restless Spirits

Stories from 1984

SARBPREET SINGH

PENGUIN

VIKING

An imprint of Penguin Random House

VIKING

USA | Canada | UK | Ireland | Australia
New Zealand | India | South Africa | China | Singapore

Viking is part of the Penguin Random House group of companies
whose addresses can be found at global.penguinrandomhouse.com

Published by Penguin Random House India Pvt. Ltd
4th Floor, Capital Tower 1, MG Road,
Gurugram 122 002, Haryana, India

Penguin
Random House
India

First published in Viking by Penguin Random House India 2020

10 9 8 7 6 5 4 3 2

ISBN 9780670093748

For sale in the Indian Subcontinent only

Typeset in Bembo Std by Manipal Technologies Limited, Manipal
Printed at Replika Press Pvt. Ltd, India

www.penguin.co.in

This is a legitimate digitally printed version of the book and therefore might not
have certain extra finishing on the cover.

This book is dedicated to the nameless victims of the violence of 1984 and the unsung heroes who responded to it with courage and compassion

If the lion slays the lamb,
Answer for it his master must.
Dogs defile this precious land,
The dead forgotten in the dust.

—*Asa Mahala 1*
(from the pen of Guru Nanak)

Contents

Phaji

She was the kind of girl who would never have got a second glance from me, for she looked nothing like a St Mark's girl. In deference to the rich and conservative Punjabi parents, whose children made up a steadily increasing percentage of each new class admitted to St Mark's each year, the school had put a dual-uniform policy in place. While the short tartan skirts with knee-length socks, which had been the hallmark of the St Mark's girl for decades in Delhi, did not go away, the girls also had the option of wearing a salwar-kameez in the school's colours with a tartan dupatta.

There had been bitter fights over the new uniform policy. School board members, who represented the elite Delhi families, those who had been sending their children to St Mark's for generations, harrumphed at the proposed accommodation. To them, it felt as if another bastion of the cream of Delhi society was under assault. Snide remarks were made in board meetings about St Mark's being turned into a 'gurdwara school'. The Punjabis, never ones to shy away from a fight, countered the claim by making even larger donations to the school and easily had their way. The Skirts and Salwars settled into an uneasy truce.

It was December 1983 and life was good. I was in the eleventh grade at St Mark's, and the captain of the cricket team. Like the rest of India, St Mark's was in the grip of cricket fever. Earlier that year, India had improbably won the World Cup, beating the feared West Indies team in an astonishing final. A young Punjabi lad, Kapil Dev, who had played spectacularly, was being hero-worshipped by young fans all over the country, especially by gaggles of screaming young women who would follow him everywhere. The fastest bowler on the team and a big-hitting middle-order bat, I was the Kapil Dev of St Mark's. Skirts surrounded me and had my full attention during recess, at the nets, during matches and, most importantly, at our monthly socials for the eleventh and twelfth grade, which were held in the smaller auditorium. The Salwars didn't even rate a second glance!

There was a well-defined social order at St Mark's. At the very bottom were the Madrasis, of whom there was a sizeable population, most of them children of government servants from the southern states who had been seconded to serve in some branch or the other of the civil service in the capital. Unlike many of my classmates who had entered St Mark's in kindergarten, most of the Madrasis spent an average of two to three years in the school, not long enough to forge deep friendships or penetrate any of the established cliques. They would be teased mercilessly for their dark skins, especially those lads whose parents forced them to wear very visible caste marks on their foreheads. Every now and then one of them would make it to the cricket team, but even that would not be enough to alter their social status significantly.

The Cats sat at the top of the pile with their disdain for all things Indian. They would not be caught dead speaking in Hindi, or God forbid Punjabi, regardless of how fluent they were in those languages. At socials, they would wear only American T-shirts, jeans and sneakers, and would be the only ones dancing easily and comfortably. Their parents were university professors, executives at multinational companies or scions of the old moneyed families of Delhi. Their jealously guarded records, sent by aunts and uncles abroad, would be the ones played at all socials. All the Skirts belonged in the Cats, as did most of the cricket and soccer teams.

The Panjus were a step above the Madrasis. Most of them came from the ranks of the nouveau riche, commuting from their large houses in faraway Punjabi Bagh. Loud and brash, with money to throw around, they walked like they owned the school, very conscious of the clout their parents wielded on the board. The Panju girls were almost universally Salwars and while the boys would show up at the Socials in groups, the girls were almost invariably absent. Of course, the boys did not dance! The Skirts were always surrounded by the Cats of the cricket or soccer teams and most of them had boyfriends anyway. Being seen even talking to a Panju boy with his greasy hair and ill-fitting clothes would have meant certain social death.

Skirts and cricket. Those were my passions in high school. I was a good-looking lad with the broad shoulders of a fast bowler, a Kashmiri complexion and nose, and I knew it. I had my pick of the Skirts. In tenth grade, Jessica Sharma, who was half-British, the captain of the girl's netball team and two years my senior, had been my girlfriend. No tenth grader had ever dated a girl from the twelfth grade before and I had become a legend in the school. Of course, those were more innocent times and high-school couples really didn't do anything other than dance together at socials, surreptitiously hold hands in movie theatres and try to steal the occasional kiss, but did it give me status! Jessica, however, had left school and was now an undergraduate at Oxford, and I was the most eligible Cat at St Mark's. Skirts surrounded me. Even girls from the eighth grade would accidentally drop their books around me or have questions about cricket stats, which of course I always had at my fingertips. The Skirts who did not have boyfriends would refuse dance after dance at the socials, hoping that I would be the one asking them next.

And cricket! I had attended a summer coaching camp conducted by a British pro who was fairly well regarded in county cricket. He had shortened my run-up a little and added a mean inswinger to my arsenal. I already had an excellent outswinger and my short-pitched balls were legend in the inter-school circuit, but with my improved action, my bowling had developed into something truly lethal. My coach felt that I would be a shoo-in for the national Under-19 team. We would have nets starting at 3.30 p.m. every day after class. Team members were required to attend three times a week, but I would go every day without fail. As long as I was batting or bowling, the two benches just beyond the netting would always be overflowing, each time with more girls that could possibly fit on a single bench. Always the Skirts. My teammates would get very excited, but I would stay calm and focused and barely give them a second glance. As much as I enjoyed being around the Skirts, this was cricket!

On that Friday afternoon in December, we were practising for a match against St Columba's, which was coming up on the weekend. I had warmed up my bowling already and it was my turn to bat. Our coach had an interesting system in place for batting practice. The weakest batsmen would start and face a variety of pace and spin. Each time a batsman was dismissed, the next strongest bat in the line-up would come to the crease and stay until someone got him out. This would continue until the entire order had batted. If there was time left, we would start all over again with the tailenders. There would be days when I and some of the other top-order batsmen would bat for hours without being dismissed, the poor bowlers swearing and groaning until it was too dark to play any more.

I was padded up and ready, eagerly walking to the crease to take guard. At the other end, nervously polishing the ball on his pants was a gangly ninth grader who was shaping up to be a decent fast bowler. But he did not have a lot of variation and usually got a terrific leathering from me at the nets. I looked at him as he started his run-up, closely watching his hand and the seam of the ball in order to pick my shot. I was going to enjoy this. My batting had been a bit sketchy of late and the St Columba's team was very strong that year, particularly in the bowling department. A solid turn at the nets was exactly what I needed before the big match. For a split second, my eyes wandered to the benches, bulging with Skirts as usual, widening in surprise as standing between them was a Salwar. The ball was a beautiful inswinging yorker that I would have been proud to bowl. It sent my middle stump flying. The bowler whooped. The Skirts gasped. The Salwar giggled. I glowered. I was in a foul mood by the time I left for home. My best friend, Ashwin, who was next up in the batting order, didn't help by batting it out without being dismissed, making me bowl twelve overs to him before nets ended.

The Inter Public School Cricket League had just introduced limited-overs matches, as the shorter version of the sport was starting to become hugely popular. St Columba's won the toss and elected to bat first. The day started out reasonably bright and sunny, but clouds were predicted and batting conditions were likely to worsen as the day progressed. I bowled a tidy length and picked up two wickets, conceding just twenty runs in my eight overs. However, Raju, our other opening bowler got hammered and the St Columba's top and middle order went on a rampage. I tried all the bowling changes I possibly could, but our spinners didn't fare better either. After we had bowled our forty overs, St Columba's had amassed a hundred and eighty-one runs, a formidable total, the highest in the league so far.

It was a home match, being played at St Mark's, which meant that we had a decent contingent of supporters in the stands. Our coach was there, of course, and a few of the teachers, but the stands were mostly filled with Skirts, many of them girlfriends of the players and their friends. Even though it was a Sunday, they seemed to be in uniform with their white T-shirts and blue jeans. I had a good view of the stands from the players' enclosure, where our batting line-up sat, a bit nervous because of the large total facing us. Our opening pair walked out to the pitch.

The sky was overcast by now and the ball was swinging. We did not lose any wickets in the first four overs, but the bowling was so hostile that our total stood at a mere six runs. And then disaster struck. The St Columba's opening bowler delivered a beautiful outswinger at full pace, and our opening bat nicked it right into the hands of second slip. As I watched in horror, my eyes drifted to the stands. I swore under my breath. Sitting in the stands in a small blaze of colour, separated from the gaggle of Skirts by a few feet, was the Salwar. The same girl who had laughed so nastily when I had been bowled out on the first ball at the nets!

I had no time to dwell on our impending humiliation. We had lost four wickets by the end of the twelfth over, and our total stood a meagre twenty-three as I walked out of the enclosure. Aswhin, who was the batsman at the other end when the last wicket fell, was the only one who had been able to offer any kind of resistance to the St Columba's attack. We decided to dig our heels in and play the next eight overs very carefully, trying to keep our wickets intact. The conditions were so perfect for fast bowling that the St Columba's captain did not make any bowling changes, letting his two top bowlers bowl out the first sixteen overs in the hope of another breakthrough. We did have a few more decent bats left, but they were inexperienced. It was pretty clear that if either Ashwin or I got out, the match would be over.

Next up was a bowler who bowled at military medium and had a decent line, but not much else. I was pretty entrenched by then and seeing the ball really well. I struck three fours in the over, all sweetly timed shots off the middle of my bat. The stands started to show some life and the Skirts started cheering. Ashwin and I continued to plunder the attack and the runs started piling up. The Skirts were starting to get raucous, which was expected, but my eyes were on the Salwar, who had sat with her lips pursed, a severe expression on her face when all seemed lost. I could see her face quite clearly because the stands were very close to one of the batting creases. Each time I struck a boundary, she would involuntarily jump to her feet, a beatific expression on her face, and dance a demure little jig.

I found myself looking at her even when I should have been watching the ball. She was dressed in a bright red but very simple-looking cotton salwar-kameez, which clearly wasn't from a fancy boutique. She had long black hair, shiny with oil, severely pulled back in a single plait that swung behind her back. Her face was more pleasant than beautiful, but every time I would hit the ball, my eyes would be drawn to the smile of pure joy that lit up her eyes and face.

We did not win the match. Ashwin was clean-bowled in the thirty-second over, trying to hit across the line of the ball. We had nearly forty runs to make in the last eight overs and five wickets in hand, but our middle order crumbled. We lost three wickets in quick succession, and though our tailenders did put up a bit of a fight, I ran out of partners and we lost the match by twelve runs. Ordinarily, I would have been devastated, but today was no ordinary day.

I was in love.

I enlisted Meena, Ashwin's girlfriend, as my spy and go-between. The girl's name was Gursharan, but she went by Sharan. She was in the eleventh grade and a science student. The first note I sent her through Meena elicited a threat to report me to the principal, which I found charming. Unless something egregious happened, the teachers and the administration would generally turn a blind eye to high-school romances. I wasn't worried. Besides, her showing up at the nets almost every day when I was batting or bowling gave me great confidence and boosted my ego, though she later told me in her matter-of-fact way that she came for the cricket. She was the biggest cricket fan in the world and apparently her room was adorned with posters of Kapil Dev and Imran Khan.

It wasn't long before we started walking back together after the nets, always talking about cricket. In addition to Kapil Dev, she was a huge fan of the West Indian fast bowlers, as was I. Our arguments would be over all-rounders. Like 100 per cent of women from the Indian subcontinent, she adored Imran Khan and secretly wanted to marry him, but I detested him, probably more out of jealousy than anything else. When I would make a case for Ian Botham or Richard Hadlee, both of whom I greatly admired, she would affix me with a withering stare and declare that I was an imbecile. Of course, I pretended to be offended but found it utterly endearing. No Skirt had ever been this passionate about cricket. I was convinced that she was the girl for me.

She laughed so hard when I asked her to be my girlfriend that I got really offended. I was, after all, the captain of the cricket team and a handsome devil to boot. No day would pass without my minions bringing me a note or two from a lovesick Skirt declaring her undying love for me in language ranging from the prosaic to the poetic. While my closest friends and I would roar with laughter as we read the notes, I would secretly be thrilled and nonchalantly inspect the authors as they invariably walked past me sometime during the school day, tossing their trendily coiffed hair. And here was Sharan, in her salwar, her slickly oiled braid, gleefully dancing as she doubled over with laughter, her shoulders shaking as she regarded me with bright, mischievous eyes.

She was never unkind, not even when she was laughing at me. She must have seen the hurt in my eyes and the wounded pride. 'Mummyji will kill me. And after she is done killing me, Phaji will kill me all over again!'

As I fretted and fumed over the next few weeks, I imagined her witch of a mother as coarse, fat and ugly, with rotting buck teeth, suspicious eyes and strands of hair on her chin, which I was convinced old Sikh women wore as a badge of honour. And her ogre of a brother who jealously guarded his sister's virtue! Surely he must be a vile and uncouth fellow who probably drove an autorickshaw or worked at a small shop, with a huge sagging belly that bulged out of his ill-fitting pants and a ridiculous printed scarf on his head that so many young Sikh men seemed to sport those days.

Sharan, however, kept coming to the nets and we kept walking back together, but of course things were not the same. Matters came to a head when she insulted Ian Botham three days in a row while singing praises of Imran Khan, with not as much as a peep out of me. 'I am sorry,' she said. 'You are the best friend I have ever had and the only boy that I have ever talked to, but you have to understand. We come from very different worlds. It is just not possible for me to have a boyfriend.' This was even worse than her laughing at me. Now I was utterly crushed. There was a social coming up in three weeks and I had been very excited about taking her as my date. No fewer than eleven Skirts had asked me, two of them even willing to dump their boyfriends if I would take them! I cursed myself for falling so hard for a Salwar. It wasn't like my friends hadn't warned me.

I do not remember having been so despondent before. The next week, I skipped nets on Monday and Tuesday, thinking that I would go the next three days. There was an unexpected rain shower on Wednesday. By the time Thursday rolled around, I found that I had no motivation at all. I got myself off the hook by lying to the coach and telling him I was sick. I did not go on Friday either. I did not see her that entire week because we had no common classes. On Monday, I got a note from her, which simply said that she would be waiting for me just before nets. My pride was hurt and I was angry. I had never been rejected before and it stung like I could have never imagined, but of course I wanted to see her.

She took in my prefect's uniform, noting, I was sure, that I had not changed into my kit for practice. For the first time, I saw a flash of anger in her eyes. 'Are you a *gadha*?' she asked. I had never been called a donkey before and was so shocked that I burst out laughing, as did she, her braid dancing as tears streamed down her cheeks. I ran off to change and was a terror at the nets that day, mercilessly hammering anyone who had the misfortune to bowl at me as my one-girl audience cheered. I poured scorn on Imran Khan as we walked back, which of course made her indignant, but she ignored me and said that Mummyji had invited me to have lunch at their house on Saturday.

I was dumbfounded. I had never been invited to a girl's house before. The whole point of high-school romances was that they were surreptitious, in a delicious way forbidden and hidden from parents. No Skirt in her right mind would ever have invited a boyfriend home. This girl was quite mad! 'But how does she even know about me,' I asked, my confusion very apparent.

'Oh!' she said matter-of-factly. 'I tell Mummyji everything.'

Shyam, our driver, had never heard of Mangolpuri. Neither had I. Sharan had told me that she lived in west Delhi's Rohini, right at the edge of Mangolpuri, as she wrote down her address on a square piece of paper, carefully torn from one of her notebooks, in her precise and elegant hand. We lived in South Extension in a home that my grandfather had built when he first moved to Delhi from Jammu decades ago. In those days, it had been in the middle of nowhere, but now South Extension was a posh colony and many of my friends who went to St Mark's lived there. I had learned how to drive, but I didn't have my driver's licence yet. I would have preferred to go myself, but I did not have the money for the taxi or autorickshaw fare, and I had never taken a DTC (Delhi Transport Corporation) bus. I had ambiguously told my mother that I was having lunch with a friend, and Shyam was passive and utterly uninterested in anything I did. I was a little nervous but excited at the same time. I did not completely discount the possibility that I might be set upon by a burly Sardar or two for daring to ask Sharan to be my girlfriend, but sometimes a man has to take a risk. After all, I was smitten like never before.

The roads were choked with traffic as usual, which seemed to get worse as we left south Delhi and wound our way to the north-western suburbs. We drove past the university and then the cantonment, which were familiar areas, as many of my friends lived there. After almost an hour of driving through totally clogged streets, we got to Punjabi Bagh, where I had never been before. Many of St Marks' Panjus lived here, but none of them were my friends, or ever likely to be. We drove past shining mansions that reeked of new money and ostentation, but the landscape changed dramatically once we got past Punjabi Bagh. The roads became narrow and the piles of trash ubiquitous.

Shyam had to stop several times to ask for directions to Mangolpuri, which turned out to be the most crowded part of Delhi I had ever been to. The streets were impossibly narrow and jammed with bicycles, pedestrians and scooters. The houses were the tiniest I had ever seen. Later, I learned that the residents were former slum dwellers who had been given twelve-and-a-half-square-metre plots each to build houses on. As we crawled through the crowded alleys, I could see little stalls selling everything imaginable, little makeshift temples and mosques, even a tiny gurdwara with the poorest and most ragged-looking Sikhs I had ever seen, spilling out.

As soon as we left Mangolpuri and crossed into Rohini, the character of the neighbourhood changed dramatically. The roads became wider and there were little patches of green laid out, ringed by neat houses on each side. It was hard to imagine that the chaos of Mangolpuri was just a block away, as we drove past the orderly rows of well-kept homes. Sharan's house was on one of the side streets, painted a pleasant cream colour with a small but well-tended garden in the front. I gave Shyam the five rupees that my mother had handed me for his lunch and told him to go find some food, waiting until the car disappeared around the corner before ringing the buzzer by the modest nameplate that simply read 'Sidhus'.

Her eyes were the first thing that caught my attention when she opened the door. They were the same colour as her daughter's, and as beautiful, but a tiny bit clouded by a film that seemed to be equal parts calmness and sadness. Mummyji was a tall, slender woman with the friendliest smile I had ever seen. In an instant I could see what Sharan would look like in thirty years. The living room was sparsely furnished and not a thing seemed to be out of place. Notable was the complete absence of the usual bric-a-brac that most middle-class homes are adorned with, sad reminders of insignificant glories past or vacations that seem less appealing with each passing year. I sat down and accepted the glass of lemonade that she thrust into my hands.

Sharan bounced into the room, almost unrecognizable, out of her school uniform, her long and freshly washed tresses gathered loosely behind her head. I am never at a loss for words, but I found myself awkwardly tongue-tied in her mother's presence, as Sharan excitedly chattered about school one moment and Imran Khan the next, pausing in between to deliver a scathing critique of my performance in the last inter-school match, to her mother's muted disapproval. I marvelled at how unselfconscious Sharan was, as if it was an everyday occurrence for the family to entertain her suitors, until the truth hit me like a punch in the gut. She had no reason to feel awkward or self-conscious. She had no romantic interest in me whatsoever.

Just as I was starting to get comfortable with Mummyji, Sharan announced that we would eat when Phaji got home, which made me feel anxious all over again. It was bad enough to have to meet the mother of the girl I was infatuated with, but I thought that I had escaped meeting her brother when he didn't emerge from the back room. Somewhat glumly, I attacked the delicious plate of fresh fruits that Mummyji had brought me, resigned to the inevitable awkwardness as we waited. Sharan's mother, ever gracious, probably sensed my discomfiture and tried her best to put me at ease, asking questions about my family and showing great interest in my future plans.

After what felt like hours, though it couldn't have been more than forty-five minutes, the door swung open. Before us stood Phaji in the flesh. Phaji wasn't exceptionally tall like his mother and sister, but he had a towering presence. He was one of the most nattily dressed Sikhs I had ever met, with his well-tailored clothes, polished shoes and a regal, impeccably wound navy blue turban on his head. His beard was neatly groomed and tied under his chin, nary a hair out of place. He had the bright, intelligent eyes of his sister, but he seemed as calm as she was vivacious as he greeted me with a firm handshake.

Phaji, I learned, had attended the elite Doon School, following in the footsteps of his father, which was not uncommon among the wealthy, landed families of Punjab, many of whom sent their sons to storied institutions such as Doon or Lawrence School in Sanawar. He was a fourth-year student at Maulana Azad Medical College and planned to train in the UK or America after he graduated. It was clear that his mother and sister doted on him, hanging on his every word as he easily talked about his plans while we ate the most delicious Punjabi food I had ever tasted.

As Sharan was deputed to clear the table, Phaji invited me to his room, the smaller of the two bedrooms at the back of the house, which was as sparsely furnished as the living room. A mahogany nightstand stood by a smallish bed, and I remember wondering how he could possibly fit on it. A bookcase, bulging with books, with a small stack of LPs on the bottom shelf, immediately caught my attention. I noticed a small turntable on the desk by the wall. Phaji waved me over to one of the worn but comfortable-looking rattan chairs, with bright cushions clad in what I know now was phulkari, which completed the furnishings of his room.

Seeing my eyes wandering to the bookshelf, Phaji asked me to check it out. I had always fancied myself as a bit of a reader. My parents had filled my room with books by Enid Blyton when I was younger, which I had devoured before I graduated to Billy Bunter and then Alfred Hitchcock's young investigators and the Hardy boys. In high school, I had mostly been reading thrillers by the likes of Alistair MacLean and Jack Higgins, as well hugely popular potboilers by Wilbur Smith and Robert Ludlum, counterfeit editions of which could be bought for almost nothing on the pavement stalls of Connaught Place. Lately, one of my female friends, a bookish Skirt, had introduced me to James Michener, reading a few of whose tomes had made me feel vaguely superior to my peers.

Phaji's bookshelf had a few titles that I had seen before, but most of the authors were unfamiliar. Phaji asked me if I wanted a book to read and, when I nodded, he mused for a moment and handed me *One Hundred Years of Solitude*. I left that day with Gabriel García Márquez and came back for Günter Grass, Kafka, Camus, Faulkner, Toni Morrison and, of course, the incandescent *Midnight's Children* by Rushdie, which Phaji gave to me only after he was convinced that I could truly appreciate magical realism, currently his favourite genre. Being the gracious lady she was, Mummyji never betrayed a hint of surprise or displeasure at my soon-to-become-regular visits to her home, always with a book in hand. She must have thought that the books were a convenient way for me to insinuate myself into their home to see Sharan.

Sharan would often come in with tea and proceed to flop down on Phaji's bed, listening intently as he held forth about his favourite authors. He asked me about my plans after high school, and I talked about my vaguely formed thoughts about studying engineering. Both my parents were college professors and my older sister, Meghna, who was at Oxford, was likely to follow in their footsteps, but I had no interest in an academic career. I wanted to live in America some day, and I had heard that an engineering degree would be my best shot at making that dream come true. Of course, Phaji's plans were much grander than mine!

Sharan's family hailed from Tarn Taran in Punjab, where they once had very large landholdings. Her grandfather, who had served in the British Army and largely been unlettered, had been a great believer in education, but Sharan's father had to leave college abruptly after his father suffered a massive stroke, placing the burden of looking after his extended family on his shoulders. A kind and trusting man, his character shaped by his years in the company of the moneyed elite in the playing fields of Doon, he allowed himself to be talked into one bad investment after another, often egged on by unscrupulous relatives, until the point that the family was left with a single, albeit fairly large, parcel of land around their ancestral home. Sharan had been an infant at the time, but Phaji had watched his father wither away as one business venture after the other failed. He had been in high school when his father passed away, but he had persuaded Mummyji to sell the last remaining parcel, so that they could move to Delhi and he could go to medical school while Sharan too attended a proper school.

Phaji had his future clearly mapped out. He was going to finish medical school in India and train as a surgeon in the West. He was going to settle down in America, where doctors, particularly surgeons, were very successful. He was going to rebuild his family fortune and carve out a great future for his sister, whom he doted on. All of this was very exciting to me. I came from a world where my peers mostly belonged to affluent families with every need taken care of. I had never met anyone close to my age who seemed to be so clear-headed, driven and motivated. I had no doubt that Phaji was going to follow through and deliver on every promise that he had made to himself, and his mother and sister. Sharan, lolling on the bed, hero worship writ large on her face as her brother talked, clearly believed that too.

As the months flew by, my friendship with Phaji deepened, as did my attachment to Sharan. I was in fine fettle on the cricket pitch and racked up record after record in the inter-school circuit. Sharan faithfully attended every match, no matter how many DTC buses she had to change. Phaji was always busy with medical school, but Mummyji did attend a few times, always thoughtfully bringing a home-cooked delicacy for me to eat after the match. Sharan easily continued to laugh away all my romantic advances, but somehow the sting had vanished. Every now and then I would feel a twinge of something indescribable as my friends bragged about their escapades with their girlfriends, but it would flee in the face of Sharan's hearty guffaws or gentle ribbing, which were an ever-present part of our deepening friendship.

In Phaji, I had found a mentor. He had a razor-sharp brain and was the most well-read person I had met. My potboilers abandoned, I read more books in those few months than I had in my previous three years in high school, by authors I had never heard of until then. Phaji's taste in music too was much more refined. My exposure to music was largely through school socials, where we danced to Boney M. and the *Saturday Night Fever* soundtrack. Phaji's stack of records introduced me to Pink Floyd, Genesis, Neil Young, Fleetwood Mac, Dire Straits, and many other artists and bands I hadn't been exposed to. We would spend hours in his room, in the comfortable rattan chairs, listening to record after record while Sharan flitted in and out, often bearing a new delicacy that her mother had conjured up for us.

And then the summer of 1984 arrived.

Meghna was in India that summer and we were back in Srinagar, at our ancestral home where my uncle now lived with his family. We had been hiking in the mountains close to Baramulla when we got word of the attack on the Golden Temple. My first thoughts, of course, were of Sharan and her family. Phaji and Sharan were not particularly religious, but Mummyji was. I knew that she visited the tiny gurdwara in Mangolpuri, a ten-minute walk from their home, every day. Most of the Sikhs of Mangolpuri were very poor. They were former slum dwellers who had been forced to move to this remote corner of Delhi when their illegal shacks were demolished before the Asian Games in a bid to beautify Delhi. Phaji, who was a bit of a snob, wanted her to go to one of the gurdwaras in Rohini, which were solidly middle class, but Mummyji, who had become very fond of her little gurdwara, would ignore her son and go early each morning for prayers and to listen to the morning hymns of Asa Di Var.

I rushed to Sharan's house when we returned to Delhi at the end of June and found Mummyji a changed woman.

She had always been a staunch supporter of Indira Gandhi, the then prime minister, and had held her up as a role model for her daughter, often talking about her graciousness, strength and tenacity that had enabled her to survive and thrive in a society dominated by men. I heard later from Sharan that even during the Emergency she had unflinchingly supported the prime minister, though she was bothered by the rumours of forced vasectomies performed on poor men in an attempt to slow down India's birth rate, and the cavalier manner in which the slum dwellers of Delhi were uprooted from their hutments in an effort to spruce up the capital's sagging image. She believed that hard decisions were needed sometimes to be able to govern, but she never imagined that her idol would launch a full-blown military attack on the Golden Temple.

In the aftermath of Operation Blue Star, we did not know what we know now. The media wrote triumphant stories of the valour of the Indian Army, which had removed a band of desperadoes, intent on tearing the country apart, from the Golden Temple complex. According to the press, the raid had been conducted with the utmost respect and sensitivity, and Bhindranwale and his followers had been killed surgically with very few civilian casualties because of the restraint shown by the army.

Phaji, in no small part because of his feudal background and upbringing, was a dyed-in-the-wool law-and-order man. He had always been embarrassed by the prominence of Bhindranwale, who to him was a rustic and simple-minded demagogue, one who had accomplished nothing other than making life very difficult for common Sikhs, particularly those who lived outside Punjab. Sharan later told me that in the years leading up to 1984, Phaji had been crushed by the burden of being a young Sikh, at a time when Sikhs were constantly vilified in the press as unruly, fractious and violent, intent on threatening the 'unity and integrity' of the nation in selfish pursuit of their political ambitions. It was no surprise then that Phaji swallowed the official narrative about Operation Blue Star without question, expressing strong support for the army and the prime minister, lauding her decisiveness.

At first, Mummyji had simply been aghast after the attack on the Golden Temple, and mostly expressed pain. As a young girl growing up in Amritsar, her life had been centred on the shrine. No day would pass without at least two visits to the Golden Temple complex. She had seen pictures of the shattered Akal Takht, the smouldering ruin unrecognizable as the graceful edifice that for centuries had symbolized the temporal power of the Sikh gurus. For more than a week after Operation Blue Star, she neither lit a fire in her kitchen nor put much more than a morsel in her mouth, her children unable to comprehend the depth of her grief. She was even unable to drag herself to the little gurdwara in Mangolpuri where she had dutifully served in the community kitchen since she had moved her little brood to Delhi. An element of anger started to creep into her heart as more reports started filtering out of Punjab through unofficial channels.

A week after Operation Blue Star, Mummyji got a phone call from her dear friend Jaskaran Kaur, who had grown up with her in Amritsar but now lived in Patiala. As much as she had been shocked by the attack on the Golden Temple, the news from Patiala devastated her completely. Jaskaran Kaur lived a few hundred feet from Gurdwara Dukh Nivaran Sahib in Patiala and had seen with her own eyes the Indian Army executing at least fifty Sikh men after lining them up against a wall inside the gurdwara. There were rumours that more than forty other gurdwaras all over Punjab had been attacked in concert with Operation Blue Star, followed by truckloads of corpses being taken to mass cremation sites in nearby villages.

Today, of course, we know that what Jaskaran Kaur had described was a part of Operation Woodrose. But at that time there was absolutely no official acknowledgement of the simultaneous attacks on multiple Sikh places of worship. Phaji refused to believe any of it. He dismissed it all as propaganda spread by diehard supporters of Bhindranwale, intent on stirring up the passions of the Sikhs. India was, after all, a democracy, he insisted, with a free press that had not one word to say about any such massacres in Punjab. While he was not happy about the loss of life at the Golden Temple, he was convinced that it had been a justifiable price to pay for restoring law and order and ridding the shrine of desperate terrorists, ones intent on tearing the nation apart.

Mummyji's devastation was complete. Phaji's cold indifference to the events in Punjab was inexplicable to her and she took it personally. Sharan was utterly miserable, desperate to somehow heal the rift between mother and son, but she lacked the maturity and the tools to make a difference. The bitter arguments gave way to silence as the weeks passed. The fire in Mummyji's kitchen had been lit again, but there was not a trace of joy left in the home that had once overflown with warmth and good cheer. Phaji started spending more and more time at his college library while Mummyji resumed her daily visits to her gurdwara in Mangolpuri.

I decided to invite myself to Sharan's home in mid-September. Of course, I still saw Sharan at the nets sometimes and at our matches, but I missed Mummyji and Phaji. I was somewhat aware of what was going on, but I was unprepared for the change when I visited her home. Mummyji mustered a smile that didn't quite reach her eyes and politely asked about my family. Sharan was dispatched to the neighbourhood restaurant to fetch samosas and gulab jamuns, as I sat in awkward silence with Mummyji. I knew what was troubling her, but I didn't dare to bring it up. For a moment, I remember wondering if my Kashmiri Brahmin background, the same as Mrs Gandhi's, had any bearing on Mummyji's changed demeanour towards me, but I guiltily pushed the thought away from my mind as Phaji walked in.

I rose to shake Phaji's hand, who was as nattily dressed as ever and greeted me like a long-lost brother. We polished off the snacks and retreated to Phaji's room, Mummyji having excused herself to lie down. We sat in the rattan chairs and chatted, Sharan sitting on the bed, listening to us but not talking much, her brow wrinkled. Phaji was completely at ease, holding forth as usual on books and music, but I don't remember a word he said because all my thoughts were on Mummyji's dead eyes.

I could not bring myself to go back to their house, even though Sharan would often tell me that Phaji was asking about me. I didn't have much interest in politics at the time, and I didn't quite understand the complexities of what had happened in Punjab in the summer. I mostly agreed with Phaji's views, which was unsurprising, given the very consistent narrative that pervaded newspapers, radio and television. I did feel tremendous empathy for Mummyji even though I found myself agreeing with Phaji about how she had allowed herself to be somewhat brainwashed by the propaganda of militant Sikhs. Somewhat selfishly, in hindsight I felt a sense of personal loss. Sharan's home had become a haven for me and now it was gone.

The summer holidays behind us, I entered twelfth grade with college admissions and a packed cricket calendar looming. My parents had signed me up for coaching classes to prepare for the college entrance exams, which were rigorous and took up whatever time I had left after nets and weekend matches. I found myself spending less and less time with Sharan who had more or less stopped coming to the nets. She would still come for home matches though and every boundary I hit or every wicket I took would be rewarded by the familiar jig complete with the flying pigtail. She would also wave from afar and smile, but I never got the opportunity to ask how Phaji and Mummyji were doing, and whether happiness had returned to their home.

My memories of that Wednesday in October are a confusing melange of clarity and muddle-headedness. I remember that I was in chemistry class when a peon knocked on the door and whispered something to Mr Chatterjee, our teacher, who was also the vice principal. Mr Chatterjee, a kind and affable man who always had a smile on his face, turned as white as a sheet and hurriedly left the classroom, mumbling that I and another prefect should mind the class in his absence. He did not return until the end of the class, but in about twenty minutes we heard the general assembly bell, the first time in my eleven years at St Mark's that I heard it ring at any time other than 8 a.m. Within fifteen minutes, the entire school was lined up in the main auditorium, arranged by grade, with the youngest children in front. The teachers were up on the stage, all in their usual positions. All of them looked grave and some of them had clearly been crying. Dr Fanthome, our principal, stepped up to the podium and began to speak. 'The prime minister,' he said, 'has been shot. She is in hospital, but there has been no word of her condition.' Dr Fanthome then led us in a brief prayer for her health and speedy recovery, and informed us that school was dismissed as a mark of respect.

My first reaction was that of jubilation. Not, of course, at the shooting, but at being let out of school on that particular day! India was playing Pakistan in Sialkot and though we had no access to a radio at school, one of the groundsmen in charge of our cricket pitch would keep the team informed. India had been winless in the series until then and I was aware that Vengsarkar and Sandeep Patil were on a rampage, tearing the Pakistan attack into shreds. I couldn't wait to get home and turn on my short-wave radio to savour the team's long-overdue triumph over Pakistan. I leaped out of the school bus and ran to my room to tune in to All India Radio. Nothing! All that was on was sad-sounding classical music. Frustrated, I called some of my friends who were also cricket fanatics, in case they knew anything about the match. That was when I learned that Indira Gandhi was dead. The match, of course, had been called off.

By early afternoon, it was common knowledge that Mrs Gandhi had been shot by her Sikh bodyguards, but there was no inkling yet of what was to come. I remember thinking about Mummyji and Phaji, and how each of them would have taken the news. I didn't quite know how I should have felt about the assassination. My parents were staunch leftists who had vigorously supported the secular ideals of Indira Gandhi's father, Jawaharlal Nehru, but they had been completely alienated by her authoritarian streak, which had surfaced overtly during the dark days of the Emergency. My father, who was home that afternoon, was visibly shaken. I was too, but my thoughts kept returning to the stories of the wanton massacre of the Sikhs earlier that year in Punjab, which Mummyji had recounted and Phaji had dismissed contemptuously as militant propaganda.

My mother got back home in the evening with disturbing news. She had heard that Sikhs were being harassed across Delhi by small mobs. Even then, I don't remember feeling very anxious about Sharan and her family. After all, this was the capital of India and not a small lawless town in Bihar! My father was convinced that these were stray incidents and that order would soon be restored as soon as the leadership recovered from the shock of the assassination. Later that evening, the news of Rajiv Gandhi being sworn in as the new prime minister reassured us all. My parents had been fearful that a vacuum in leadership could cause the fear and anarchy to escalate. It was heartening to have someone who seemed very sensible and untainted by scandals or corruption at the helm.

School, of course, was cancelled the next day, as were local colleges. We spent the morning glued to our television, watching the crowds as they made their way to pay their respects to Mrs Gandhi. The camera would focus on the solemn throng that filed past Mrs Gandhi's body, many in it bearing flowers and sobbing uncontrollably, and then breaking away to show obstreperous and unruly crowds of men who seemed to be chanting angrily. As we strained to hear, we realized with a shock that they were shouting '*Khoon ka badla khoon se lenge*' (We shall avenge blood with blood). It didn't strike me at the time, but it was a huge departure for Doordarshan, the official Indian TV network, known for its unimaginative, plodding and heavily censored coverage, to broadcast something that could even remotely be perceived as inflammatory!

And then the phone calls began. Mostly from my parents' colleagues; fellow academics who lived all over Delhi. Sikhs were being attacked in their homes across the city and the police was nowhere in sight. As we heard story after story of Sikhs being beaten up and harassed, my heart began to sink. I imagined the untold horrors that could be descending upon Sharan, Phaji and Mummyji. I wondered if they had any safe place to go to. They had moved to Delhi only a few years earlier and had no family to speak of. Their local gurdwara would be a natural choice, but we knew by then that Sikh places of worship all over the city were under siege. I tried Sharan's phone number a hundred times, feeling sick with worry each time the call went unanswered. When my mother asked about 'my Sikh friend in west Delhi', I broke down and asked if I could go to Rohini to see if she was okay.

My parents are not the bravest of people and have always had the fear of confrontation and violence that characterizes so many intellectuals. As I expected, my mother tried to dissuade me. When it was clear that I would not give in and announced my decision to board a DTC bus to go to Sharan's house, my mother relented and sent for Shyam. I would be allowed to go, but not on my own; my mother would come with me.

We made it to Sharan's house quickly because the highways and streets were deserted. Buses, taxis, autorickshaws, all of them were conspicuously missing. We saw the occasional car or a couple of men on scooters or motorcycles, but Delhi was mostly a ghost town. By now, Shyam was very familiar with the area Sharan lived in. He got us there without having to navigate the narrow lanes of Mangolpuri. He parked right outside the little house and I rang the doorbell, feeling a relief I had never experienced before as I looked into Mummyji's kind eyes. Her face looked drawn and tired, her eyes puffy from crying. She looked at me in surprise, for surely this was not a day for visits. She looked even more surprised as my mother got out of the car and walked up to her front door.

Mummyji regained her composure very quickly upon seeing my mother and graciously invited us inside. Sharan greeted me with a wan smile as she walked past me to give my mother a hug, whom she was meeting for the very first time, and then disappeared to fetch Phaji. Even though Phaji couldn't possibly have stepped out of the house for at least a day and a half, he was as impeccably dressed and well groomed as ever. It took him about a minute to completely charm my mother. Soon enough, they were chatting easily as I fidgeted awkwardly, feeling a little foolish for dragging my mother halfway across Delhi on a day such as this. Sharan and her family were obviously fine. They had heard rumours about Sikhs being attacked, but most of the attacks had been in remote colonies, miles away, and could very well be in a different world. When I expressed some concern over their safety, Phaji, a picture of calm and equanimity, assured me that no harm would come to them. There have been Hindu–Muslim riots aplenty, he said, but whoever has heard of Hindu–Sikh riots! He added that he had heard Rajiv Gandhi speak on the television after being sworn in and had felt comforted by the new leader's rhetoric, especially when he had invoked his dead mother and asked for calm in her name.

Not one to ever shirk the responsibilities of a gracious hostess, Mummyji dispatched Sharan to the kitchen to slice up vegetables. She emerged from the kitchen soon bearing a tray laden with piping hot pakoras. Sharan followed with a plate of laddoos. Mummyji explained that since all the shops were closed, the only sweets she could offer us were the laddoos, which had come from their neighbours—the Mishras—who were celebrating the arrival of their first grandson. Mummyji also prepared a plate for Shyam who was waiting outside in the car. Sharan took it to him as we dug into the delicious pakoras. With a pang, I realized how much I had missed Mummyji's delicious food and, even more, the quiet warmth of her hospitality the past few months.

We ended up staying longer than we had expected. Phaji had a few things to say about the assassination of the prime minister and all of us sat quietly and listened to him. He felt ashamed, he said, that two strapping young Sikhs had seen it fit to pump a grandmother full of bullets. His family, he said, had been Sikhs for generations and could trace their ancestry back to one of the first Khalsas to be initiated by the tenth Sikh guru. His forebears had never shirked from battle and had a proud tradition of serving in the armies of the Khalsa, the Sikh Empire of Ranjit Singh, the British Raj and independent India, but never could anyone have raised their hand at an elderly woman, no matter what the circumstances. All the while, Sharan maintained a diplomatic silence, avoiding eye contact with everyone, but I could see conflicting emotions playing on Mummyji's face.

Around five, my mother got up to leave. Mummyji, clearly touched by our concern for her family, hugged us both and promised to call if they needed any help. As Shyam drove us back through the still and somewhat deserted streets, we could see increased signs of activity. I felt a vague sense of unease that I could not explain, until I realized what was so unusual. There wasn't a single woman in sight! There were small clumps of men starting to form everywhere, mostly younger men, and I vividly remember thinking about the small packs of feral dogs that seemed to roam every neighbourhood of Delhi unimpeded. We got home without incident and spent the evening watching the news on Doordarshan.

It was a little past midnight when the phone rang.

My father got to the phone first and handed it to my mother. Later, we learned that Sharan had been forbidden by both Phaji and Mummyji to call us, but her fear for her brother's safety gave her the courage to defy them. They had barricaded themselves in Phaji's room, she said. She had slipped out on the pretext of having to use the bathroom. Phaji had nothing to defend his mother and sister with, except a blunt two feet-long ceremonial sword that had been part of his late father's wedding accoutrements. Mangolpuri, which was a few blocks away, had turned into a killing field. All through the night, well-intentioned non-Sikh neighbours had knocked on their door, asking them to seek safety elsewhere. But none had offered them shelter, fearing for the safety of their own families. It was only a matter of time before the violence spilled over Mangolpuri's boundaries. Looting seemed to be the primary motivation for the armed gangs that were roaming the streets of the resettlement colony and they would inevitably seek greener pastures. My mother asked Sharan if they could go to the gurdwara and learned that the mobs were everywhere and that, in fact, the carnage had started with attacks on neighbouring gurdwaras where many Sikh families had sought refuge.

I had to bang on the door to Shyam's quarters for a while before he came out, muttering curses under his breath. Again, as expected, my mother forbade me from going with my father and Shyam, but I would have none of it. My mother handed my father a small bag bulging with hundred-rupee bills as we got into the car. We were stopped seventeen times before we got to Sharan's house. I know for sure because I counted. The pattern was more or less the same. Many streets had been partially blocked off with barrels and makeshift barriers, making it impossible for cars to speed away. There were uninterested-looking policemen at many of the barriers, idly standing by and making no attempt to stop the swaggering youths, most of whom were drunk and armed with iron bars, all strikingly of the same length. 'Any behenchod Sardars in the car?' was the question asked every time before our clean-shaven faces were probed by flashlights that seemed to move past them with great reluctance. Invariably, our trunk would be searched as well, its emptiness eliciting the foulest curses from our interrogators. As we crossed Mangolpuri, getting closer to Sharan's neighbourhood, I could see a pall of smoke in the light of the street lamps.

I knew that they would not open the door. I went to the back of the house, to Phaji's window, and rapped on it lightly with my knuckles. The thick curtains parted a bit, just enough for me to discern Sharan's intense eyes, piercing the darkness.

Mummyji and Sharan, who had let us in, quickly opening the front door for just a second, started to pack a small suitcase, but my father stopped them, asking Mummyji instead to put her jewellery into our car's toolbox, which he had brought in and emptied. Sharan, who was crying quietly, collapsed into one of the chairs in the living room, her face buried in her hands as her mother tried to comfort her. My father stood by helplessly, looking at them until the sound of footsteps made him turn, bringing him face to face with Phaji, resplendent as ever in a peacock blue Patiala turban, nary a fold out of place.

Phaji's first response was, 'Never!'

My father begged and pleaded as I stood miserably, looking at Mummyji's face one moment and Phaji's the next. 'Take Mummyji and Sharan, and let me take my chances. I am sure the army will be called in soon and nothing will happen here.'

Mummyji took Phaji into the back room and shut the door. I could hear her speak rapidly in Punjabi, her exasperation apparent. Then I heard her sobbing. When the door opened, Phaji strode out, somehow managing to look defeated and defiant at the same time.

What were the odds of a barber being found at this hour? It so happened that Shyam had been born into a family of barbers and had plied his ancestral trade in his native Saharanpur until he moved to Delhi as a young man. He looked somewhat contemptuously at the scissors that Sharan brought him, but mumbled that they would do. Of course, there was no razor or shaving cream in Sharan's house! I was dispatched with Mummyji to the Mishras and tried my best to look inconspicuous as she made her unusual request before a befuddled Mr Mishra when he opened the door to our quietly persistent knocking.

Phaji sat in a chair in the little hall behind the living room. Mummyji had had the foresight to spread a large bed sheet under the chair. My father sat in the living room, and I wanted too as well, but something inside me forbade the escape. Phaji sat stone-faced in the chair, staring straight ahead, refusing to make eye contact with anyone. I could hear muted sounds of sobbing emanating from the crumpled heap in the corner that was Sharan. Mummyji stood silently, leaning against the wall, silent, viscous tears that seemed to move as deliberately as drops of mercury sliding down her cheeks.

So much hair! More than I ever imagined a single head could hold. I could taste the horror rising in my throat every time a fresh clump of shorn hair floated down to the growing pile on the sheet. By the time I returned from the bathroom, my diaphragm was twisted and hurting from the retching. All of Phaji's hair was gone. With the stony look and steely glint frozen on his countenance, he very deliberately began to unwrap his carefully groomed beard, which to my amazement seemed to reach his belly. Shyam, somewhat unceremoniously, used his free hand to gather and straighten Phaji's now flowing beard and began to hack at it with the scissors. When all that was left was an unruly, uneven stubble, Phaji got the first shave of his life, Shyam's hands flying dexterously, even tenderly, across his face.

Visibly proud of his handiwork and glad to discover that his skills were still intact, Shyam handed Phaji a mirror, which he quietly waved away as he stood up. I must have been gawking at him because I found Mummyji, her eyes dry and composure regained, gently nudging me.

Phaji had shrunk. With a shock I realized that he was shorter than me without his turban, but that was the least of it. The Phaji I knew had been broad-shouldered with a confidence of one born to command, almost bordering on the arrogant. The man who stood before me looked very ordinary, even diminutive. Somebody one would pass by in the street without a second glance. My heart lurched as I looked at him through Sharan's eyes, and his mother's. The enormity of what had happened began to sink in.

My mind in turmoil, I almost forgot to be anxious on the drive back home, until we were stopped. And we were stopped so many times that I lost count. The mobs seemed more drunk and more boisterous. I was terrified each time someone would poke their head in the back, looking for Sikh men. Phaji had an innocuous and ordinary-looking haircut, but he had a receding hairline, which would be unusual for one so young, unless one's hair had just been cut after having been in a tightly wound topknot for twenty-four years. Also, he had a prominent tan line running across his forehead, marking the part that had not been covered by his turban. His lower cheeks and chin, which had always been covered by his full, heavy beard, were much paler than the rest of his face. Fortunately for us, our interrogators were uniformly drunk and in the half light and shadows of their flaming torches, the very visible evidence of Phaji's antecedents stayed hidden.

Mummyji, who had exhibited impressive calm and maintained a studied silence through our harrowing journey, broke down and wept, clutching her children to her breast, as soon as we got home. 'Our lives,' she tearfully told my mother who had been on tenterhooks awaiting our return, 'are in your hands.'

I slept fitfully but stayed in bed till very late, largely because I didn't want to face Phaji or Sharan or Mummyji. I need not have worried. There was no sight of them when I finally ventured out of my room. My parents were poring over the newspapers, anxiety writ large on their faces. Rumours were flying fast and furious. The most persistent one was that Sikhs were out on the streets, dancing and distributing sweets to celebrate the assassination of Indira Gandhi. Another one was that the Sikhs had poisoned the municipal water supply in Delhi and were readying a massive response to the attacks against them. Our neighbourhood, thankfully, had stayed calm during the violence. A small mob had tried to attack a Sikh home a block away from ours, but the Gurkha watchmen who patrolled our colony at night had chased it away. My mother stayed at home to look after our guests, but my father stepped out to attend a public meeting in central Delhi, which had been organized to protest the violence and organize relief efforts.

Around noon, I finally saw Mummyji and Sharan. While
Mummyji was calm and composed, with not a hair out of place,
Sharan looked like a wreck. My sister's clothes seemed to fit her
quite well, but to my eyes, unaccustomed to seeing her in anything
other than a Punjabi suit, they looked strange on her. Her eyes
seemed puffy and swollen, but I could not tell for sure because she
made fleeting eye contact with me, an utterly unfamiliar emotion
briefly flickering on her face. She silently went into the kitchen
to help my mother make rotis for lunch, not saying one word
the entire time. I awkwardly tried to hover as the three of them
worked together silently with an incongruous sense of purpose,
but my mother and Sharan totally ignored me. Mummyji was her
usual polite self, but it seemed that on that day the potatoes and
cauliflower that she was stir-frying required intense concentration.

I desperately wanted to talk to Sharan. Comfort her. Tell her
with naive sincerity that everything was going to be okay, but she
ate hurriedly and retreated to the guest room with a plate of food
for Phaji. Mummyji and my mother were comparing notes about
the difficulty of finding good domestic help in Delhi, chatting like
they would on a normal social call. I remember feeling inexplicably
angry at their banal exchange and so excused myself to return to
my room.

In my room was plenty of evidence of the role that Phaji
had come to play in my life—the books that I would have never
bought or read had I not met him, the records by the bands that I
had never even heard of, ones that were to have the coolest kids
flocking to my room when I went to college. Sitting miserably on
my bed, I could think of nothing but the events of the previous
night. More than anything else I had ever wanted until that day,
I wanted to somehow comfort Phaji and Sharan, who were just a
few feet away on the other side of the concrete wall I was staring
at, but my legs had turned to lead. It almost felt like we shared a
shameful secret. One we had buried as deep as the toxic skeleton
that inevitably lay in every family's closet.

And then it hit me like a ton of bricks. My heart almost stopped as I belatedly understood the look I had caught on Sharan's face. The hurt I could understand, but the accusation seemed terribly unfair. It crushed me.

It was evening by the time my father returned with terrible news. What was happening in Delhi was just starting to become apparent, even though Doordarshan, All India Radio and the newspapers told a very different story. Terrible massacres had occurred in many parts of the city, particularly the trans-Yamuna colonies in the eastern part. My father had gone from the public meeting to a makeshift camp that had been hurriedly put together for the survivors from Trilokpuri. He told us that there was not one male Sikh, not even a teenager or an older man, among the survivors. Each and every one of them had been hunted down and killed. Some of his female colleagues, who were also at the camp, had heard rumours that almost every young woman had been gang-raped, often within the sight of a policemen who stood by, sometimes laughing! A retired Indian Police Service (IPS) officer, a fellow Kashmiri and a good friend of my father's, had news to share that was even more frightening. An end to the violence was nowhere in sight. The highest levels of the new government had decided that more bloodletting was necessary to 'teach the Sikhs a lesson'. A decision had been made to not deploy the army yet, which is often the only force equipped to deal with such widespread violence.

Of course, we didn't share any of this with Sharan, Phaji or Mummyji. My parents and I were very uneasy, but we had every reason to believe that we would all be safe. Our little enclave was home to many wealthy and well-connected families who could easily get the attention of the city councillors or even members of Parliament (MPs). There was absolutely no possibility of the kind of violence that had ravaged places like Trilokpuri happening here.

We did not see either Sharan or Phaji at dinner. Mummyji spent an hour in the kitchen with my mother and let slip that

Sharan seemed to have a fever. She took a plate of food back for
her and Phaji after hurriedly eating with us.

I lay in bed, tossing fitfully again, utterly exhausted but unable
to sleep. Every time I would doze off, I would wake up sweating
in the grip of a recurrent nightmare. Sometimes we would be
in our living room, sometimes in Sharan's. My parents and I
would be sitting, frozen and unable to move. In the centre of
the room would be a white sheet, spread upon the floor with a
chair on it, its back towards us. Shyam would be hovering over
the slight figure slumped in the chair, an enormous, shining pair
of scissors in his hands. Grinning maniacally, his teeth would not
be stained red with the paan he chewed all day but would be
brilliant and sparkling white. Tufts of jet-black hair, seemingly
as light as feathers, would be floating down surreally as Shyam
whirled like a dervish, scissors snapping. The figure in the chair
would turn and look at me, at times piteously and at other times
in rage. Sometimes the eyes boring into me would be Phaji's and
sometimes they would be Sharan's.

And then my nightmare was invaded by a sound, quite like the
buzzing of angry bees that seemed to get louder and louder until
the loud rapping on the door woke me up and I realized that it was
very real. I leaped to my feet and peered out of my window, which
overlooked the front of our house. In the half light of the street
lamp just beyond our gate, I could see around fifty men crowded
into our front yard. They looked exactly like the fellows who had
searched our car on our way to Sharan's house and back. Many of
them were carrying iron rods and a few even had rusty-looking
tridents that they were waving excitedly. The Gurkha watchmen
stood at the periphery, unable or unwilling to deal with the mob.
I stood transfixed in horror, watching them as the rapping on the
door turned into a loud banging.

I ran downstairs to find my parents and Mummyji in a
perturbed huddle by the main door, wincing at every loud thump.
In hindsight, I realized what a challenge the situation must have

been for my father, the most mild-mannered and genteel of men, and how unequal he must have felt to it. As the banging became even more insistent, my father seemed to visibly straighten as he whispered to Mummyji to go back to the guest room and asked me to go with her. Mummyji left reluctantly, but I was going nowhere. I went up to my mother as my father, wearing his incongruously fancy silk dressing gown over his night-suit, stepped out on to our front stoop, hurriedly shutting the door behind him. My mother and I rushed to the door, our eyes pressed to the glass panel, through which we could more or less see what was happening outside.

The buzzing of the crowd seemed to stop momentarily at the sight of my father, and we could see the bulky form of the man who had been banging on our door retreat into the crowd. 'What is going on, Gullu?' I heard my father say. I realized with a start that the leader of the mob was none other than the *halwai* from the sweet shop in the Part-I market, whose samosas and jalebis were the toast of South Extension. I had known him as a jovial giant of a man, whose massive belly quivered as he laughed, which he did constantly as he bantered with the stream of customers lining up for his piping hot creations. This, however, was a new Gullu.

'There are Sardars in your house, Kaul Sahib,' Gullu said, setting off the angry buzzing again.

My father tried to brazen it out at first, insisting that there was nobody in our house other than me and my mother, even haranguing Gullu in indignation, at the suggestion that our house be searched. But the mob was having none of it. A couple of young roughnecks sidled up to Gullu, speaking to him in loud whispers, even as they looked at my father. Gullu put a pudgy hand on their shoulders, restraining them and whispering back as he inclined his head towards the street. My father doggedly insisted that there was nobody in the house and that he would be damned if he was going to let anyone enter, until he saw who the two toughs had in tow as they elbowed their way back to the front of the mob.

I realized with horror that it was Shyam.

Shyam's face was flushed and he was staggering a little. It was obvious that he had been drinking. Shyam's family had served us Kauls for generations, which probably explained the sheepishness with which he looked at my father, who now looked utterly defeated, his fake bravado gone. An inexplicable expression of insolence and defiance seemed to briefly flit across Shyam's face as Gullu and the toughs eyed my father triumphantly.

Ever the believer in the innate goodness of his fellow men, my father tried to reason with them. 'They are friends of my son's,' he said. 'Good, kind people. You know that they had nothing to do with Mrs Gandhi's death. They are just children, Gulluji. You have children too. There has already been so much bloodshed. Take these boys and go home. The guilty will be punished, but this family is innocent.'

'Innocent?' said Gullu with quiet menace. 'Kaul Sahib, our mother has died and these behenchods are celebrating?'

'What are you taking about, Gullu Bhai? This is a kind and decent family. They have been mourning the death of Mrs Gandhi. They didn't light a stove in their home to cook out of respect for her.'

'*Chootiya bana raha hai, saala!*'

My father winced at the insult and stiffened, angrily protesting that he wasn't lying, but Gullu waved him shut, turning towards Shyam and gesticulating at him.

'They were celebrating,' Shyam said triumphantly. 'I know because I was at their house yesterday. The behenchods were distributing laddoos. I know because they gave me some. The little bitch brought them to me herself and I threw them into the drain when she left. And they made me give the pup a haircut and a shave. Just to fool everyone,' Shyam spat venomously.

The mob seemed to go berserk after Shyam's little speech. 'Kill them all! We won't stop until they are all dead! Blood for blood!'

the men started to murmur, starting to inch towards the house. My father, his face as white as a sheet, stood directly in their path, unyielding.

There was a loud thump and something struck Gullu smack in the middle of his eyes. As the mountain of flesh that was his body slowly quivered to the ground, I heard a mocking sally in Phaji's cultured voice.

'Yes, you motherfuckers! Your mother is dead and now you can watch me dance with joy.'

Brick after brick was then hurled with unerring accuracy from our rooftop balcony. In a manner of minutes the crowd had melted away, leaving Gullu lying in a heap in our front yard. My father called his old friend, the retired IPS officer, and within an hour a police detail was stationed outside our house.

Gullu was dead.

Later, we learned that he had a heart condition and the shock of Phaji's well-aimed brick had triggered a massive cardiac attack. Phaji was arrested and held at the local police station overnight and was speedily produced before the Additional Chief Metropolitan Magistrate the very next day. My parents hired Mr Puri, one of Delhi's best attorneys, to defend Phaji. We were assured that the mitigating circumstances around what had happened would be considered. However, bail was denied and Phaji was remanded to Tihar Jail, awaiting trial.

Sharan was ill. Her fever had spiked and she had become very weak, only tenuously aware of what was happening. Mummyji was a tower of strength, tending to her daughter and comforting my parents who blamed themselves for not having protected her family more effectively, and spending every hour she could with Mr Puri, working on Phaji's defence.

The news of Phaji's death came through a phone call. A day before his trial, he was found hanging in his cell with a leather belt. Nobody could explain how he had managed to acquire a belt inside his cell, but his death was ruled a suicide.

Mummyji and Sharan stayed at our house until Phaji's funeral. Their own home had been ransacked and torched by the mobs that had been devastating Mangolpuri right around the time of their escape.

Sharan did not look at me as she was helped into her uncle's car that was to take them back to Punjab. Mummyji put her arms around me and, reading the anguish on my face, simply said, 'Give it time, son.' But I knew it was false comfort and I would never see either of them again.

The last thing that Mummyji did before they left was to forgive Shyam, who had wept at her feet in shame every day after the night he had betrayed her and her family.

The General

Liv was eighteen then. She was back home for spring break in her freshman year at Amherst College when, out of the blue, she announced that she was going to be a human rights lawyer. I was slicing vegetables for dinner and not really paying attention to her, but I remember cutting myself as the knife in my hand slipped when I heard her mumble something about disappearances in Punjab. Amherst College didn't have many Sikh students, but the much-larger University of Massachusetts Amherst (UMass) had a Sikh students' association. Liv had been going to their events, I learned, much to my surprise.

Of course, Liv had known her father was a Sikh, but after his disappearance, in my anguish and rage, I had cut every tie with my husband's Sikh friends. Pregnant with Liv, I had left New York and returned to my parents' home in Sudbury, Massachusetts, where I had eventually found a teaching job in a neighbouring town. The only thing that connected Liv to her dad was her last name, which I did not have the heart to change despite me going back to my maiden name. She had my husband's dark-brown eyes but my red hair and pale, freckled skin. Nothing about her was even remotely Sikh, and I was fine with that.

There was a gurdwara in Milford, maybe twenty miles from our home, but in the years that had passed since I moved back from

New York, not once did I have the faintest desire to take Liv there. My dad, who had always been very fond of my husband, disagreed and felt that Liv needed to learn about her father's people. He was her father and his memory deserves respect, he would say. But I was so bitter in the early years after my return that I would not hear of it. As far as I was concerned, the Sikhs were responsible for shattering my universe. I wanted nothing more to do with them. I was singularly focused on raising Liv, doing my best to give her a happy childhood. Anything that led her to her father's memory would only bring her pain.

Raja, as my husband was known, had been estranged from his family. His father was a small businessman from Delhi, and I think his family owned an auto-parts store. The plan had always been for Raja to get his American MBA and return to India to set up an auto-parts factory. Raja had told me that his family was very traditional and it was no surprise that they were mortified when they learned that he had accepted a job in New York after graduating, instead of returning home. They were very disappointed but also proud of his success. Raja used to tell me that his salary, when converted into Indian rupees was a small fortune and the subject of many triumphant conversations within his extended family, much to his mortification.

The bragging abruptly turned into shame when Raja told them that he had removed his turban and shaved his beard too. He had not travelled to India during his time at Northeastern University and had moved to New York right after graduation to start working with Salomon Brothers. They had, of course, no way of knowing that he had shed his identity just a couple of months into graduate school. It took him more than two years to pluck up the courage to tell them, and I could tell from his expression after the phone call that it had gone worse than he had anticipated.

His calls to India became less frequent and when he did call, he only spoke to his mother and brother, but never his father. And when he told them that he was going to marry his American girlfriend, his mother stopped taking his calls as well. Raja was an intensely loyal person and I never heard him utter one word against his parents, not even in anger. I was, of course, furious because his pain was quite apparent. He had always been very attached to his parents. I simply could not understand what the big deal was. Besides they didn't know me at all! How could they possibly judge me and treat him like this.

I graduated from Northeastern a year later and followed Raja to New York. He had been sharing a small apartment in the Village with three of his friends. We soon found a one-bedroom in Brooklyn and, in the fall, I started grad school at New York University (NYU). Raja's gloom had lifted by then and he was pretty much back to his happy, gregarious self. I suppose my joining him in New York had helped. I didn't have many friends in New York, but Raja had plenty. Many of his friends from Delhi University had come to the US around the same time as him for grad school and several of them worked in or around the city. Raja's best friend while growing up, Yogesh, who went by Yogi, also worked in New York. Yogi and Raja had grown up in the same neighbourhood and were both alums of St Stephen's, which Raja had told me was one of the elite colleges in Delhi. Yogi's girlfriend, June, an incredibly sweet Midwestern girl who wrote a column for *Vanity Fair*, became one of my closest friends. Raja and I spent almost every weekend with Yogi and June, often hopping from one Delhi University party to another.

'So there was this talk by a human rights activist who lives in Nepal. He was at UMass to talk about his new book about disappearances in Punjab.'

I snapped out of my reverie and regarded my daughter balefully. 'And that interests you because?'

'Well, I met this guy at the Ekta Bhangra party at Smith. He is at Hampshire College and he invited me.'

Liv seemed unwilling to share any more information about the 'guy' and I did not want her to sense my anxiety. I had never discouraged her from dating when she was in high school. My anxiety would have seemed perplexing to her, but I couldn't restrain myself.

'So is he from India?' I heard myself asking.

'Nah. He was born in Chicago. His name is Nihal. He's a Sikh and really cool.'

I wept angrily when I was alone. I suppose I should not have been surprised. It was inevitable that Liv would seek out other Sikh kids, but I was unprepared.

During my junior year at Northeastern, I had decided to take a kundalini yoga class. Of course, I did not know this at the time but the instructor, a grad student from California, was a Sikh. She went by Ellen, but I learned later that she was also called Dharma Jyot Kaur. We became very friendly and I started to really enjoy my yoga class. In April, during my junior year, several months after I had started in her class, Ellen invited me to a Sikh celebration at the chapel in Ell Hall. Free Indian food, she had said.

That was when I first met Raja. He was with a bunch of other Indian grad students who were serving food after the event. Some of them had long beards and wore orange turbans. Raja, however, had a day-old stubble and an orange bandana tied around his head. I remember asking Ellen, who was sitting next to me, who that cute guy was. Ellen had laughed and said she would introduce me after we had eaten.

I started hanging out with Raja. He was different from any of the guys I had dated in high school or college. He was the kindest and most gentle person I had ever met. Pretty soon we were dating and it quickly turned serious. I thought it cute that I was the first girl he had ever been with. He, however, would get a little upset whenever something I said reminded him that I had been with other guys before I met him. He also seemed to get incredibly sad when I finally invited him home to meet my parents. My mother had a bit of trouble dealing with an 'Indian boyfriend', but Raja and my Dad got along famously right from the first meeting.

Much to my annoyance, every time I brought him home, he and my dad would end up tinkering with the vintage cars that my dad was always rebuilding in his garage.

When I asked him why he got so sad each time he came home, he was evasive at first. Much later, he told me that the kindness my family treated him with made him think of how his family would react when they learned that he had a white girlfriend.

Raja was wrapping up his MBA and had started interviewing for jobs. He also had a research project for the summer, which paid him enough to survive. I, meanwhile, had a retail job at the Prudential Center. I didn't know it then, of course, but those were to be our happiest days together. I would commute in from Sudbury and hang out with him at the really ratty apartment that he shared with several other grad students. We would spend most weekends at my parents' in Sudbury. My mother had warmed up to him as well; how could she not! We would often drive to an Indian store on Route 9 in Framingham to buy spices and Raja tried to teach both my mom and me how to make biryani, which was his favourite food.

By the end of the summer, he had a job with Salomon Brothers and I was ready to start senior year. The next year would be a flurry of weekend trips to New York and long phone calls every day. I just loved the city and was happy to spend most of my weekends there. Every now and then, Raja would catch a bus to Boston and we would hang out in Sudbury.

I was intensely happy about the way my family had accepted Raja, and I really wanted to get to know his family but when I suggested that we make a trip to India, Raja looked completely horrified. 'You can never understand, Meg! The shock of seeing me without my turban will kill my father. And if we go together, it will be a huge scandal.'

I guess I didn't understand. It was pretty obvious to Raja that I was hurt and more than a little insulted at the suggestion that his family would consider me so 'inappropriate'. But I could see how uncomfortable the topic made Raja, and so I dropped it completely. His new job kept him super busy and I had a job on campus and my thesis to juggle along with a long-distance relationship. I really wanted to believe my mother when she would tell me that things would sort themselves out eventually.

Liv, meanwhile, had been chattering about her friends and classes as we drove back to Amherst, but I was barely paying attention. I hadn't slept a wink. Instead, I had tossed and turned until the early hours of the morning and then gone to the basement to fetch a cardboard box that was filled with happy pictures from my years in New York with Raja. Liv has never seen these, I said to myself, my guilt razor-sharp, as I looked at photographs from parties and hikes, and us at concerts with Yogi and June. I hadn't even realized that I was crying.

The car swerved as the words 'California' and 'internship' registered and I looked at my daughter as I struggled with the car. 'So Nihal interned at this really cool organization called Ensaaf last summer, and he knows the director well. He's pretty sure he can talk to her and get me an internship there this summer, Mom. They have done a lot of work documenting the events of 1984 and fighting for justice. It totally fits with my law-school plans and I think it will look great on my resume.'

I didn't say a word, but I knew I would make a terrible poker player. 'I guess you probably don't know much about 1984, Mom, but some really terrible things happened to Sikhs in India, and twenty years later, there is still no sign of justice. This is important work and I really want to get involved. This means a lot to me, Mom. I guess it's hard for you to understand, but please be supportive. I really want to do this.'

I drove back in a daze. I did know a thing or two about 1984.

I was off for the summer and Raja too had taken a few days off. The last semester at grad school had been brutal and Raja had been under a lot of pressure at work. We hadn't even had the time for a short honeymoon after our simple marriage ceremony at the registrar's office in Brooklyn. Now, we had decided to go to the Poconos. Raja told me that when he was a kid, his family would go to Kashmir in the summer, where one of his aunts lived, and that he loved the mountains. In the Poconos, we didn't turn on the TV in our hotel room even once, and we certainly didn't have any reason to buy a newspaper.

It was past midnight on 6 June when we returned to Brooklyn. The next morning, Raja left early for work. He had taken three days off and knew that a pile of things would be waiting for him. I had chosen to sleep in. As I was drinking my first cup of coffee, I opened the *New York Times*. I had never seen the word 'Sikh' in any newspaper until then, much less the front page of the *New York Times*, and a story immediately caught my attention: '308 people killed as Indian troops take Sikh temple', read the headline.

I had visited a gurdwara only once. Raja had taken me there a few months earlier during a major celebration. Yogi and June, and a couple of Raja's Sikh friends had come too. The gurdwara, which was in Queens, had been jam-packed and everyone had seemed really friendly. The meal after the service, which Raja had told me was commonplace at gurdwaras, had been delicious. We often ate at Indian restaurants, and there were plenty in New York, but I had never tasted such good Indian food anywhere else. Raja was not very religious then, and after that one visit, he never talked about going again. The gurdwaras had services on Sunday and we always had plans with friends on most weekends.

The article was surprising. There had been armed Sikh militants inside the gurdwara, and there had been a standoff in which hundreds had been killed. I remember being surprised on reading that forty-three other Sikh places of worship had been attacked in order to flush out Sikh terrorists. It was all vaguely disturbing because it implied that gurdwaras were violent places that provided sanctuary to armed men, who, according to the report, routinely committed murder. Until that moment, Raja's being an Indian and a Sikh had been irrelevant to me. We were just two young people in love.

Of course, none of that had changed, but in some inexplicable way Raja's identity seemed to have acquired a disquieting undertone.

Raja had heard about the attack too, but he didn't seem particularly concerned when he came back home. 'Oh yes,' he had said, when I showed him the article. 'There has been trouble brewing for a few years. There have been a few lunatic Sikhs who have been stirring up trouble and hiding in gurdwaras. The biggest troublemaker is this guy called Bhindranwale, who is like a Sikh Ayatollah. But now that they have killed him, things will settle down.'

The phone rang in the middle of the night. I am a light sleeper and the slightest noise always wakes me up. There was silence at first when I groggily said hello. And then a voice in an Indian accent said, 'Raja, Raja.' My heart sank. There had never been a phone call from Raja's family until then, ever since we had moved into our apartment. Raja had never really introduced me to his family, or told them about the wedding, and now his mother had heard my voice on the phone in the middle of the night. In a panic, I shook Raja awake and whispered to him, 'I think it's your mom.'

Turning on the lights, I could clearly see the worry on Raja's face during the entire conversation. He was speaking in Punjabi with a few words in English thrown in. I heard the words 'army' and 'terrorists' many times, as well as the name of the leader of the militants, Bhindranwale. Calls from India were very expensive then and Raja had told me that his parents were very frugal. As Raja got increasingly perturbed and his face turned ashen, it felt like the conversation had been going on for hours, but the call really had lasted barely ten minutes.

'Did she ask about me?'

Raja shook his head, looking dazed.

'What's the matter? Is everything okay with your family?'

Apparently, Raja's mother had been trying to call for more than a day. Two of her sisters lived in Amritsar, their homes a few hundred yards from the Golden Temple. 'The news reports are lies,' Raja said to me. 'Thousands have been killed and truckloads of bodies are being taken away from the Golden Temple. They attacked with tanks. They demolished the Akal Takht.' I had no idea what the Akal Takht was. Later, Raja explained that it was an ancient structure of great historical significance in the Golden Temple complex. That was where Bhindranwale and his men had been hiding.

Raja barely slept after that call, and I stayed up with him. Even though he was exhausted, I insisted that he go to work. I bought a bunch of newspapers but couldn't find much news. The *New York Times* had a story about Sikh terrorists holding out at the Golden Temple, firing at Indian soldiers during a visit by the Indian President. The story also mentioned that Sikh terrorists had killed at least fifteen more people and that thirty more Sikh terrorists had been rounded up. Of course, at that time I did not really comprehend how significant the attack had been, particularly to the Sikhs. I certainly did not understand Raja's reaction because, to me, it seemed that it was just a law-and-order situation. There were armed terrorists holed up in a place of worship and the government had taken action to flush them out!

Raja came back early from work that day, the anguish evident on his face. He said he would not feel all right if he didn't visit the gurdwara in Queens. I said that I would come as well. The Richmond Hill gurdwara was swarming with people. When we got there, a group of Sikh minstrels were playing an instrument, which I later learned was called the harmonium, and singing. The songs sounded mournful. As I sat down, an orange scarf covering my head, on the women's side of the congregation that Raja had nudged me towards, I saw that many had tears streaming down their cheeks.

After the music ended and the service concluded with the handing out of a sweet pudding, people got up to speak. The initial speeches were in Punjabi, of which I did not understand a word, but I could tell that the speakers were angry. There was a lot of raising of the fists and a loud call and response at the end of each speech. I heard the name of the Indian prime minister Indira Gandhi and Bhindranwale being mentioned several times in each speech.

The final speech was by a nebbish-looking Sikh, who was probably Raja's age. He was tall and gangly, and wore a large blue turban on his head. He had a long, flowing beard that reached till the middle of his chest. He was dressed in flowing white robes and he wore an ornamented strap across his chest, at the end of which dangled a wicked-looking dagger. Of course, Raja and I didn't know this then, but Dr Rachpal Singh was to play a huge role in our lives. Much to my surprise, the young Sikh began to speak in English, with an unmistakable Texan drawl. Years have passed, but I still remember his words.

'I was born and raised in this country, and I am a proud American, but I am proud to be a Sikh no less. Today is a shameful day for India, which prides itself on being the largest democracy in the world. For what the Indian government did is simply unforgivable. What kind of democracy attacks its own citizens with tanks and heavy armour? What kind of democracy kills thousands of its own citizens in cold blood? We have still not fully understood what has just happened at the Golden Temple, but one thing is clear: the news coming out of India has been carefully controlled and the news reports you have read in the *Times* and elsewhere are inaccurate. There have been mass killings at the Golden Temple and many other gurdwaras all over Punjab. Young Sikhs are being rounded up and killed. I have spoken to at least thirty people who have received calls from Punjab. Our people are being terrorized. My father came to this country forty years ago to start a new life. He became an American citizen, but he was always an Indian first, then a Sikh and finally an American. My grandfather and great-grandfather served in the army. My family has sacrificed many men in the wars that India has fought since Independence. Until yesterday, I was a proud Indian American. Today, I want nothing to have to do with India, never again. Why would I want to associate with a nation that mercilessly kills my brothers? Today, I commit myself to justice for the rest of my life. Today, I have untied my beard and I swear that I will never tie it again. Tomorrow I shall go to work as a Sikh who has dedicated his life to righting this injustice. And I urge every young Sikh, man or woman, here today to do the same. We have been tested and we will be tested again. Do not be afraid. Do not fear that your turban will make it hard for you to find a job. Do not fear that your flowing beard will make you stand out as someone foreign. Let this be your first act of defiance! If you have cut off your hair, grow it back. Return to the fold. Unless all of us do this and make ourselves strong on the inside, I swear that we will never win this fight. Show the dogs who attacked us that we are not afraid. Bhindranwale has been martyred. And for what? For being a staunch Sikh! For condemning all the vices that so-called Sikhs are steeped in today! Drugs. Alcohol. No more! Let his sacrifice not be in vain my brothers. Let us all return to the fold. If something good is to come out of this tragedy, then coming back to the faith has to be the first step.'

Raja was deep in thought and didn't say a word during the subway ride back home. He had bought a stack of calling cards from a little shop close to the gurdwara. When he called his parents, I sat there looking at his anguished face as he spoke in Punjabi. Neither of us slept that night.

The next day, we went back to the Richmond Hill gurdwara, and the following day too. Raja didn't speak to anyone there. We just sat and listened to the minstrels, ate after the service and came back home. Raja started calling his parents every day and didn't volunteer anything about the animated conversations, which were always in Punjabi. When I asked, his answers were terse. Soon, I stopped asking.

It was Monday, 11 June 1984. Raja had taken the day off to go to a protest at the United Nations (UN) headquarters. We had spent several hours on Sunday at the gurdwara, and there had been posters about the protest everywhere. I had been a little surprised when Raja had declared that he was going. Though he did not ask me to come, I decided to tag along anyway. A large crowd had gathered, with many men and women carrying signs and placards, protesting the attack on the Golden Temple. Many of the protesters were older than us and seemed to know each other well. Raja and I made our way towards a group of younger people who were listening attentively to a speaker. It was Dr Rachpal Singh.

Rachpal was holding forth on how important it was for young Sikhs to learn about their faith and embrace it fully. He and a few other young Sikhs were starting a study group that planned to meet every Saturday at someone's home. He had a stack of flyers with his phone number and a posh Briarcliff Manor address on them, where the first meeting was to be held. Raja was one of the first to grab a copy.

I wasn't sure if Raja really wanted me to go to Briarcliff Manor with him. It has been many years now, but I can still remember the sinking feeling in the pit of my stomach. Every aspect of my existence was wrapped around Raja, but ever since he learned of the attack on the Golden Temple he seemed to be pushing me away. I was, of course, distraught, but I also experienced a twinge of resentment. How was any of this my fault?

I decided to go with him. When I told him, he simply grunted.

The first meeting of the study group was at a lovely home in Briarcliff Manor, a fancy town in Westchester County, where the well-heeled lived. There were more than twenty cars parked outside when we arrived. Raja parked our battered Nissan away from the late-model BMWs and Audis in the driveway. The kitchen alone seemed bigger than my parents' tiny home in Sudbury. A lavish spread had been laid out on the granite counters and our very gracious hosts pressed plates into our hands. Raja, somewhat brusquely, shook his head and walked towards the sound of someone singing. A little red-faced at his rudeness, I stayed to eat and chat with the grey-haired woman who had welcomed us. I learned that her husband was a surgeon and that they had lived in Briarcliff Manor for a decade after moving from Dallas. Rachpal was their older son. Their daughter was away at medical school.

The large room, from where the sounds of singing were coming, was a library with more windows than I had ever seen in a room. Bookcases filled with leather-wrapped volumes lined one wall. The room had been stripped of all furniture and the floor was covered with expensive-looking oriental rugs. It had been set up like a miniature gurdwara, where in one corner the most handsome Sikh I had ever laid eyes on was playing the harmonium and singing. Rachpal sat to his left, playing the drums. About thirty people sat in the room, cross-legged, listening. All the women wore expensive-looking Indian clothes, making me feel frumpy by comparison. A few of the men sported turbans and full beards, but most of them had orange bandanas on their heads and were for the most part clean-shaven.

As I looked around curiously, my eyes found Raja. He was sitting with his back ramrod straight. His eyes were shut and I could see that his cheeks were glistening with tears.

The young man sang for about half an hour, after which Rachpal delivered a fiery speech in Punjabi. While I did not understand what he said, I caught enough English words to know that he was talking about the attack. Raja was drinking in every word.

Later, a sumptuous meal was served and a few people, particularly some of the older ones, left after that. The others gathered in the library again. The theme of the first session was sacrifice and Rachpal's friend kicked things off by reading a chapter from a history book that was in English. It was a vivid description of brave Sikhs from the eighteenth century, who fearlessly stood up to the marauding armies of an Afghan king who had attacked their homeland over and over, and targeted the Golden Temple on numerous occasions. The discussion that followed was in Punjabi. I was lost again. Rachpal explained to me that as a group of young Sikhs in the US, they were trying to understand what was demanded of them in the aftermath of the extraordinary attack on the Golden Temple.

Raja's gloom seemed to have lifted a bit and on the drive back he was almost himself. He had been very impressed with Rachpal and his friend, and declared that he would go to attend every study-group session.

Yogi and June had invited us to dinner on Sunday evening. Given Yogi's excellent cooking, I was looking forward to it. Raja and I had not been talking much after our return from the Poconos. I was also stressed out because I could see his anguish but felt completely helpless. The phone calls to his parents had continued and his agitation only seemed to increase each time he hung up. Much later he told me that his parents were begging him to return. His mother had also begun asking him about me and whether we were really married. I was dismayed when Raja said he didn't want to go to Yogi and June's. Yogi always made Raja laugh and I felt that it would be good for Raja to talk about something other than the attack. And I really wanted to share my anxieties with June. The change I was starting to see in Raja was making me nervous.

Ultimately, I had to throw a huge tantrum before Raja grudgingly agreed to go. Yogi was his usual gregarious self, greeting Raja with a string of abuses in Hindi, which they never translated for me. Usually Raja would respond by punching him or swearing at him, but that day, he just looked blankly at Yogi. When Raja went to the bathroom, I quickly told Yogi and June what had been going on and asked them to treat Raja with kid gloves. But Yogi being Yogi, of course, launched into a frontal assault as soon as Raja returned. 'Now I know the reason for your long face, you fucker. You should be thrilled that that *behenchod* Bhindranwale and his terrorists are dead! Aren't you the one who was so angry that the Golden Temple had become a refuge for criminals!'

Raja looked at Yogi coldly and said, 'Let it go, Yogi. This is not a joke.'

'Fuck that, Raja! *Tere behenchod barah kyun baje hue hain!*'

Now that was a phrase I understood. Yogi used to say it all the time to Raja, who would always crack up in response. After the very first time I met Yogi, Raja had explained to me that this was a harmless ethnic joke that played on the stereotype of Sikhs being amiable buffoons. The canard went that at midnight all Sikhs go mad and behave irrationally. Raja had told me that the Sikhs were a sporting lot who never took 'Sikh jokes' personally, which I understood as being the Indian equivalent of 'Polish jokes'. Raja, in fact, would often be the first to crack them.

Well, that day Yogi encountered a Raja that he had never met before. Nor, for that matter, had I. 'Do you think it's funny, Yogi? Are you amused that the Indian Army attacked the Golden Temple? Do you find it funny that thousands have been killed? Is it a joke that the Akal Takht was attacked with tanks and destroyed? Do you know that there have been mass executions all over Punjab? Hilarious, right? That truckloads of bodies have been taken from the Golden Temple and secretly cremated? Yes, laugh, you Hindu bastard. Laugh. Your Brahmin bitch has taught us Sikhs a lesson. Rejoice.'

Yogi looked at Raja, his face ashen. 'What's happened to you, Raja! What is this Hindu–Sikh shit? We have been joking like this since we were five!'

Raja looked at Yogi, stone-faced. 'That "Sardaron ke barah baj gaye" joke? Do you think that's funny, Yogi? Never fails to crack you up, right? Do you really want to know what you are laughing at? I just found out myself. Let me tell you. It's quite hilarious actually.

'In the eighteenth century, as the Mughal Empire was collapsing, Afghan warlords started raiding north India repeatedly. They would swoop down from the mountains, pillage and plunder, and then return with booty and captives. Who do you think they enslaved? Mostly young Hindu girls. Nobody dared to confront them, except roving bands of Sikhs. The Sikhs would attack at midnight, when the Afghans would be raping the captured women.

They would make off with the Afghans' plunder, free their captives and bring them back home.

'Does any of this sound funny to you, Yogi? Well, it sounds fucking hilarious to me. Because all these years you and other miserable Hindus like you have been laughing at your great-grandmothers being violated by Afghan cock.'

I did not speak to Raja for the next two days and later called June to apologize. Yogi refused to talk to me and I sensed coldness in June's voice too. Yogi and Raja never spoke after that. June and I stayed in touch and still talk on the phone occasionally. She got married to Yogi and they have two kids who are a little younger than Liv.

At one point, Raja started coming home late. In the past he did meet some of his college friends for drinks after work and often he would ask me to join them, especially if their wives or girlfriends were around. I knew he had been withdrawing from his college friends after the attack and one day I just bluntly asked him where he went, on the days he came home late. He said that had been meeting some young Sikhs, including Rachpal, after work, sometimes at a cafe and sometimes at the Richmond Hill gurdwara. He hadn't invited me to join him, and I knew that it would be awkward, which is why I didn't ask to go either.

That weekend, Raja brought two visitors home. One was Rachpal and the other was the extremely handsome Sikh Raja and I had first met at the study-group meeting in Briarcliff Manor. His name was Harjinder and he worked at an electronics store in Jersey City. I learned that he was in the US illegally. A professional Sikh minstrel, he had been invited to sing as part of a group at the Richmond Hill gurdwara, but instead of returning to India with his fellow minstrels, he had disappeared into the Sikh community around Richmond Hill. A mesmerizing singer and very charismatic, he had become a permanent member of Rachpal's study group and a bit of a rock star. He had photographs with Bhindranwale, the militant leader who had just been killed.

In one of them, he had a bandolier strapped around his chest and a Sten gun slung across his shoulder.

Harjinder, Rachpal and Raja had become inseparable. Raja continued to come home late every night and I stopped asking where he went, knowing that my questions would irritate him. He had stopped shaving and was letting his hair grow, which worried me because he had told me that his Wall Street employer had a dress and appearance code that, while unwritten, was strictly enforced. In fact, I wasn't the least bit surprised when Raja declared that he was returning to his Sikh identity. The following week, there was to be a ceremony at Richmond Hill in which several Sikhs would be readmitted into the fold. Raja told me with great pride that finally he was going to become an Amritdhari Sikh or a Khalsa. When I asked what that meant, his answer was not entirely clear.

The next day, I went to the New York Public Library. I learned that the Khalsa was an order created by the tenth guru of the Sikhs, Guru Gobind Singh, in 1699. All the reference books provided slightly different interpretations, but I remember feeling terrified after reading them. Weapons, self-sacrifice, a regimen of daily prayer, a rigid code of conduct—all of these things would have seemed alien to the man I had married just a few weeks ago, but my world had changed profoundly after the attack on the Golden Temple. I went home in a daze. I really didn't want to worry my parents, and I had absolutely nobody to talk to.

And then, of course, there was Raja! The decision to become a Khalsa had completely transformed him. It seemed as if the old Raja was back. There was a spring in his step and it was after weeks that I was seeing him smile and laugh. Worried as I was, I could not help but feel happy for him. All kinds of thoughts, ones I did not dare to share with him, ran through my mind. His appearance would be so different. He would have a beard and a turban. In New York, nobody cared, but whenever we left the city we would now attract even more attention as an interracial couple. After an incident at a bar in Sudbury, while we were both in grad school, we had formed an unspoken rule. We simply avoided places where we were likely to encounter bigotry. Surely his very alien appearance would only make it harder. I was determined to support Raja, no matter what; after all, it was his right, but a small part of me did feel betrayed. I had not bargained for any of this. I often found myself wondering if I would have fallen for him had he had a turban on his head and looked so different, before I would guiltily bury such thoughts.

Harjinder and Rachpal came over for dinner a night before the initiation ceremony. I was completely nonplussed when Harjinder pointedly observed that it was common for a couple to be initiated into the Khalsa together. It would be challenging for Raja to follow the code of conduct if his wife did not observe the rules as well! My family was nominally Episcopalian and while we had never been religious or churchgoing, I had never considered the possibility of becoming a Sikh, much less a Khalsa! Raja, who was the kindest and most easygoing person, had never said that he expected this from me. I found myself getting annoyed at Harjinder's presumptuousness, and I suppose it showed. Raja looked Harjinder in the eye and calmly told him that this would always be my decision.

My husband was a changed man! It took a little bit of getting used to, but in a few weeks his appearance did not seem alien or unfamiliar any more. He was clearly thrilled at his transformation; how could I not be happy! I actually began to think that he looked very distinct and dashing in his neatly tied peaked turban. The only thing I hated was the foul-smelling green glop that he brushed into his beard each morning to groom it, something he had picked up from a store in Jackson Heights, before tying on a black scarf to set his beard, which made him look positively villainous!

I also breathed a sigh of relief when Raja told me that his boss at Salomon was being very supportive. I had been terrified that he would lose his job. We had a mortgage to pay and a week after his initiation, I discovered I was pregnant. It was not planned, but Raja was ecstatic when he found out. I was not sure how I felt.

I certainly did not feel ready to be a mother yet. Raja, however, was convinced that it was a gift from God. A reward, he said, for returning to the faith. He was convinced that our son, for he absolutely knew it would be a boy, was blessed.

That weekend, there was tremendous excitement at the study group, which was meeting at a house in Chappaqua, New York. The meeting was delayed as a distinguished guest was expected, and Harjinder was asked to continue singing until he arrived. The guest was the most dapper-looking Sikh I had ever seen. He was easily six feet tall and sported a navy blue turban that was adorned with some kind of military medal. He was dressed in an impeccably cut, expensive-looking suit. His tie matched his turban and his grey beard was very elegantly groomed and held in place by what looked like a hairnet. All eyes were on him as he walked through the assembly to bow before the scripture, before sitting cross-legged to listen to Harjinder and Rachpal.

After the religious service was over, Harjinder, who seemed to know the visitor, ran up to him with a smile and reverently bowed to touch his feet in traditional Indian style. The visitor smiled and stopped him, enveloping him in a bear hug instead.

The visitor's name was Patwant Singh Khuller, and he was a retired general from the Indian Army. A powerful orator, he held the assembly spellbound as he spoke for the next forty-five minutes. The speech was in Punjabi, but I caught several references to Indira Gandhi and Bhindranwale. For the first time, I heard the accursed word 'Khalistan', which was to become the rallying cry for Rachpal's study group. I also thought I heard him say Madison Square Garden several times. The assembly was abuzz and I was dying to learn what he had spoken about as we ate after his speech.

Major General Khuller was a highly decorated veteran who had shown great gallantry in all the wars India had fought. He said that he had become thoroughly disillusioned with the Indian government because of the shabby treatment the Sikhs received in the army, often looked on with suspicion and routinely passed over for promotions. He had been mesmerized by the rhetoric of Bhindranwale who had promised to return the Sikh faith to its pristine purity and glory, and gravitated to him like many other ex-army men. He had been initiated into the ranks of the Khalsa by none other than Bhindranwale himself, with Harjinder present at the time. According to Major General Khuller, Bhindranwale had had a premonition that he would be killed by the Indian government and had charged the General's former colleague, another war hero named General Sahbegh Singh, with fortifying the Golden Temple in anticipation of an attack. Major General Khuller had been anxious to do his part and seek martyrdom himself, but Bhindranwale had a different mission for him.

Major General Khuller was to go to America and organize the Sikh diaspora for a freedom struggle aimed at carving out the independent Sikh state of Khalistan. The General had left India illegally before the attack on the Golden Temple and had been smuggled into the US, as his passport had been impounded by the Indian authorities. He had entered through Mexico and had been taken to Yuba City in California where he met Iqbal Singh Sidhu, the largest peach farmer in the US, who initially bankrolled the General's US operation. Through the very well-connected Iqbal Singh, one of America's wealthiest Sikhs, the General had reached out to prominent Sikhs in every US State and Canadian province.

The following weekend, a massive rally was to be held at Madison Square Garden in New York City. Thousands of Sikhs from the US and Canada were to converge upon New York to formally launch the movement for an independent Khalistan.

While my heart lurched when Raja told me this, Rachpal, Harjinder and he were jubilant. The study group had been looking for an opportunity to do something. To express the rage they felt at the attack and channel it in a useful manner. The General was a godsend and here was their opportunity.

The study group met after the General had left. A couple of the older members expressed some anxiety. They did not know the General. He had literally appeared out of nowhere and seemed to be flush with funds. His rhetoric was impressive, but the path he proposed seemed dangerous and irrevocable. Every Sikh in the diaspora had deep ties with India. They had extended family there. Who knew what the consequences might be.

Then Harjinder had got up to speak. He had known the General for years and could vouch for him. In fact, he had been present when the General had become a Khalsa, in a ceremony that Bhindranwale himself had presided over. Harjinder mocked and berated the naysayers, offering examples of brave Sikhs who had again and again sacrificed themselves when their faith demanded it. 'They put their lives on the line!' he thundered. 'What do you have to lose? Nobody is going to take away your fancy mansions or your luxury cars! We have been offered a great opportunity to serve. How can we possibly step back?'

A vote was taken. The study group unanimously decided to back Major General Khuller and do everything possible to make the Madison Square Garden rally a success.

I barely saw Raja that entire week. He took two days off and spent every minute at the rally headquarters, which was a Sikh store owner's large house in Jackson Heights. Harjinder introduced Raja to the General who quickly took a liking to him and, in just a few days, much to my dismay, Raja became the General's right-hand man.

I had nothing against the General. In fact, he was one of the most courteous and affable men I had ever met. Raja would bring him home often and make biryani for him, which the General loved. While Raja cooked, the General would regale me with charming stories about life in the upper echelons of the Indian Army: stories of elaborate balls, bridge parties, polo matches and cricket that sounded very glamorous to someone brought up in a blue-collar home in Massachusetts. He talked proudly about his wife, who was a well-known philanthropist dedicated to social causes, and of his collection of Sikh military memorabilia, which he had started as a young second lieutenant after he was first commissioned. He showed me pictures of himself in full military regalia, with his wife, who looked very elegant in a sari, taken outside their lovely home in Chandigarh.

It did not seem very odd at the time that he didn't say much about the struggle that he had been sent to launch. After all, I was a young girl, and an American to boot, and perhaps he felt that I would find the topic uninteresting. I was intensely curious about his plans, particularly because they seemed likely to affect my husband. But whenever I tried to probe, he would deftly steer the conversation away to a more innocuous subject.

Raja, Rachpal and Harjinder, along with the rest of the study group, were fully immersed in the complex logistics of putting together the Madison Square Garden meeting. I found myself getting sucked in as well, as Raja's do-all assistant. On the day of the rally, I was given the task of making sure that the speakers were lined up backstage and ready to go, just before their slots came up. It was not an easy task because each speaker seemed to have a lot more to say than their slot allowed, but I did get a ringside view.

There were thousands in the audience, mostly men, but several women too. The women were dressed in saris or the tunics and loose pants that Punjabi women wear, with colourful scarves covering their hair. Some of the men were middle-aged and very well dressed. Many of them sported turbans. The most rambunctious section of the crowd was a group of young men, none of them in turbans. Most of them had closely cropped hair and a vaguely military bearing, and they cheered or booed speakers with great gusto.

The General was one of the first speakers. There was silence in the arena when he began to speak in a clipped accent that sounded vaguely British. Later, Raja told me that the General was not very comfortable making speeches in Punjabi. He had started by telling the gathering who he was and spoke at length about his distinguished military career. He had emphasized that he had been an Indian patriot his entire life and fought valiantly in multiple wars to defend his country. He had then voiced a litany of complaints at how poorly Sikh soldiers were treated in the Indian Army and indignantly talked about how senior Sikh officers had been mistreated during the Asiad. Raja explained to me later that he was talking about the security precautions taken during the last Asian Games held in Delhi, as a result of which several senior Sikh officers had been manhandled and treated insultingly by low-level police personnel in the neighbouring state of Haryana.

He had then moved on to a complex set of issues and demands that he introduced as the Anandpur Sahib Resolution, which I barely understood. Finally, he had talked about how he and several former Sikh military commanders had gravitated to Bhindranwale, driven by a sense of injury and hurt pride. The General was eloquent and persuasive, and the massive crowd had listened in rapt attention. His voice had begun to shake with emotion and he seemed to tear up when he got to Operation Blue Star and the attack on the Golden Temple. 'It was incomprehensible,' he said, 'that the Indian Army would brutally attack the most prominent place of Sikh worship.' The heart of our faith was what he called it. He lamented the loss of life and praised the valour of his old comrade, General Sahbegh Singh, who had perished in the battle at Bhindranwale's side.

'Sant [Bhindranwale] knew what was coming. That is why he commanded me to leave India and come to America. I am here to fulfil his dream. I am here to carry out his mission. I am here to lead the fight for Khalistan, an independent Sikh state. The time has come. Only in our own state will we, the Sikhs, experience the glow of freedom that is our birthright.'

The arena erupted in cheers, the loudest coming from the group of young men in the audience. When the cheers subsided, Iqbal Singh Sidhu took the podium. He was a burly, rustic-looking man with none of the polish of the General, but he seemed to command respect. He spoke at length in Punjabi and I barely understood a word of what he said. The cheers though were very loud when he sat down.

Speaker after speaker followed, most speaking in Punjabi and some in English. There were Sikh community leaders, as well as scientists and academics, all of whom expressed outrage at the attack and strong support for an independent nation for the Sikhs.

And then there came a speaker who seemed to set the stage on fire. I had had a good look at him as he had been standing by my side, waiting for his turn. I had been informed that he was from Vancouver. My order of speakers told me that his name was Ajmer Singh Bajwa. He was a somewhat portly man with a straggly beard, quite unlike most Sikhs I had encountered. He was dressed in flowing light-blue robes and had a golden sash across his chest, from which hung a long dagger. His turban too was very different from the peaked turbans that Raja, Rachpal, the General and Harjinder sported. It was round, white, very tall and circled by a metal band. His speech was very short, but it seemed to have electrified the crowd. For a moment it seemed that his words had stunned the crowd into silence, and I am sure I heard some whisperings and a few voices saying 'no, no', but then the crowd thundered, applauding and cheering. The hard-faced young men were on their feet and leading the arena in a chant of 'Khalistan' as the man in the tall turban left the stage.

Raja was not close by. He had been assigned the task of making sure that collection boxes were being passed around. I turned to Rachpal, who was backstage as well. 'What on earth did that man say?'

Rachpal looked at me, managing somehow to look jubilant and sheepish at the same time. 'He said that the Indian government had already killed fifty thousand Sikhs. He scoffed at those who suggest that the Hindus and the Sikhs are brothers. He said that we will not rest until we slaughter fifty thousand Hindus.'

The rest of the rally was a blur to me. What had Raja got us into?

Iqbal Singh Sidhu was elected the president of the World Sikh Congress and the General, its secretary.

I know that several resolutions were passed because I helped proofread them before they were sent for printing. The World Sikh Congress was established on that day. It was to have thirty members, ten each from the US, Canada and Britain, and was to be based in New York. A fund would be set up to defend 'all those Sikhs facing persecution in India' and a committee would be set up to track rights violations in India. Prominent Sikhs serving the Indian government were asked 'to disassociate themselves from that regime'. Sikhs in the diaspora were asked to boycott Indian government events and stop flying Air India.

The Indian government was asked to return control of Sikh religious places to Sikh organizations. All government-sponsored work to repair the Golden Temple was to stop as the Sikhs would do it themselves. The Indian government was asked to provide accurate statistics on those killed, wounded and arrested. Civil liberties in Punjab were to be restored and press restrictions were to be lifted.

None of this sounded unreasonable to me, but I was still reeling from Rachpal's translation of the very violent speech that had so roused the crowd. I decided to confront the General that evening, much to Raja's embarrassment.

The General was unflappable. 'Hot air, my daughter,' he said. 'Just a young fool, blowing steam. You need to understand the ethos of the Sikhs. We are a chivalrous people. Throughout our history we have protected the weak and the oppressed, and we have suffered for it. Our movement will never attack or harm the Hindus, or any other community for that matter. The notion would be anathema to any Sikh. I have served India my entire life and most of my friends are Hindus. My own son-in-law is a Hindu. Please do not be alarmed by the rantings of a lunatic. This is not who we are. We will be unyielding on justice, but we will never target anyone.'

My husband was in the thrall of this man and I desperately wanted to believe him. But the voice of the man in the tall turban still rang in my head. The disquieting response of the crowd would not let me sleep.

In the months that followed, the General moved to Washington, D.C. Lobbying Congress was to be an important component of the strategy. Harjinder had moved with him, and Raja, Rachpal and I would often drive down on weekends to see them. The General had acquired a very posh home in Potomac. When I asked Raja how he might possibly have the funds for that, my husband reacted sharply. 'He is committed to the cause, and he is its most visible symbol. Do you think his supporters will let him live in poverty? He has to entertain diplomats and congressmen and senators. Think of him like the head of a state in exile!'

It was after one of our trips to Potomac that Raja had dropped a bombshell. The World Sikh Congress was starting to get a lot of traction and the General was having difficulty keeping up with the constant demands for him to travel to Sikh population centres across the US and Canada. He needed a full-time assistant: well educated, well spoken, someone who would not spook the Sikh professionals, mostly doctors and academics who were the primary funding source for the World Sikh Congress. Raja was ecstatic at the General choosing him. He had already given his notice at Salomon.

I was livid and fought hard. We had a baby on the way. A mortgage to pay. We had agreed that I would look for work when the baby was ready for preschool. Raja had been well paid and we did not need a second salary. My poor husband was so dazzled by his cause, 'the movement' as he called it, that he had plunged us into uncertainty without a thought. I asked him what he would be paid and he sheepishly said, 'Nothing. I will be a volunteer. How can I possibly take precious funds from the movement for my personal use!'

I did what I had to do. The New York City school district had a shortage of teachers and I started looking for work as a substitute teacher. Raja started travelling constantly. Every weekend, he would drive to a different gurdwara, some hundreds of miles away, in our beat-up car. He would come back with shopping bags filled with cash, which he would count meticulously. The collections would be documented in a ledger and either Raja or Rachpal would run the money and records down to Potomac. I started getting substitute-teacher gigs and was soon making enough money for us to scrape by. The biggest expense was my medical care; we did not have health insurance any more. We lived very frugally. I bought groceries at the cheapest supermarket and we never ate out.

I now regret the hard time I gave Raja. I was always upset and cranky and ready to pick a fight. Of course, some of it was hormones, but a lot of it was frustration too. Just a few months ago, we had been a happy couple dreaming of a family and a home in the suburbs, with a big yard where our children would play. I had not asked for any of this. Raja was obviously very happy doing what he was doing, but I could not be happy for him. The General became the symbol of everything that was wrong with our lives and I resented him with all my heart. I refused to go to Potomac with Raja on his very frequent trips and made it very clear that the General was not welcome in our home any more. Raja, if anything, had become more attentive and solicitous towards me. He could see how much his transformation had affected me and tried to make it up to me, never reacting when I lashed out at him. I bitterly regret never letting him know that I could see how much he loved me and that it touched me to the point of breaking my heart. I was just too angry.

I was in my eighth month when Raja went away on a two-week-long trip. He was travelling with the General, making a huge push to raise funds for the movement in California and Vancouver, both home to very large and relatively affluent Sikh populations. When he returned, I was shocked to see that his turban was missing, as was his beard. For just a second, it looked like my old Raja was back, but his somewhat sheepish smile told a different story. 'I have been given a mission,' he said. My heart sank.

The General had been very successful in his fundraising efforts and a large war chest had been raised, which needed to be put to work. The movement needed guns. It needed money for bribes. The cash that had been collected was useless sitting in the US. Someone had to take it to the front lines, and that someone was Raja! I asked him if he was mad. Did he not care that he was going to be a father in less than a month? How could he take such a risk? Trying to smuggle a hundred thousand dollars in cash into India was madness. The government was very aware of the events in New York and the activities of the World Sikh Congress. We had heard rumours that the Indian government had watch lists, and for all we knew Raja was already on their radar.

Raja had clearly been coached well but all his attempts to reassure me failed miserably. 'See, this is why I cut off my hair again and shaved my beard. I still have my Salomon Brothers business cards. I have the perfect cover! I will present myself as an analyst travelling to evaluate investment opportunities. The General is going to get me several invitation letters from large companies. The money weighs just seventeen pounds and has been sown into the lining of my suitcase. Look, it is undetectable! The General is having me picked up at the Delhi airport in an army jeep, which will take me to Chandigarh. In just one day, I will be done with my mission. I am not even going to see my parents. That will have to wait until my hair and beard have grown back. I will visit the Golden Temple and then go to Anandpur Sahib to be taken back into the Khalsa fold. You won't even know I'm gone! I will be back in a week. There is nothing to worry about. Our due date is still four weeks away, and remember what your doctor said? The first baby never comes early.'

I desperately wanted to believe him, but I could not get rid of the sinking feeling in the pit of my stomach. He looked so dashing in his navy blue suit and favourite red tie when I dropped him off at JFK. It's just a week, I told myself unconvincingly as he disappeared into the throng of passengers and visitors streaming into the airport.

He called me after he landed in Delhi. He told me that his uncle Tarsem Singh was feeling much better, which was our code for his having got through customs safely. My heart was still in my mouth, but I began to breathe a bit easier. I called Rachpal and told him that Raja had made it to Delhi. Raja called again in eight hours. He had brought his uncle Tarsem Singh to Chandigarh and had dropped him off at his home in Sector 10. I finally breathed a sigh of relief. Raja had delivered the money and was safe. I called Rachpal again.

The phone rang in a few minutes. It was the General, sounding jubilant. 'You were worried about nothing, my daughter. The plan was flawless, and before you know it, Raja will be back. You should be so proud of him. Your husband is my bravest soldier! He did not take even a second to think before volunteering for the mission. You have no idea what an impact this will have on the movement. Your husband is a hero!'

I don't quite remember what I said in response. For the first time in months, it seemed, I slept well.

I don't know how I got through the next five days. Raja had planned to visit many gurdwaras and historical Sikh sites before returning to Delhi. I knew his schedule was going to be hectic. I was disappointed when he didn't call but not unduly worried. He hadn't been back in years and I knew how excited he was, particularly about being initiated back as an Amritdhari in Anandpur Sahib, where he had told me the Khalsa had been born hundreds of years ago.

I drove to JFK and decided to park. I wanted to see my husband the second he stepped into the arrivals hall. The display at arrivals showed that his flight had arrived. Soon, there was a steady procession of people clad in Indian clothes pushing heavily laden luggage carts. I did not start to get worried until the trickle of Indian passengers had almost dried up. Maybe his luggage got lost.

Maybe he was being questioned at immigration. But there was no reason for him to be stopped. He was a US resident. He had got his green card within months of our getting married.

After waiting for more than an hour, my anxiety growing, I went upstairs to the Air India counter. The agent at the counter, a bright-eyed young girl, was very polite but not helpful. 'I cannot give out passenger information, Madam,' was her first response. When I insisted that I needed to know if my husband had made it on the Air India flight, she called her supervisor. I was asked if my husband and I had the same surname. We did not. I still used my maiden name. The supervisor was sympathetic but would not let me know if Raja had boarded the flight.

I was worried but hadn't panicked yet. I was sure he was on the flight. If he wasn't, surely he would have called me from Delhi. Raja knew what a worrywart I was. He must have been detained because of some mix-up at immigration or customs, I tried to tell myself, reassuring myself that he would be here soon. Another forty-five minutes passed and there was still no sign of Raja. Completely at a loss, I wandered in the arrivals area, wondering if I should call my parents. My eyes fell upon a kindly looking woman, probably close to my mother's age, wearing an official badge. She had just emerged from the arrivals gate. It turned out that she was an airport security supervisor.

When I explained the situation to her, she went back inside to check if Raja had been detained. It was the longest fifteen minutes of my life. When she returned, the expression on her face made my heart lurch. 'I checked with both immigration and customs and was told that they are not holding back any passengers who came in on the Delhi Air India flight. I then had the Air India folks check the passenger manifest. Rajinder Singh Duggal was listed as a passenger on the flight, but he never checked in. He was tagged a no-show.'

I really don't have a clear recollection of the weeks that followed. I was on the verge of delivering, and I was flat broke.

The first thing I did when I got home was to call Rachpal who shut me up when I mentioned that Raja had not made it. 'Not on the phone,' he said. Within an hour, he was at my door. Raja had delivered the money to his contact in Chandigarh and then boarded a bus for Amritsar to visit the Golden Temple. That was all that Rachpal had been able to find out. I told him that I wanted to speak to the General, but Rachpal told me that he was in Canada on a fundraising trip. He also warned me that the World Sikh Congress was under scrutiny and that in all likelihood all our phones were tapped. Under no circumstance was I to ever discuss any of this on the phone. He promised to take me to Potomac to see the General in person when he returned from Canada.

I remember getting a stack of quarters and calling my parents from a payphone. I had told them nothing and I never really called often. My mother sounded worried and asked if there were complications with the baby. I started sobbing.

The next morning, my mom and dad were in Brooklyn. My parents are simple people. Their lives until then had been very predictable and contained. All this talk of Khalistan and violent movements and secret missions must have shocked them, but I honestly don't remember how they reacted. My dad went to a payphone to call his brother, my uncle, who is an attorney. He came back looking even more worried. Raja had broken several laws by smuggling such a large amount of money into India. We would have to tread very lightly.

Perhaps he went home, my mom mused. The thought had occurred to me as well. I knew that Raja's parents would never accept me. I knew how attached he had been to his family and how much the estrangement bothered him. It was entirely possible that he had gone home. Perhaps his mother had threatened to kill herself. Perhaps they had convinced him never to return to the US. Perhaps they were planning to get him married to a Sikh girl. Perhaps he had abandoned me and our unborn child. I started to cry.

My dad went to the bodega at the end of our block and brought back a paper bag filled with quarters. My hands shook as I dialled the unfamiliar international number and put in more quarters than I could ever imagine the payphone could take. How we remember these details! I can still hear the clink of the quarters before the call connected. An unfamiliar voice said hello. Neither of Raja's parents spoke very good English and someone, most likely his brother Narinder, was summoned. He had a thick accent, but he seemed to understand me. There was an awkward silence when I introduced myself as Raja's wife. I heard him say something in Punjabi, presumably to his parents. 'Hello,' he said again, very awkwardly. 'Myself Narinder. Raja Phaji's brother.'

'Is Raja there?' I asked.

'Raja?' He sounded incredulous. 'But Raja Phaji is in Amair-ka.'

'Yes, he was, but he went to India on a short visit. He was in Punjab. Amritsar and Anandpur Sahib. Did he come home to Delhi?'

Once again, I could hear Narinder talking to his parents in Punjabi. 'He did not come home, ji. We have not seen him since the day he left for Amair-ka.' The coins ran out at that point and a voice prompted me for more. I had plenty of coins but didn't want to talk to Narinder any more. My knees were shaking and, for the first time, I experienced terror. I was pretty sure Narinder had not been lying. Where was my husband?

My dad called my uncle again, who had made several calls to an attorney he knew at the State Department. Even though Raja had a green card, he was still an Indian citizen and the State Department really could not do much. We were asked to call the office of the Overseas Citizens Services in Washington, D.C. I was, of course, not going to tell them anything about Raja's connection to the World Sikh Congress. I finally managed to get through to them after hours of trying. They were not helpful at all. The best they could do was to get me an appointment at the Indian consulate in the city.

We were led into a poky, airless room at the end of a long corridor in the consulate. After we had waited for more than an hour, two men abruptly entered and sat down, without a word of apology for keeping us waiting. One of them was middle-aged and kindly looking, sweating in his ill-fitting suit, with buttons that strained against his large belly. His hard-faced younger companion had close-cropped hair and looked vaguely familiar. Later, I realized that he looked somewhat like the men in the large group that I had seen chanting vociferously during the Madison Square Garden rally. The middle-aged man introduced himself as Vice Consul Sharma. His companion was not introduced.

Vice Consul Sharma handed me a form to fill, in which I had to enter Raja's details, our contact information and the circumstances of his disappearance. I also had to provide a notarized copy of our marriage certificate, which was then attached to the form. After I explained that my husband had gone on a trip to India to visit Sikh religious places and not returned, their interest seemed to perk up. The younger man left with the form and did not come back for half an hour or so. When he returned, he spoke rapidly in an unfamiliar language, which I assumed was Hindi. I caught a few words and my heart began to pound. I was pretty sure he had mentioned the World Sikh Congress. Vice Consul Sharma listened carefully and then looked at me, tight-lipped.

'Madam,' Vice Consul Sharma said gravely, 'your husband's name is on a watch list. He has been consorting with some very evil people who are trying to do India harm. We will wire Delhi, but so far there is no information about his whereabouts. If we hear anything, we will inform you, of course, but please be advised that as an Indian national, he can be arrested if he has engaged in any antinational activities. Are you aware of any such activities, Madam? Do you know why he went to India?'

'Of course not,' I snapped. 'He is an investment banker. He had gone back to visit Sikh temples in Punjab. He wanted to become a full-fledged Sikh again, to make his parents happy.' My mom told me later that she was very impressed with my performance, but I was convinced that the men saw through me. My husband was in trouble. I had nodded in a daze when Vice Consul Sharma had asked if I would answer some of his colleague's questions.

Puri, the colleague, who was probably close to Raja's age, spoke impeccable English. I realized that he sounded similar to the General. He was not unkind, but very businesslike. He asked me if Raja was active in the movement for Khalistan. I looked at him as if I had not understood and asked him what that was. He looked at me with the hint of a condescending smile that infuriated me. He opened a thick folder that he had brought with him and placed it before me. 'Do you recognize any of these photographs?'

I leafed through the photographs, many of them grainy. Most of the faces were unfamiliar, but I was not surprised to see photos of several of the speakers from the Madison Square Garden event. His face hardened when I kept shaking my head. 'Are you sure?'

'Yes, I am absolutely sure that I have never seen these men before.'

'These are terrorists. Hell bent on harming India and killing innocent people. You need to know that.'

I looked at him impassively, starting to get angry.

'Are you a Khalistani yourself? Do you support these violent criminals? I have to warn you. It could get you into a lot of trouble.'

'I'm a US citizen, asshole,' I muttered, as I stormed out of the room, my parents following hastily.

I decided to call Rachpal from a payphone, but there was no answer. I asked my dad to drive us to Briarcliff Manor. I was crying the entire time as we left the city behind and drove into the manicured towns of Westchester County. A late-model Mercedes-Benz was parked in Rachpal's driveway, as was his MGB convertible. They were home! Why were they not picking up the phone? Rachpal's mother, Mrs Brar, greeted us when we rang the doorbell. Today she was elegantly dressed, not in Indian clothes but in a trendy blazer and slacks. She welcomed us in as I introduced my parents and bustled to bring us hot Indian tea and cookies, despite our insisting that it was unnecessary.

'Raja is missing,' I said, 'and I need to talk to Rachpal. He really is the one who got him into this mess.' The words tumbled out before I could stop them and I saw Mrs Brar's lips tightening.

'I am very sorry to hear that, my dear, but what could Rachpal possibly have to do with all this? You are welcome to see him, of course, but he is not home today. He is away with his study group, preparing for his boards.'

I asked her to make sure that Rachpal called me the minute he returned. As we walked to our car, I turned back to look at the Brars' magnificent mansion. I could have sworn that I saw Rachpal looking at us from an upstairs window. In a second, he had ducked out of sight.

The phone rang that night. It was Narinder. Raja's parents were as worried as I was. I could not tell Narinder anything about the General, or the World Sikh Congress, or Rachpal, or our visit to the Indian consulate. In despair, I started crying. Narinder mumbled unconvincingly that everything would be fine and then hung up. I had been desperately hoping that Raja would somehow show up at his parents' home in Delhi. The only person who knew anything about Raja's trip was the General. I had tried to call him several times from a payphone, but nobody had picked up.

My dad offered to drive us to D.C., and since none of us could sleep, we left at 5 a.m. I was relieved to see the General's Cadillac parked in the driveway. I rang the doorbell, my hands trembling and my parents behind me. The General opened the door, resplendent in a Chinese silk dressing gown that he wore over expensive-looking pyjamas. Instead of his customary peaked turban, he wore something that looked like a bandana. His beard was encased in a black strip of cloth, like the one Raja used to groom his beard. The General seemed as affable as ever and greeted me warmly, even effusively. 'Come in, daughter. Come in. As you can see, I am not quite ready to receive guests yet, but you are like family.' He shook hands vigorously with my parents and led us into his very well-appointed living room.

He seemed genuinely surprised when he learned that Raja had not returned. Had Rachpal not told him? The General sounded reassuring. 'I am sure nothing is wrong, my dear. If anything had happened I would have heard. I know he got to Chandigarh safely and I know that he delivered the package. Your husband has already struck a huge blow for human rights and freedom, daughter! You should be very proud. And I know he got on the bus to Amritsar because my nephew drove him to the bus stand.'

'But where is he then?' I asked, refusing to be mollified by his smooth assurances. Why did he miss his flight? Why did he not go to his parents' home? Why has he not called? He must know that I am beside myself with worry. We have a baby on the way. He was supposed to be back well before my due date.'

And then everything poured out of me. 'Ever since you arrived, my husband has changed. Your movement is more important to him now than his family. He changed his appearance. He took a huge risk by smuggling money for your movement into India. He put himself in harm's way. He quit his job. We have no money. I can't even pay this month's rent. We have no health insurance and the baby is coming soon. Where is he? Why is he doing this?'

The General looked at me sympathetically. 'I don't have those answers, my daughter, but rest assured I will get them for you. In the meantime, this should help take care of your immediate needs. He went up to a writing desk and came back with a wad of hundred-dollar bills. Please take this, my daughter, while I try to find out what is going on. The movement will always take care of its soldiers,' he announced grandly, almost seeming to pause for applause.

I wanted to fling the money at his face, but I am ashamed to admit I didn't. We had less than two hundred dollars in our bank account. I wrote down my telephone number, as well as my parents' in Sudbury, and handed it to the General before we left.

I have no recollection of how I got through the next few weeks. My parents stayed on with me in Brooklyn, sick with worry. I spent entire days calling Rachpal's number, then the General's and then Harjinder's over and over again. Rachpal was never at home and the other two phone numbers just kept ringing. I went back to the Indian consulate several times but was turned away. The vice consul was never available. I left messages for the Overseas Citizens Services every day, but they went unanswered. Finally, I got a call back from a very rude woman who told me to stop calling. My husband was not a US citizen and they could do nothing. I called Raja's home in Delhi every other day, hoping against hope that there would be news. There was nothing.

When my parents suggested that I return to Massachusetts with them, I resisted. A part of me still believed he would be back. I had never been superstitious, but I started believing that if I gave up and left Brooklyn, it would somehow make his return even less likely. 'How would he feel, Mom? If he came back and found the apartment locked and me gone?'

But my due date was approaching and my mother had to go back to work. She had used up all her vacation and could not stay on any longer. I went back with them. Two weeks later, Liv was born. We had resisted finding out whether we were going to have a boy or a girl. Raja had been sure that it would be a boy. I was oddly happy that it was a girl. For some reason, it seemed that I would have felt Raja's absence even more acutely if it had been a boy.

My baby gave me no joy. She was a constant reminder of how my life, which had seemed perfect just months ago, had turned into this surreal nightmare. As the weeks passed, resignation started to set in. When my dad suggested that he go to Brooklyn to clear out the apartment and terminate the lease, I simply nodded.

Three months later, the searing pain turned into something that was hard to describe. I was depressed, of course, but I clearly remember how angry I was. Sikhs were pretty rare in Boston then, but the mere sight of one was enough to bring my rage bubbling to the surface. I would curse Rachpal and the General and the World Sikh Congress. I did not care about the attack on the Golden Temple. I had no sympathy for the Khalistan movement. I hated them all. They had robbed me. My poor, gentle father was aghast and tried to reason with me. My mom asked him to leave me alone.

I was a single mother with a child to raise. My parents, without any hesitation, dipped into their savings. Breaking my lease had been expensive. I needed childcare so that I could look for a job. Formula. Diapers. Who would have thought that having a baby would be so expensive? Of course, none of this would have been a problem had Raja not disappeared, I would keep thinking and the paroxysms of rage would continue.

Finally, I got a job, teaching third grade in a school in the neighbouring town, and started to put my life back together again. Liv was changing every day it seemed and pretty soon became the centre of my existence, much to the relief of my parents. I had stopped ranting and raving, but still seethed inside. The General had not called once in the six months that had passed since our conversation. One weekend, I left Liv with my mom and got into my car. I was going to Potomac. I told my parents that I was going to spend the weekend in New York, visiting friends.

There was a 'for sale' sign outside the General's home.

I drove straight to Briarcliff Manor. Rachpal would have some answers. I was not going to let him blow me off this time. At least he would know where the General was. The mansion looked as gorgeous as I remembered it. I was greeted by a woman in her mid-thirties, who was planting flowers in the front in muddy jeans and boots. Her smile was friendly and questioning. 'Don't the Brars live here any more?' I found myself asking. 'Oh, the former owners? That nice Indian couple? They moved back to Texas.'

I don't remember when I gave up, but I did. Liv was my life now. My poor, fatherless daughter. We lived with my parents for five years. I had saved enough money by then for the down payment on a house in Maynard, where I now had a permanent job teaching elementary schoolchildren. Maybe I was trying to compensate for Raja's absence, but I filled Liv's life with everything that I could possibly think of. She was a super bright and happy child. She was never very athletic, but she did well at school and had many friends. Singing and acting were her passion, and I was convinced that she was going to pursue that as her career, right from when she was in middle school.

I really wanted her to go to Northeastern, but it turned out that my daughter was smarter than I had ever been. She got an almost-perfect score on the SATs, and when she got a full scholarship at Amherst College, going there was pretty much a no-brainer. I would have preferred to have her closer to home, but Amherst was not that far and I could always drive up to see her.

Of course, I still thought about Raja. I had resolutely resisted every attempt by my parents and friends to get me to 'meet' someone else. There were times when I felt intensely lonely but perhaps, deep inside, I still nurtured a hope that my husband was out there somewhere. Liv had settled in well at Amherst and, after a long time, I had started to feel that my life had returned to some form of normal. And now she had turned it upside down again! I had tried so hard to shelter my daughter from my pain and my rage, and now she wanted to intern with a Sikh organization that was seeking justice for 1984! I went to my mother's home in the evening and cried after a very long time.

Kids know how to get their way and Liv was an only child. Very ill at ease, I put her on a plane to San Francisco. One of my cousins lived in Sunnyvale and she had very graciously offered to put Liv up for the ten weeks that she was going to spend interning with her human rights organization. We talked every day on the phone. On the one hand I was happy that she seemed very engaged and was clearly enjoying her work. But why could she not have found something else to do in the summer!

We were driving up to Amherst again. The fall semester was about to begin. 'Oh, by the way, Mom, I'm like seeing Nihal.' Of course, she was! My hands gripped the steering wheel tighter, but I did not say anything. Later that evening, I lay on Liv's bed in her room, trying to make sense of what I was feeling. Why was I panicking? Liv was just dating a Sikh boy. She was not about to get married to him. Even if she did, there was no Khalistan movement now for him to get involved in. There was no reason for him to vanish like Raja had. What had happened to me was inexplicable, but it had been an accident of fate. It was ridiculous to imagine that my daughter would somehow relive my experience. I knew it was stupid of me to feel so anxious, but I could not help it.

My eyes were drawn to Liv's desk. She had always been an organized kid, and her desk was tidy. There was a stack of papers that she had probably brought back from California. In the middle of the desk sat a thick paperback. It seemed to be somewhat shabbily put together. The cover was not particularly well designed. The graphic, which looked like a map with an overlay of photographs, looked fuzzy and unattractive. The white spine of the book was starting to fall apart. On it was printed the title of the book in black ink. *Reduced to Ashes*. The subtitle was 'Insurgency and Human Rights in Punjab'.

So this was the book that had started Liv's journey, the source of my intense discomfort. I remember that somewhat oddly; it made me think of the kundalini Yoga class that started mine. I really did not want to read it, but I still picked it up.

It was at 3 a.m. that I realized I had been reading for several hours. The book, which seemed to be deeply researched, was about the disappearance of Jaswant Singh Khalra, a human rights activist from Punjab. Khalra had spent years meticulously documenting the cremations of young Sikh men who had been killed by the security forces in Punjab because of their alleged association with the Khalistan movement. Most of them seemed to have died under mysterious circumstances in what were described as 'encounters' with the police.

I had raced through the early sections that talked about Khalra and his disappearance, and then presented a short, but very cogent, account of the history of the Sikhs in modern India and the convoluted politics that led to the attack on the Golden Temple in 1984. The description of the attack immediately transported me back to the Richmond Hill gurdwara where Raja and I had heard Rachpal speak for the first time. In the years that had passed, I had often wondered if Rachpal had been telling the truth when he had inflamed the Sikhs of New York with the graphic descriptions of the attack. It was all in there.

I was also aware of the assassination of the then Indian prime minister Indira Gandhi by her Sikh bodyguards, several months after the attack. I had also read about the massacre of thousands of Sikhs in Delhi and other cities in retaliation. In Raja's circle, there had been much jubilation at the prime minister's assassination, which had quickly turned to dismay as terrible stories of the pogrom that followed filtered in. By then, I had already become hostile towards the General and the movement, and had started to wonder if the tales of the carnage in Delhi had been embellished to aid in the movement's recruitment efforts. But it was all there in the book, meticulously researched and presented with a complete lack of rhetoric and backed up by references.

By then my head was reeling, but I could not stop reading.

The fourth section of the book was like a punch in the gut. On some of the pages were grainy black-and-white pictures of young Sikh men. Many of them had the long, flowing beards that declared that they had been initiated into the Khalsa like my Raja had been briefly. Some had no turbans and others sported turbans but trimmed beards. Some looked defiantly at the camera while others looked meek and even frightened. The book in my hands shook as I read about one of the youngest men whose case was documented. He was really a boy, only eighteen, wearing a turban with not even the hint of a beard or a moustache.

The case histories were eerily similar. Men who had been brought in for questioning by the police, suspected of supporting the movement. Men who were interrogated and then simply disappeared. Men who had been identified as having been killed in 'police encounters', a euphemism for staged executions. The eighteen-year-old, a year younger than my Liv, was a Khalsa who according to the report had no political affiliations at all. His name was Sawinder Singh and he was a tailor's apprentice. He and his companion had been gunned down by the police while they were cycling across a bridge at the end of which was a police outpost. Two days later, a prominent Punjabi newspaper had reported that two 'unidentified militants' had been killed in an encounter.

There were women as well. A twenty-four-year-old girl named Kamaljit Kaur, who had been sleeping on her roof, which I understood people often did in India to escape the summer heat, was accidentally shot dead by the police during a raid in the neighbourhood. Her body was surreptitiously taken to a cremation ground attached to a prominent temple in Amritsar and cremated. Three newspapers reported that she had been killed in a police encounter, suggesting that she had been a terrorist!

The short case histories had poignant details. They mentioned the 'informants', presumably the family members who had talked to the investigative team that had written the book and told them about their loved ones who had disappeared. Fathers, mothers, wives, brothers and sisters whose loved ones had been snatched away and had often vanished without a trace.

Just like my Raja had.

It was six in the morning. I hadn't even realized that I had been crying. For the first time in nineteen years, I felt something other than anger. I was not alone. Thousands of miles away, there were many other women who, perhaps like me, were waiting like I had been. Still waiting for their Rajas to return.

I called in sick and slept through the day.

I did not tell Liv about any of this. We talked about other things when she called. She had a heavy workload this semester and hated some of her professors. She was spending most weekends with Nihal, which didn't bother me as much as it used to. When she announced that she was going back to California during her winter break to work with Ensaaf again, I didn't try to discourage her.

Several weeks after I had read the book, I decided to go to the Milford gurdwara. I have no idea why I decided to do so. I felt a very familiar sense of unease as I took off my shoes and tied a scarf around my chin. The gurdwara was small. Much smaller than the Richmond Hill gurdwara where Raja's transformation had begun. I went inside and sat in the back of the women's section. A group of young girls were singing and a really tiny boy accompanied them on the drums. I was charmed and my sense of unease started to dissipate.

I started to come back regularly. I never really talked to anyone, but the people were very kind. Nobody asked why a white woman was in their midst every Sunday. When I would go to the basement for breakfast, I would be charmed by the little children, scurrying to their Sunday school classes, lugging impossibly large backpacks. I really looked forward to hearing the young girls sing, but my joy was always tempered with a tiny bit of guilt. Why had I stolen all this from Liv?

On the Sundays that I was unable to go, I would miss the gurdwara tremendously. With some trepidation, I went to the gurdwara's kitchen one morning, where a flock of chattering women were making rotis for the midday communal meal, the langar, which was served at the conclusion of the service. I was greeted with shy smiles and a couple of the women made room for me. In a couple of months, I was making rotis like a pro. Raja would have been so proud.

Something had changed, but I couldn't quite figure out what it was. And then I realized what it was. I did not miss Raja any less, but my anger was gone.

One Sunday at the Milford gurdwara, I was sitting upstairs, lost in my thoughts and not quite paying attention to the music. From the corner of my eye, I saw a couple enter the sanctuary, two children in tow. They caught my eye because I had never seen them there before and also because the woman was white. She looked a few years younger than me and was dressed in a beautiful Indian outfit. The man, tall and lanky, and dressed in an expensive-looking suit, looked vaguely familiar. After the family had gone up to the scripture to pay their respects, they turned. With a shock, I realized that it was Rachpal.

I did not stay until the end of the service that day. I had wanted to vent my rage and frustration at Rachpal, the General, Harjinder and everyone else involved with the movement for years. But now that Rachpal was sitting twenty feet away, I wasn't quite sure if I wanted to talk to him.

I didn't go back for several weeks. I missed my Sunday routine intensely, but I did not want to run into Rachpal again. After years, I had found some measure of peace, but I still felt the familiar rage building inside me. Rachpal was the one who had drawn Raja into the movement. Who knew what terrible things my Raja had had to suffer and here was Rachpal with his fine-looking family, thriving. How was any of this fair? And I had not forgotten how heartless Rachpal had been when Raja vanished. Raja had been his friend. His comrade in arms. Why had Rachpal been such an asshole!

'Hello, Rachpal. It's been a while.' After all the agonizing, it was all I could bring myself to say when I saw him with his family in the foyer of the gurdwara. Rachpal looked at me carefully and his face turned ashen. 'Meg?' His wife looked at her husband and then at me with an uneasy smile. Rachpal awkwardly put his arms around me and I burst into tears.

Rachpal and Lauren had just moved to Boston from Texas. She was a doctor as well and they had both accepted positions at UMass Memorial in Worcester. Rachpal was a cardiac surgeon and Lauren an oncologist. They had two children, a boy and a girl, and they had just moved to a new home in Southborough, not too far from Milford.

I wanted to be resentful, but I could not. When they invited me to their house-warming event, I decided to go. It was a religious service on a Saturday and it seemed that the entire Milford gurdwara was there. I was starting to like Lauren a lot. We had chatted several times at the gurdwara and she had joined our roti-making gang with her daughter, Jess, who was a lovely child.

I stayed on to help Lauren after all the guests had left. We were drinking coffee in her designer kitchen when Rachpal returned. The Sikh minstrels who had sung at the event were from the Medford gurdwara, close to Boston. Rachpal had gone to drop them off.

'Can we talk, Meg?' he asked when he saw that I was still there. Lauren excused herself saying that the kids needed supplies for a school art project, and that they needed to go to the Target in the next town.

'I was just a kid, Meg. And I was scared. Raja's disappearance freaked me out as much as it did you. I had no answers. I asked the General. Over and over. But he had nothing to say. Raja delivered the money. That much I know. But what happened to him after will always remain a mystery. The General suggested that Raja had gone underground. That he probably wanted to be directly involved in the movement. That he probably went to Pakistan for arms training. I didn't believe him for one minute. Raja and I talked constantly. We made plans. He never once said anything about picking up a gun. And besides later we learned that everything the General was telling us was bullshit.'

I looked at Rachpal uncomprehendingly.

'He was an agent of the Indian government, Meg. I knew something was off, even before Raja went to India. We had driven down to Potomac one weekend to bring him that week's collection from New York. Raja was with me. When we got to his house, we didn't ring the bell. We had a key to a side entrance, which we used because he would often not be home when we went to D.C. with the week's collection. When we walked into his living room, he was listening to classical music and drinking Scotch! He must have seen how freaked out we were. "What's the matter, lads?" he had asked us coolly. "Have a drink."

'When I managed to blurt out that the Khalsas who had taken amrit and been initiated were forbidden to drink, he looked genuinely puzzled. This was a man who claimed that he had been personally initiated by Bhindranwale! "Is that so, lads?" he asked. "Sant Bhindranwale didn't mention this to me during my initiation!" I told him that if any of the Amritdhari Singhs saw this, he would be lynched. "Ah!" the General said. "Clearly, I need to be more careful."

'We were shocked. Raja actually thought it was funny. "These old soldiers!" he said. "They love their booze so much. Just let it go, Rachpal. Don't tell anyone. So what if he drinks in secret? He is doing good work and the movement needs him." Now I wish I had not listened to Raja. Maybe things would have turned out differently.

'Shocking as this was, it actually got much worse. You probably don't know this, but we were raising serious money. The World Sikh Congress had set up chapters in every state. People were mad and wanted to do something. The money just kept pouring in. The General got outed when he went on a fundraising trip to Ohio. This was a couple of months after Raja vanished. He met with a professor, who was the key organizer in Ohio, and asked him for the names and addresses of all the Ohio donors. Now that was super suspicious. Why on earth would he care who had donated! The professor stalled him, but called the World Sikh Congress organizers in other states. It turned out that he had been asking for donor lists everywhere!

'It all unravelled in a few months. My dad is very well-connected with the Indian embassy. One of his college buddies, a senior diplomat, tipped him off that the Indian government had detailed lists of everyone in the US and Canada who was making large contributions to the movement. Their names had been put on a terror watch list, and if they ever went to India, they would be arrested. The government was also compiling lists of their family members who were still in India to use as leverage.

'So my dad got a bunch of the greybeards together, including the professor from Ohio, and they went down to Potomac to confront the General. Guess what! He had vanished without a trace. The money was gone. The complete truth came out much later. The General had been a plant all along. He had been tasked with infiltrating the movement even before the attack on the Golden Temple. The Indian government had been paranoid about overseas Sikhs and their support for Khalistan. The General's mission was to trap as many Khalistan supporters as he could and discredit the American and Canadian Sikhs as supporters of terrorism. And he did it! Brilliantly! Oh, and by the way, Harjinder, who vouched for him? He disappeared too, around the same time. It turns out that he was a major in the Indian Army. He had been assigned to RAW [Research and Analysis Wing], their dirty tricks division, and sent to the US to assist the General.'

'But this is impossible, Rachpal! You and I were both at Madison Square Garden. We heard him speak. He literally launched the World Sikh Congress and the Khalistan movement. How could he be an Indian agent? Was the entire movement just bullshit then?'

'We will never know, Meg. A lot of us were genuinely hurt after the Golden Temple was attacked. My dad had always laughed at the Khalistan movement until then. There had been a few kooky Sikhs in the diaspora who had fashioned Khalistan passports and currency. My dad used to find that hilarious, but that was before 1984. When it became apparent that the Sikhs could be targeted with impunity in India, his thoughts changed. The pogroms in November only confirmed our misgivings. I guess we were easy targets for recruitment. There we many like us who were seething and wanted to respond in some manner. When the General showed up and launched the movement, we suddenly found a sense of purpose. But I can tell you that after the General was exposed, most of us ran for our lives. We had no clue what we had got ourselves into. There were rumours that the lists of donors had been shared with the US and Canadian governments, and that we were being put on terror watch lists at home as well. It was scary as hell. That's why my dad decided that we would move back to Texas and lay low. We cut ties with everyone who had even remotely been involved with the General. Thankfully, we were left alone.'

'And my Raja? Was his name was on a watch list too?'

Rachpal looked at me. 'Yes, Meg. All our names were. We were the General's foot soldiers. We recruited for him. We raised money for him. Our names must have been at the top! Why do you think Raja was not stopped at the airport? They knew exactly who he was and what he was carrying. A hundred thousand dollars in India in those days was a lot of money. I am sure it didn't make it to the movement! Raja was a dupe. We were all dupes. Nobody knows where the money went, but once it was delivered, Raja was probably a loose end.'

Silent tears were running down my cheeks. Swimming before my eyes were the fuzzy black-and-white photographs from the book. Raja's image belongs in there too, I remember thinking. I felt a sudden rush of love for all the women in Punjab who had been carrying those images in their heads for years.

Liv needs to know, I said to myself, as I left Rachpal's house.

The Curfew

It has been thirty-five years, but the sting of the slap is still fresh on my face.

I had just returned to our home, on the outskirts of Saharanpur, after the inquiry. I had forgotten how small and shabby the house I had grown up in was. Five years ago, the son of an almost-illiterate shopkeeper had left this house to enter the lofty portals of the Lal Bahadur Shastri National Academy of Administration in nearby Mussoorie. There were a few others like me at the academy, who wore cheap polyester pants and plastic sandals, and were not truly comfortable conversing in English, but I was different from them. I was never intimidated by the boys who had attended the Doon School or La Martiniere, who wore Levi's jeans and Nike shoes and played squash in the evenings when I would be discussing politics with the locals over chai and samosas at the little tea stall just outside the campus.

My mother had been the guiding force in my life ever since my father had passed away. Our little fabric shop in the heart of the *fuara*, or fountain, in Saharanpur, steeped in the foul stench of the nearby *ganda nala* that carried the city's sewage, was jointly owned with my uncles. It had been started by my grandfather and oldest uncle after they staggered into Saharanpur in 1947, fleeing the bloodletting in Lahore, where they had owned a flourishing business. My father, who had always been a timid man, had worshipped his brothers, and during his lifetime had never dared to ask them for anything, beyond what he got each week for the upkeep of our household. The shop itself was successful and probably worth a lot of money because of its location and the amount of business it generated, but there was no prospect of my mother ever getting a fair share. My uncles were not unkind, but with my father gone, the weekly allowance did start to shrink.

I do not know how my mother managed to make ends meet, but she did. She even managed to send me to Pinewood School, where all the rich people of Saharanpur sent their children, when I entered the eleventh grade. I was unhappy to leave my friends behind when I was pulled out of the government-run school that I had attended since first grade, but I was an obedient son and knew that it would bring me a step closer to making my mother's dream come true. Her son was to be an officer in the elite Indian Administrative Services (IAS). I was probably four or five when she had informed me that this would be my destiny. Partition had robbed my father of an education, as the family struggled to survive, but she was adamant that her sons would be educated at the schools and colleges that the children of the elite attended.

After Pinewood, I got admission in Hindu College in Delhi. We had no family in the capital and I was sick with worry about my living expenses, but once again my mother somehow managed to find the money. Wrapped up in my academic cocoon in Delhi, I didn't comprehend the extent of my mother's sacrifices. She had been diagnosed with cancer while I was still at Pinewood, but she hid it from both me and my brother. Our neighbour, who had been accompanying her during her visits to the government hospital, inadvertently let the cat out of the bag one day, when my brother was at her house. That's how I found out. I am ashamed to say that while I was concerned, I was so consumed by my studies that my worries about her illness soon retreated to the far corners of my mind.

The government hospital was a terrible place with mediocre doctors. There were better treatment options in Delhi, but they were expensive. Every penny we had was going into my education and my brother's. The few times I expressed my anxieties, my mother put on a brave face and told me to focus on my studies. Not once did I consider interrupting my studies and getting a job. I was only too willing to believe her when she swore that her prognosis was good. There was never any doubt in my mind that I was going to enter the IAS, but I failed the Civil Services exam on my first attempt. Most of my classmates at Hindu College who had got in had signed up for expensive coaching classes, but I had not even told my mother about them because I knew we could not afford it. I was ready to throw in the towel and start searching for clerical jobs because I was eager to help. My younger brother was now at Pinewood and tuition seemed to go up every year. But my mother would have none of it. She knew that I could sit for the exam five more times, and I was only twenty-one, which meant that I had ten more years before I would be too old to apply. Of course, she paid for the coaching and a year later, I entered the academy at Mussoorie.

My father's family, and especially my mother's, came from a proud tradition of Arya Samajists. Her grandfather, Lala Kishan Chand, was the younger brother of the legendary Lala Hans Raj who had founded the Dayanand Anglo-Vedic College of Lahore. From its humble beginnings as a school dedicated to the principles of the great Dayanand Saraswati, the college went on to be known as one of the finest in Lahore.

Lala Kishan Chand was a successful cloth merchant and a leader of the Lahore Arya Samaj. It was on his knee that his favourite grandchild, my mother, learned about the glorious traditions of Vedic India. We never had any idols in our home, which resounded with Vedic chants every morning and evening to accompany the sweet-smelling ritual flame of the *agnihotra*. Ours was the only home in our little colony where sweepers and other untouchables would always be offered water or tea.

More than anything else, my mother's ideals helped me hold my head up high during my two years at the academy. The snobbery of the elite boys, directed at those like me who wore cheap clothes and listened only to Hindi film songs, seemed to me like a modern version of the caste system, which the Samaj unequivocally rejected. The other boys from the mofussil towns came to regard me as their leader, as I always stood up for them when they were bullied or ridiculed. The two years at the academy flew by and there was no one prouder than my mother when I graduated near the top of my class. At twenty-five, I was a freshly minted IAS officer with a dazzling career ahead of me, awaiting my first posting.

I had never heard of Hoshangabad until the postings were announced, and I was deeply disappointed. I was young and naive and had simply assumed that my class rank would get me a plum posting. Kerala was particularly sought-after in those days, as were places like Pondicherry where everything worked and you could do your job with minimum political interference, building a clean record in your early years that would come in handy as your career progressed. A small district town in the backwoods of Madhya Pradesh was definitely not my dream posting, but it could have been much worse. Without political patronage or a powerful, well-connected family and the inability to grease palms, I could have easily ended up in Bihar, which was utterly lawless, or Punjab, which was a flaming mess because of the 'Sikh problem'.

Hoshangabad, my first posting as Additional District Collector (ADC), turned out to be much better than I had expected. It was a sleepy little town on the banks of the Narmada, where nothing really happened. My senior officer, Ramesh Pradhan, was an excellent mentor who took me under his wing despite our backgrounds being dramatically different. The youngest District Collector (DC) in the entire civil service, he was the scion of a prominent Delhi family that had counted barristers, judges and political leaders among its ranks for generations. He had been educated at the Lawrence

School and St Stephen's and was clearly destined for greatness. He and his wife, Mallika, who also came from an equally storied background, presided over the social scene in Hoshangabad like royals. The monthly parties at the DC's residence were legendary, with entertainment provided by the finest classical musicians from Gwalior and Bhopal. Mallika had decided to take charge of me and find me a suitable wife, often instructing me about the intricacies of Hindustani classical music as I mentally groaned and tried to hide my yawns, insisting that I needed to be less of a philistine if I was to land a wife who would help propel me further as my career advanced.

The Superintendent of Police (SP), Ajoy Sengupta, was a young officer as well, and a rising star in the Indian Police Service. A close friend of the DC's, he introduced me to bridge, which apparently was another essential qualification for advancement. Playing cards was considered a grievous sin by my mother, and I always remember feeling a twinge of discomfort when I sat down at the table covered with green felt with SP Sengupta and our opponents. Occasionally, our opponents would be army officers from the Pachmarhi Cantonment, who would visit Hoshangabad to break the tedium of life in a military camp.

Life in Hoshangabad was truly idyllic. The workload was light and nothing untoward ever happened there, unlike districts in other states that were often racked by communal violence, terrorism or ethnic rivalries. My career was off to a great start and I was building a solid track record, which would help me get a good posting when my stint here ended. I was fully accepted as an equal by my fellow civil service officers and, for the first time in my life, I truly felt like I belonged. My mother had taught me to never be ashamed of my humble background, but now I felt that I could stop feeling like an imposter among the elites and truly savour the success that her sacrifices and my hard work had brought.

And then, at 9.20 a.m. on Wednesday, 31 October, everything changed.

On that morning, I was in the neighbouring town of Itarsi, looking into the rape of a minor untouchable girl, which the family claimed was being hushed up by the police and the local member of the legislative assembly (MLA) who was from the ruling party. I was at the Station House Officer's (SHO) office, reviewing the first information report (FIR) that had been filed after the alleged rape. I was seated at his desk, as he stood nervously by my side, sweat streaming down his face and his huge belly flowing over his regulation belt, when the phone rang. I nodded curtly when he looked at me. He then picked up the phone, stiffening to attention, as he recognized the voice. 'DC Sahib,' he grunted as he handed the phone to me. I was surprised because I was scheduled to meet Ramesh for lunch in less than an hour to plan the visit of a Soviet delegation that was touring the state. If a conflict had cropped up, I would have expected his personal assistant to call. In a nervous voice that I had never heard before, he simply said, 'Get to the Residence right away.'

Ramesh sat in his study, shell-shocked. Ajoy Sengupta and Biswas, the other ADC sat with him, their faces ashen. Ramesh waved his assistant away as he ushered me in and gestured, asking him to shut the door. 'They shot her,' he said. 'The bastards shot her.'

The official communiqué that had come in over wireless was terse. Earlier that morning, as Mrs Gandhi was walking from her Safdarjung Road residence to her Akbar Road office, two of her bodyguards, both Sikhs, had attacked her. She had suffered multiple bullet wounds and been taken to the All India Institute of Medical Sciences (AIIMS). The press had already reported that her attackers had been Sikhs and rumours of retaliatory attacks on Sikhs in Delhi were beginning to spread. DCs were directed to put the police on high alert as the anti-Sikh violence was expected to spread beyond Delhi.

Ramesh had grown up playing in the corridors of power. His mother was a close friend of Mrs Gandhi's and Sanjay had been like an older brother to him. I do not know if it was his blue blood or his training, but whatever it was, I felt deep admiration for him at that moment. His composure was astonishing as he directed Ajoy to put together a detailed plan for police bandobast, asking questions about police station locations and personnel strength.

Hoshangabad was home to more than ten thousand Sikhs who had managed to stay isolated from the violent events of Punjab. There had been no protests of note even in June, when the Golden Temple had been attacked by the army to flush out a group of terrorists who had occupied part of the complex. At that time, the Sikhs had congregated in large numbers at the Gurdwara Shri Gurugranth Sahib Atihasik, the main Sikh place of worship in the city. Their leaders had called for restraint and the community, mostly small businessmen and labourers, had for the most part stayed calm. If any trouble were to start in Hoshangabad, the gurdwara would be the most likely flashpoint as Sikhs were to be found there at all hours. The rest of the Sikhs were scattered around the city, though there was a small shanty town on the outskirts of the city—Hargobindpura—which was home to several clans of Sikligar Sikhs. They had their own little makeshift gurdwara and, because of their 'low caste' status, tended not to mix too much with the rest of the city's Sikhs.

Ajoy was directed to send a large police contingent to the main gurdwara, and another one to Hargobindpura. It was a well-known fact in the civil-service community that the poorest localities were always the worst affected when communal clashes broke out. Biswas was given administrative oversight over plans for the main gurdwara, in case an extraordinary situation arose, and I was assigned the defence of Hargobindpura and a few other localities nearby. The district offices were to be our headquarters, but Biswas and I were told to accompany the police patrols periodically until the danger of communal clashes was behind us.

I rushed back to the district guest house, which had been my home for the past two years, to change before Mishra, one of Ajoy's deputies who had been assigned to me, picked me up. Hoshangabad district did not have any accommodation for single civil-service officers and when I first arrived here, I was billeted at the guest house as a stopgap measure. The guest house was a stately bungalow, which dated back to the British Raj and easily was the finest place I had ever lived in. Besides there was a steady stream of visitors whose company I enjoyed, often army officers from Pachmarhi Cantt who made excellent drinking buddies. Today, the only guest I encountered as I rushed through the dining hall to my room was Captain Paramjit 'Pickles' Cheema, who was going back to his home in Patiala on leave and was in Hoshangabad to catch a train later that night.

Pickles had become a good friend over the past year. A tall, handsome and gregarious Sardar, and a huge bridge fanatic to boot, he was often a guest at our bridge games at the Officers' Club. I suppose my anxiety must have been apparent on my face, or perhaps it was my refusal to banter with him, which prompted him to ask what was wrong. The news of the attack on the prime minister was still classified and I could tell him nothing. I wished him a good journey and a great furlough and sprinted to my room to quickly change and grab a sweater. It was the end of October and the nights were starting to turn chilly earlier than normal.

As I drove around the city in DSP Mishra's jeep that afternoon, there did not seem to be any visible signs of trouble. In tea shops, people were huddled around transistor radios, listening to All India Radio that was playing devotional music non-stop. At 11 a.m., AIR had broadcast that Mrs Gandhi had been attacked, but there was no word of her condition. Later, we learned that the BBC World Service had announced her death as early as 1 p.m. As the afternoon turned into evening, the city seemed tense but calm. DSP Mishra and I had driven through Hargobindpura at least four times by the evening. Each time, the streets seemed to be less busy, and by 7 p.m. some of the shops around the little gurdwara were shuttered, which was unusual. One of the constables in our patrol, who lived nearby, told us that the evening was usually the busiest time of day with throngs of people, both Sikhs and non-Sikhs, visiting the gurdwara to partake in the langar, or communal meal that was served every night.

By 9 p.m. or so, the first reports of sporadic violence began to filter in over the police wireless. Later, we learned that Doordarshan had announced that Mrs Gandhi was dead. Stones had been thrown at the houses of prominent Sikhs all over the city and three auto-parts shops, owned by Sikhs, were looted in nearby Itarsi. The police response was swift and, in an hour or so, the city was calm again. Mishra and I handed over the command of our patrol to one of his inspectors and went back to the guest house for dinner.

Pickles was in the dining hall when we arrived. His face was grave and there was no sign of his usual jovial self. It didn't occur to me then, but I imagine that the prime minister's assassination by her Sikh bodyguards must have been very difficult to deal with for this Sikh who had dedicated his life to the defence of the motherland. Pickles wasn't leaving for Punjab until the next night. We had a few drinks and chatted for a while before retiring to our rooms. The only dim ray of hope for us, I remember, was the swearing-in of Rajiv Gandhi as the new prime minister. The younger cadre of the civil services had been rooting for him ever since he took his first hesitant steps into the world of politics. He was young, modern, urbane and, most importantly, clean. The very antithesis of the archetypal corrupt politician whose excesses were the bane of every IAS officer's existence.

Ramesh had called a breakfast meeting the next morning. Once again, Ajoy, Biswas and I found ourselves in his office. The constant patrolling had been effective and Ajoy reported that there had been no violent incidents overnight. We were directed to continue the patrols and vigilance, and all of us left after a hasty breakfast.

The morning was largely uneventful. By around 10 a.m., the shops around the Hargobindpura gurdwara had reopened and little children were playing in the streets again. I drove through the city with Mishra's patrol, chafing a little at what seemed to be a colossal waste of time. The crisis seemed to be over and Ramesh's zeal was starting to feel a little excessive, as in neighbourhood after neighbourhood we saw people going about their normal business. We stopped for lunch at a dhaba that the policemen often frequented and chatted with several locals, all of whom seemed to be somewhat on edge because of the assassination.

A middle-aged man at the table next to ours, who turned out to be a schoolmaster, was holding forth about the 'Punjab problem', a dozen young men listening in rapt attention. The dhaba was packed and noisy, but I could hear snatches of the discourse. The Hindu, according to him, had been completely emasculated by the nation's pandering to minorities in the name of secularism. His vitriol was initially directed at Indian Muslims, who according to him had a much greater allegiance to Pakistan, rather than their own country. His arguments, albeit expressed more directly and crudely, were no different from the ones put forth by many of my brother IAS officers over drinks. As a nation, he felt, we were far too tolerant of minorities, who instead of being grateful at the warm and inclusive embrace of Hindu India, acted out, often violently, in support of ever-escalating demands that seemed designed to take even more from the majority.

'Take the Sikhs, for instance,' he said. 'We have let them thrive in our country. They are few, yet they are so wealthy. We let them serve in numbers far out of proportion in our army. We have made a Sikh our President. And how do they reward us? With terrorism! Threatening to break the country apart. Pulling innocent Hindus out of buses and slaughtering them. Assassinating police officers and journalists at will. We risk the lives of our soldiers to protect their gurdwaras from their own terrorists and how do the motherfuckers pay us back? By killing our prime minister? We are all impotent. Eunuchs, all of us,' he blustered, the young men hanging on to his every word.

Despite my disgust at his crassness, I could not help but listen with feelings of grudging admiration at his directness and clarity. There was something to be said for standing up to the violence we had been living with for a decade, especially in Punjab. I had always had many Sikh friends growing up in Saharanpur, those who I had played with every day. While their families were always kind and generous with their hospitality, I could never get rid of a vague feeling of unease around them. Taunts about the cowardice of Hindus were common and somehow I was made to feel small because I came from a family of cloth merchants. When I would complain to my mother, she would ask me to shrug it off, saying that this was how Sikhs had always been.

I found myself reflecting on the stories my mother used to tell me about the Arya Samaj in Lahore and its brilliant attempts at ridding Hindu society of its superstitions, while trying to create intense pride in its glorious past. Lahore had been dominated by Sikhs for generations, but traditionally the Hindus and Sikhs had been close. So close that many Punjabi Hindu families often raised their eldest son as a Sikh. All of that changed in 1873, when the Sikhs began to distance themselves from Hindus and started creating Singh Sabhas, or societies of Sikhs, in Punjab and elsewhere. The Hindu faith was vilified as being superstitious and backward. My mother would proudly tell me about her grandfather, who clearly understood that the time had come to protect and preserve our own identity. He became the prime force in Lahore behind regular *shudhi* or purification ceremonies in which Sikhs would be encouraged to publicly renounce their identity by cutting of their long locks and shaving their beards, as they returned to the Hindu faith. I wondered what my great-grandfather would have made of this surreal day.

I was snapped out of my reverie by Mishra. Disturbing reports were coming in over the wireless. We needed to get back to patrolling. Small groups of mostly young men were starting to form all over the city, as condolence meetings were announced in every ward and council. The reports said that the mood was turning ugly and slogans were being shouted against Sikhs. In several condolence meetings, Sikhs had been jostled and harassed, and there were already reports of three Sikh men being beaten up severely, close to the paper mill. There were many areas where there was potential for further trouble and it started to feel like the police force was being stretched too thin. Our own patrol became less systematic as we lurched from one neighbourhood to another, driven by the ever-escalating stream of wireless reports.

The administration had focused on known troublemakers and junior leaders of the ruling party, fearing that they might try to whip up anti-Sikh sentiments, but unbeknownst to us, there was a much more powerful force at work that we had no control over. I learned later that day that Doordarshan, the national television network, had been broadcasting live footage of mourners around Teen Murti Bhavan in Delhi, where the fallen prime minister's body lay in state. Angry mobs were clearly heard chanting 'Khoon ka badla khoon se lenge', we will avenge blood with blood. In fact, some claimed that Bollywood megastar, Amitabh Bachchan, who was very close to the Gandhi family, was featured on television inciting rage against the Sikhs, an allegation that continues to dog him to this day.

By 8 p.m. that day, violence had broken out all over the city. The constables in our patrol team dispersed several small mobs around Hargobindpura, who were shouting slogans and hurling rocks at the little gurdwara, even as the priest and his family sheltered inside. At one deserted intersection, we prevented a group of young thugs from seriously injuring an elderly Sikh whose motorcycle they had stopped. The wireless crackled constantly as central command struggled to send patrols to new eruptions of rioting. We found ourselves returning to the gurdwara repeatedly as the mobs had clearly made it their primary target in the area.

With two constables, armed with ancient bolt-action rifles, visibly standing guard outside, Mishra and I took off our shoes.

With our handkerchiefs precariously perched on our heads, the ends tucked behind our ears, we entered the small gurdwara. It was nothing more than a shack made of corrugated iron, completely unlike the beautiful one in Saharanpur on Gurdwara Road, which I often visited as a lad. We were astonished to find the door unlocked. A Sikh man in his late thirties, wearing a blue turban and a startlingly white, crisply ironed kurta-pyjama, was seated on the beautifully canopied dais, chanting a prayer with his eyes closed. The gurdwara was empty. A teenaged girl, who I remember was exceptionally beautiful, stood behind him in a very simple salwar-kameez, gently plying the traditional whisk you see at every gurdwara over the scripture, as her father continued to chant, oblivious of our presence. A woman, clearly her mother, sat on the floor on a white *dari* or rug and by her sat a young lad, probably seven or eight years old, with wide, mischievous eyes that took in Mishra's uniform and his holstered sidearm, his hair in a topknot covered with the tiniest of white handkerchiefs.

We waited, somewhat impatiently, for Pritam Singh, the Granthi and custodian of the gurdwara, to finish his chanting, after which he led his tiny congregation in prayer, all of them rising to their feet. When the prayer was completed, his wife dispensed piping hot prasad from a steel bowl into our hands, as delicious and comforting as the prasad of my boyhood gurdwara visits. We told Pritam Singh that we would leave an armed constable behind to protect the gurdwara and his family. We found ourselves in the odd position of being reassured by him that nothing would happen. Mishra tried to persuade them to leave the gurdwara because it was likely to be targeted again, but Pritam Singh would have none of it. 'I have lived here for twelve years,' he said, adding, 'Pammi was only three years old when we came here and Kaka was born here,' pointing to their little room by the side of the gurdwara. 'Nobody will harm us, DSP Sahib.'

Leaving a constable behind, Mishra and I continued our patrol. From the wireless bulletins, it seemed that the city had settled into an uneasy equilibrium. New attacks would start and then, as the patrols responded, the small mobs would melt away. Our own patrol broke up fifteen to twenty attacks without the constables having to fire their weapons. I was on high alert, my ear glued to the wireless. Biswas and I had a very specific role in the patrolling. We were, of course, not required, or for that matter, helpful in any way in terms of the actual duties of the patrols. While Article 19(1)(b) of the Indian Constitution gives citizens the right to 'assemble peacefully and without arms', it also clearly states that the right is 'subject to reasonable restrictions in the interest of the sovereignty and integrity of India and public order'. Section 141 of the Indian Penal Code (IPC) describes the process for dealing with an 'unlawful' public assembly that attempts to use criminal force with the aim of resisting the law, committing mischief, seizing property or harming other citizens. In such instances, the police are empowered to use force in a very measured way, under the instruction of an executive magistrate. As ADCs, both Biswas and I were executive magistrates and had been empowered by Ramesh to make decisions on the use of force, including firing at crowds, if the situation warranted. As we drove through the city, dispersing mobs and either breaking up or pre-empting attacks, I dreaded that call on the wireless, asking me to make the decision to open fire at the mobs, which only seemed to be inevitable.

Around 11 p.m., I received a message on the wireless, summoning me back to the DC's residence. I transferred to one of the other jeeps in Mishra's patrol and, twenty minutes later, was ushered into Ramesh's study. Ajoy and Biswas were already seated, their faces grim and lined with worry. I suppose my face must have look similarly drained as well. It had been a scant twelve hours since Ramesh's assistant had ushered me into this room the last time, but it felt like a lifetime had passed. The three of us looked at Ramesh, expecting to be debriefed as his face registered a complex interplay of emotions. 'We have received new orders, gentlemen, from up above. The police force is to stand down with immediate effect,' he said quietly, not really looking at any of us.

Ajoy was the first to break the stunned silence. 'But, Sir, we have been engaging with mobs constantly all over the city! If we stand down, there will be violence, possibly fatalities.'

Ramesh seemed to be looking at the wall behind us as he responded. 'These are our orders, gentlemen. If any FIRs are filed, deal with them case by case, as per normal process. I am going to get some rest, and I suggest you do the same.'

Back at the guest house, I tried to eat but felt that I would vomit. I asked the bearer to pour me a stiff drink and moved from the dining room to the lounge. To my surprise, I found Pickles there, nursing a drink as well, an elegant dressing gown draped over his broad shoulders. 'All trains through Delhi have been cancelled,' he said. 'Something big must be going on, but my brother officers in military intelligence have no inkling of what it is either, unless they are being very tight-lipped about it.' I asked if he was worried about his family, but he said that as far as he knew Punjab was completely calm.

I tossed and turned for several hours, my brain fevered with worry. Every time I drifted off, I would have violent nightmares and would wake up with a start, my face covered with sweat. Was it anger I had seen on Ramesh's face, mixed with resignation? Was it directed at the orders, which seemed almost surreal under the circumstances? Surely, I must have misinterpreted his expression, but I could almost have sworn that I also saw grim satisfaction. It must have been four or five in the morning before I fell into deep slumber, so deep that the bearer, I later learned, had to use the master key to open my door and shake me up. 'ADC, Sirji,' he said, fearful of my response at being so rudely awakened, 'DSP Sahib.'

Mishra's ashen face was enough to spur me into getting dressed hurriedly, without even showering. A few minutes later, we were driving to Hargobindpura in his jeep.

Mishra and I didn't need to take off our shoes or cover our heads. We walked past the two young constables, boys really, who stood outside the charred remains of the gurdwara. The silk canopy above the raised dais was in tatters, and the book that had rested in its aegis, swathed in file silks, was half burnt, ripped pages scattered on and around the dais. The unmistakable smell of urine and faeces, mixed with the stench of singed hair and burnt flesh, assailed our nostrils as we walked in. A trail of purplish red on the cotton sheets, which were sparkling white no more, led from the smashed door of the little room on the side to a corner of the gurdwara, where the charred remains of three bodies lay, one of them heartbreakingly small.

'The girl,' said Mishra quietly, 'is nowhere to be found.'

The attack on the gurdwara had occurred at 3 a.m. or so. The FIR had not been filed until 9 a.m. The FIR is what officially sets the wheels of criminal justice in motion. Usually, the victims of a crime are expected to file an FIR with the local police station, but anyone who knows that a crime has been committed may file one too. In this case, the FIR had been filed by Parveer Chandra Bharia, a tribal leader and the only city councilman from the Communist Party of India (Marxist-Leninist) [CPI (M-L)], after he learned of the attack. It was a mystery why not even one Sikh resident from Hargobindpura had come forward to file the FIR. Surely, they must have known that the gurdwara had been attacked and the Granthi killed!

Mishra instructed the SHO of the local police station to start investigating. We then drove to P.C. Bharia's home nearby to talk to him. Bharia turned out to be an intense young man with very dark skin and an earnest manner. He had been awakened just after 5 a.m. by a persistent banging on the door of his tiny house. Two lads, members of the CPI(M-L) youth wing, stood outside, sweat streaming down their faces, shaking. 'Gurdwara, Sirji, gurdwara,' was all he could get out of them at first, since the boys were too fearful to talk. He gave them water and sat them down, and it was only after he had reassured them many times that nothing would happen to them did their story begin to emerge.

The boys, it turned out, often went to the Hargobindpura akhara, a wrestling pit owned by the schoolmaster's brother. Some of them would wrestle, but mostly they went to listen to the schoolmaster who would be there most nights, holding forth on some topic of 'social interest'. He would often speak about the virtues of *brahmacharya*, or sexual abstinence, for young men, and sometimes he would tell stories from the Mahabharata or the Ramayana, always managing to connect them to what was going on in the city and the country. The mood at these gatherings was always festive and by late night bottles of country liquor would invariably be passed around.

Last night, the schoolmaster had been talking about Punjab and the Sikhs. In the past few months he had often talked about the Sikhs and how they had betrayed the nation by turning from being the sword arm of the Hindu faith, which he claimed had been the intent of the tenth Sikh Guru—Guru Gobind Singh—to becoming traitors to their nation and mother faith. The schoolmaster had spoken eloquently and using simple, powerful language made a case that it was finally time to teach the Sikhs a lesson. The Hargobindpura gurdwara, which was the pride of the local Sikhs, would be a good place to begin, he had said. According to him, the Sikligar Sikhs were doubly worthy of punishment because they were former low-caste Hindus who had abandoned their glorious faith for false promises of equality. They had become belligerent and uppity and would refuse to defer to the higher castes any more, as generations of their forebears had. He had sent a couple of lads to the gurdwara, who had come back to report that there was an armed guard outside.

Around 11 p.m., a white Ambassador with a red beacon atop had pulled up at the akhara. The boys did not know who the heavyset middle-aged man, dressed in sparkling white khadi or homespun and the familiar white cap on his head, who stepped out of the car was, but Bharia was pretty sure that it was Raghunath Sharma, the local state legislator and a leading light of the Party. He had disappeared into one of the back rooms of the akhara with the schoolmaster for a few minutes, after which he had got into his car and left. Just before the car drove off, the uniformed driver had opened the trunk and carried two large cardboard boxes into the akhara, laying them close to where the schoolmaster sat in a high-backed cane chair, quite like a judge haughtily presiding over his courtroom.

There had been fifteen or so youths in the akhara most of the evening, including the two CPI(M-L) lads. But by midnight, the crowd had swollen to forty or fifty. Many of the new arrivals seemed older and somehow looked more hardened than the schoolboys who usually attended the gatherings. The cases were opened and the bottles of XXX Rum, a staple of army and police canteens, were freely handed out. One of the schoolmaster's favourite lads, who had been sent to reconnoitre the gurdwara, returned and whispered into the schoolmaster's ear, who then beckoned to Ghanshyam, the best-known young thug in Hargobindpura who had been gleefully swigging away at an impossibly large bottle of rum. In a couple of minutes, the schoolmaster was gone. It was 3 a.m. by the time the cases of rum were emptied.

Bharia had rushed to the local police station as soon as he heard what had happened. He was just a junior politician and he was used to the insolence of the police, but he was taken aback at the SHO's attitude, who seemed to be more interested in Bharia's motivation for filing an FIR rather than what had happened at the gurdwara. When it was clear that Bharia would not give in, he reluctantly handed out a form. When Bharia insisted that the SHO immediately start a search for the Granthi's daughter, a salacious grin had appeared on his face. 'The girl,' he said, 'was sleeping with half of Hargobindpura. She has simply taken advantage of the confusion and eloped with one of her lovers.'

Mishra and I looked at one another, dumbfounded, as Bharia finished his story. 'It is not over,' he said. 'The mob has tasted blood. A much larger attack is coming tonight. The homes of the Sikligar Sikhs will be attacked after sundown. Ghanshyam is busy rounding up toughs from all over Hoshangabad, and even Itarsi. Unlimited rum and plunder are being promised with a guarantee that the police will not interfere.'

My first instinct was to talk to my superior officer. I called Ramesh's office but was told that he was at the Residence. I tried the office phone at the Residence, as well as the Pradhans' personal phone, but nobody picked up. As horrified as I was at what had already occurred, I was sweating profusely at the thought of what might happen in Hargobindpura that night. In desperation, I called Ajoy and managed to track him down on the police wireless. Ajoy completely agreed with me that the Sikhs of Hargobindpura needed to be protected, but added that his hands were tied. Only the DC could give orders to restart the police patrols, and he had unequivocally told us to stand down!

I did not give up hope. Ramesh Pradhan was my mentor and one of the fairest and most decent people I had ever known. I was certain that if I could see him face to face and explain what had happened, and was likely to happen, he would do the right thing, no matter what orders he had received. It was, after all, our responsibility to protect all the residents of Hoshangabad. I had Mishra drive me to the Residence. The DC's assistant was in his office, but he had not seen Ramesh all day. I made my way down the familiar corridor to the door that led to the private quarters. It was locked. Getting a little desperate now, I went back to Ramesh's office and had his assistant call every possible place that he could be at. Nothing. The DC of Hoshangabad was missing.

I called Ajoy again but could not reach him either, not even on the police wireless. I asked Mishra if he would resume patrolling Hargobindpura on my orders, but he demurred. As much as he wanted to help, he was an experienced IPS officer and understood that chain of command was sacred. I quickly dismissed the thought of calling the chief minister of the state or the MP who represented Hoshangabad. Both were from the Party and, even in the best of times, it was impossible for junior IAS officers to get the ear of powerful politicians.

Feeling nauseated, I had my driver take me back to the guest house. I had not eaten for sixteen hours now, but I simply couldn't stand the thought of food. The only image lodged in my mind, which refused to go away, was of the tiny charred skeleton that I had looked upon with horror earlier that day. How many more would there be by the time the sun came up tomorrow!

Pickles was in the lounge when I settled down with my salted lime. I suppose my face must have reflected how I felt. When he asked me what was wrong, my horror, anguish and anxieties poured out at once. So intent was I on expressing my outrage that I almost missed his question, which he asked quietly. 'Have you considered calling in the army?'

I racked my brains, going back to the academy in my thoughts; to the mind-numbing lectures about the Criminal Procedure Code (CrPC). Under normal circumstances, the civil administration has the resources to deal with unrest and disturbances, but on rare occasions it is permissible to call in the army, which tends to be more disciplined and effective than the local police. The army often gets called in during instances of sectarian violence when the administration feels that the police are incapable of or unwilling to act impartially. This decision is always made by the senior magistrate, in the civil administration, which in this case would have been Ramesh Pradhan.

I summoned my vehicle and rushed to the district headquarters, looking for Biswas. Though as ADCs we held the same rank, Biswas was much older than me and a very experienced civil servant. He was no greenhorn fresh from the academy; he was a twenty-year veteran from the Bihar cadre who had been seconded to the IAS. I was sure that Biswas would know what to do. If the army was to be called in, I felt that in Ramesh's absence Biswas would be the right person to make that decision, particularly because he was a sensible fellow and constantly a source of excellent, practical advice whenever I encountered new situations.

Biswas was nowhere to be found either. Nobody had seen him at the headquarters and his assistant suggested I try his residence. The little bungalow that Biswas and his family lived in was also deserted. I started to feel a growing sense of unease as I drove to the police headquarters, looking for Ajoy. En route to Biswas's home I had received a call from Mishra on the wireless. One of his informants in Hargobindpura had come forward to report that a big attack had been planned in the neighbourhood at sundown. Weapons and cases of rum were being assembled at the akhara and toughs from all over Hoshangabad district were pouring into Hargobindpura. Party workers were fanning out, shouting slogans and swearing revenge on the Sikhs. The word on the street was that the police was going to stand down for one more night and a golden opportunity for rape and plunder was at hand.

I was not surprised at all when Ajoy was nowhere to be found either.

It was already 3 p.m. and sundown was only a few hours away. My sense of foreboding was starting to turn into panic. I have to confess that I did consider going back to the guest house to disappear like the other officers. Clearly, they were following official orders. In a certain sense, I could understand their actions. While civil servants are nominally expected to act with autonomy, particularly in dangerous situations, in reality they are at the mercy of their political masters. An informal hallway conversation, followed by a transfer to the backwaters, has destroyed many a career. I thought of all the sacrifices my mother had made to make me who I was today. And then I had a sudden moment of clarity.

As far as I could remember, my mother would constantly talk to me and my brother about right and wrong. She had always been a treasure trove of stories about heroes and villains. Stories she had heard sitting on her grandfather's knee. Stories of courage and sacrifice. Stories from the Puranas and the Ramayana and the Mahabharata. Stories of men who did the right thing every time they were confronted with difficult choices. In the most difficult of times, I would always go back to the dialogue between Lord Krishna and Arjuna before the start of the great battle. A voice in my head reminded me that it was never okay to back down from a righteous war, no matter what the consequences. The Sikhs were wrong to pick up guns and nothing could justify the cold-blooded killing of an unarmed, elderly woman, no matter what their grievances. Yet, the Granthi of the Hargobindpura gurdwara and his family were completely innocent and should have been protected. Just like the hundreds of Sikhs living in Hargobindpura needed to be protected. I was sure my mother was by my side at that moment when I cast my self-doubt aside. I knew what needed to be done.

I went back to the guest house but not to hide. I rousted Pickles, who was taking an afternoon nap, and asked him to call his Commanding Officer (CO) at the cantonment. I explained the situation to the General Officer Commanding (GOC) who had many questions about the police as well as the violence that had already occurred. The GOC seemed to be a no-nonsense kind of person and, after he had quickly understood the situation and established that I had the credentials to be having this conversation with him, asked me a simple question. He asked if I would be willing to put the orders in writing.

My hands were trembling as I loaded the official letterhead with my name and title on it into the ageing typewriter at the guest house. Slowly, using two fingers, as there was no time to summon my assistant, I typed out the orders, signed them and handed them to Pickles, who had been drafted by the GOC to carry them to the Pachmarhi Cantonment. It was a good three- to four-hour drive to Pachmarhi from Hoshangabad, and I was sick with worry. The GOC had said that it would take at least an hour to get a column ready and dispatch it. When I explained to him that the attack was imminent at nightfall, he agreed to dispatch the column before Pickles arrived with the written orders. He assured me, however, that the column would not enter the city until he had the written orders in his hand. He would give his team the go-ahead on wireless only after that.

The next four hours were the longest of my life. I got periodic phone calls from Bharia, whose lads were my only source of information, for each time I called the Hargobindpura police station for an update I was blandly assured that all was well— 'Sab theek hai, ADC Sahib.' As the afternoon turned into evening, Bharia reported that there were now at least three hundred men at the akhara, drinking and raising hell. He did not know how many other gathering points there were for the toughs who had been drifting into Hargobindpura and the surrounding areas all afternoon. Bharia himself hadn't dared to show his face on the street because word was out that he had filed an FIR about the attack on the gurdwara. The schoolmaster had spoken a couple of times at the akhara and denounced all 'comrades' as traitors who seemed to be unaffected by Mrs Gandhi's murder and were siding with the Sikhs. Bharia's lads, however, were able to slip in and out of the crowd without arousing any suspicions.

Bharia had reported that there was utter terror in the Sikligar Sikh colony. Every man, woman and child knew what had happened to the Granthi and his family, even though not one had dared to visit the gurdwara all day. As rumours had swirled about the impending attack, a few families had left or sent small children and the elderly away, to get them out of harm's way, but most had stayed. First of all, they had nowhere to go and their meagre possessions that they had scratched together their whole lives were all they had. They must have had some hope that the administration would come to their aid. If they had known that the DC and the SP had both chosen to stay absent and ignore the impending attack, they surely would have fled.

There were also rumours that the Sikligars had been arming themselves. The Sikligars had traditionally been burnishers of weapons, and several of them still made sickles and knives in the dozen or so forges that Hargobindpura was home to. While they were no doubt afraid of what was coming, they were also determined to protect their homes and families. They were particularly fearful of what awaited their wives and daughters. In the twelve hours that had passed after the attack on the gurdwara, there was still no word about the Granthi's daughter despite the perfunctory investigation by the Hargobindpura SHO, who was forced to go through the motions as an FIR had been filed.

At 6.45 p.m., with no word from the army column, I got the last call of the day from Bharia. It was dusk and the attacks had begun. Fifty young thugs had left the akhara, drunk and rowdy, and had entered the main Sikh colony in Hargobindpura. They had filled the narrow street, hurling abuses at the Sikhs who were cowering behind closed doors. The mob had come to a stop outside a two-storeyed home, larger than most of the surrounding homes and extremely well kept, the three television antennas that rose from the roof and the row of scooters parked neatly inside the compound, just beyond the locked iron grates, promising rich plunder. The mob had flung bricks and stones at the house but achieved little because every window and door was covered by a metal grill. The thugs had been staggering around in a drunken stupor in front of the gate when five Sikh men, two of them young lads, had charged out of a side gate in the compound, brandishing swords and thundering at the tops of their voices. The patriarch of the family, Madho Singh, who I met later, a heavyset man in his late forties, had wielded a sword in each hand and managed to land several blows before the mob took to its heels and vanished into the little lanes that criss-crossed Hargobindpura. Bharia had warned that the mood at the akhara was really ugly. He feared that a much bigger attack was about to begin.

I could stay at the guest house no longer. I summoned my vehicle and rushed to the Hargobindpura police station. It was only

7 p.m., but as I got closer to the heart of Hargobindpura, the streets were deserted. Usually the markets would be teeming at that time and there would be hundreds thronging the row of food carts that offered delicious and cheap snacks of every kind. Every shop was shuttered and there was not a single vendor in sight. Even the stray dogs that usually played in the piles of trash on the street and blocked every sidewalk seemed to have sensed that something was awry.

To my surprise, when I walked into the police station, it was buzzing with activity. I counted at least a dozen constables and three sub-inspectors, all of whom were being issued weapons from the armoury. I was relieved. It seemed that the top brass and politicians had finally come to their senses and the nightmare was soon to be over. I nodded at the SHO and asked if he had enough men to protect the Sikhs of Hargobindpura. There was insolence writ large on the SHO's face as he looked at me. 'Protect the Sikhs? First these motherfuckers kill our mother and now this? Do you even know what's going on, ADC Sahib? These bastards have gone mad. An FIR was just filed against Madho Singh and his sons. Do you know what they did? A group of young men were walking in the street, peacefully protesting the murder of the prime minister, when these savage bastards attacked them with swords! Four boys in hospital, ADC Sahib. The Sikhs are trying to trigger a communal riot and my orders are to disarm them to prevent further violence.'

It took me a few minutes to collect myself and call Mishra from the SHO's desk. By then, four police patrols had already left with instructions to raid all the forges in Hargobindpura and confiscate anything that might be used as a weapon. Mishra sounded distant on the phone. He confirmed that he had given the order to disarm the Sikhs. When I asked him under whose authority, he remained tight-lipped. I was dumbfounded. Surely he must have cleared it with Ajoy, and possibly even Ramesh. Surely they had to know that stripping the Sikhs of their meagre weapons would be a sure death sentence.

Sick with worry, I simply did not know what to do with myself and decided to go back to the guest house. Just as my car was pulling in, I saw the approaching headlights of an army Jonga. The column had arrived and not a minute too soon!

We drove to the eastern outskirts of Hoshangabad where a convoy of green Nissan trucks was waiting. The GOC had sent an entire battalion—five hundred men—under the command of Major Suri who had driven to the guest house to get me. The convoy started to rumble behind us as we drove through the deserted streets towards Hargobindpura.

We drove past the charred shell that had been the gurdwara and turned into the Sikligar colony. The main road that ran through the colony was deathly calm and the stench of burnt human hair hit our nostrils the minute we entered. Major Suri's Jonga was in the lead and I was in the front passenger seat. Major Suri had sent his driver to the back and was driving himself so that both of us could command a good view of the streets. We could see smoke pouring out of one of the houses a little farther down the road. Major Suri halted the column as we pulled up next to it. Three partially burnt bodies lay just outside the wide open iron gates that seemed to gape drunkenly at the street. The four jawans who had run inside came out with a mountain of a man on a stretcher. His kurta was blackened with smoke and soot, his flowing salt-and-pepper beard was badly singed and he was without a turban, almost bald, much to my astonishment. I had always imagined Sikhs with full, heavy heads of unshorn hair, but without his turban Madho Singh looked almost like my uncles who had gone bald fairly young, or perhaps our family *purohit* with his tonsured head and long beard.

Major Suri looked at me grimly as we stood over the charred remains and asked the question I had been dreading. I simply nodded and got back into the Jonga with him. Whenever the army is given permission to use force, the magistrate who authorized the action is required to accompany the column. This was not going to be easy. Gurung, one of the captains under Major Suri's command, took over the lead of the column in his Jonga while his non-commissioned officer (NCO) rigged up a portable public address system. Fifty jawans, carrying light machine guns (LMGs), fell in behind the Jonga, two abreast, and Major Suri and I brought up the rear. The rest of the force was split into four patrols and dispatched to other neighbourhoods in Hoshangabad where there were sizeable Sikh populations. The flag march had begun on the streets of Hargobindpura.

Every two hundred metres or so, Captain Gurung would announce on the public address system: 'Section 144 of the CrPC is now in place in Hoshangabad. You are advised to go home immediately. Assemblies of five or more people are now illegal. For your own safety, you need to go home and stay there.' Gurung's announcements seemed a bit ridiculous because the streets were totally deserted, but they were required by law. We marched through the main streets of Hargobindpura and arrived at Bhagat Ravidas Chowk, usually a busy intersection. Like the other streets, it was deserted too, but we found an overturned autorickshaw, which had been set on fire, still smouldering. We could hear a hubbub from a narrow, winding alley that opened into the square. Captain Gurung dismounted from his Jonga and unholstering his service revolver led ten jawans into the alley. Major Suri and I followed on foot too since the alley was too narrow for the Jonga.

As the alley wound its way deeper into Hargobindpura, becoming even narrower, our small column was hemmed in between tiny homes, not more than huts really, mostly with thatched roofs. The hubbub was much louder now and we could hear an occasional scream and sounds of laughter mixed in with a constant torrent of filthy abuse. Over the shoulders of the jawans in front of us I could see that we had reached a small square where a narrow street intersected the alley. A group of youths, thirty or so, had crammed into the square and formed a rough circle, crouched around a shapeless form. Some of the youths had bamboo staves and a few carried iron rods, the kind you often see around

construction sites, cut into small lengths. They were prodding at
the form with their sticks, punctuating abuses with kicks. I could
now make out that in the centre lay a man with a long beard.
His body was bathed in blood and he was sobbing as he curled
up trying to anticipate where the next kick would come from. A
discarded length of maroon fabric lay close to his head and I could
see tufts of what looked like freshly shorn hair everywhere.

Captain Gurung shouted several times to get the attention of
the mob, but it was just too noisy. Finally, he raised his revolver
into the air and fired a single shot. There was stunned silence for
a second and then the mob, to my surprise, erupted in cheer.
Drunken salutes. Cries of 'Hindustan Zindabad!', 'Long live India',
'Indira Mata amar rahe!', 'Mother Indira, forever immortal' rang out.
The leader of the youths, who looked like he must have been in
his early thirties, staggered up to Captain Gurung and started to talk
in an exaggeratedly conspiratorial tone. 'Sirji, we have fucked their
mothers today. The bastards had swords, but after SHO Sahib took
their weapons away, we just fucked them in the ass. Sirji, there is a
foundry at the end of this alley. The bastards there still have some
weapons and there are four girls inside. Enough for us and your
jawans, Sirji. If you can just take their weapons away, we will take
care of the rest.'

I am sure Captain Gurung must have been as dumfounded
as me. Two of the jawans trotted back to the trucks to fetch
a stretcher to carry the gravely injured Sikh away, while the rest
of the jawans, guns drawn, formed a ring around him. Once he
was safely out of the square, Captain Gurung addressed the crowd
and firmly told them to go home. He reiterated that Section 144
was in force and that the youths were subject to arrest if they did
not disperse. When it became clear that the army wasn't there to
disarm the Sikhs, the youths sullenly started leaving the square,
slinking down the alley in small groups.

The column followed the lads, weapons drawn. As we marched
down the meandering alley, we started to hear the low, ominous

hum of a mob again. Around a sharp bend, we saw a much larger mob, almost a hundred strong, made up mostly of young men. Some of them were carrying flaming torches and were gathered around a small brick house. There was a six-foot wall around the house and a heavy wrought-iron gate was the only way to get inside. The gate was padlocked from the inside. At the back of the house stood the largest Sikligar foundry in Hargobindpura, owned by Maiyya Singh, the patriarch of the community. Later, we learned that seven families had been sheltering behind the locked gates. There had been thirty-seven people inside, including twelve women and eleven children. The mob knew that there were young women inside and that, more than anything else, fuelled their frenzy.

Ghanshyam was in the thick of the mob, directing the attack. Two of the biggest wrestlers from the akhara were pounding the wall with jackhammers. It was only a matter of time before the wall would give in. Every time a hammer struck the wall, the drunk crowd cheered. Captain Gurung tried to make himself heard above the racket and even fired three rounds into the air, which got the mob's attention but only for a second before the pounding continued. Captain Gurung looked at Major Suri in despair and Major Suri looked at me. I nodded my head almost imperceptibly.

The ten jawans took positions at the back of the alley, their backs pressed against the walls of the little houses, their guns pointed at the crowd. Captain Gurung stood to the side, drew his revolver and took aim. There was a loud crack as Ghanshyam dropped to the ground, blood streaming from his head. The stunned silence felt impossibly long, but it really lasted only a second. Then a cry of rage exploded from the mob. They picked up all the bricks and stones they could find and started hurling them at the jawans, several of them finding their marks. Captain Gurung calmly raised his revolver, pointed it down to aim for the legs of the brick-throwing lads and shouted just once, 'Fire!'

After the crowd stampeded and cleared the alley of its own accord, running pell-mell in every direction possible, we could see five forms crumpled on the street, by the brick wall. The other four were young. Later we learned that they were all students from the local degree college. The jawans had fired low, as they had been trained, but the ricochets off the wall and the street had been lethal. I sat on the steps of Maiyya Singh's home, my head in my hands. There would be no more trouble in Hoshangabad. The riot was over, but the cost had been high.

The chill in the air was palpable when I entered the district headquarters the next day. I certainly did not expect to be congratulated, but I was unprepared for the open hostility I encountered. My own assistant would not look me in the eye and Ramesh's assistant could not tell me anything about his whereabouts. I sent for a copy of Hoshangabad's only English language daily. 'Five Hindu youths killed in unjustified army action,' screamed the headlines.

I learned that Ramesh had been summoned to Delhi to explain what had happened. I did find it rather odd that I was not debriefed before he left. After all, I had signed the orders to call the army in and I had first-hand knowledge of what had happened on the ground. I was summoned to his office after his return, and I found his demeanour to be distant and chilly. I was suspended with pay, he informed me, pending the outcome of an investigation into the events that led to the firing.

I was disappointed and angry but not surprised. After all, I had acted in direct opposition to the orders I had received from my senior officer. I felt like I had helped save many innocent lives, but there was no getting away from the fact that five men had died as a result of my actions. Civil services rules dictated that an inquiry had to be conducted within a week of my suspension. It was announced that the inquiry in this case would be led by S.K. Sinha, a senior IAS officer and home secretary to the state government.

I truly did not know what to expect. S.K. Sinha was an experienced civil servant who had a reputation for fairness, but the days that followed the prime minister's assassination had been emotionally charged. There was great public anger against the Sikhs and many in the government and administration felt that the Sikhs 'needed to be taught a lesson'. The inquiry was swift and, to my surprise, very few witnesses were called. The schoolmaster, who apparently was very well connected, politically, was one of the star witnesses. Mishra and the Hargobindpura SHO were called to testify too, as was Ramesh. Conspicuously absent from the witness list was Bharia.

The results of the inquiry made national headlines. It was determined that calling in the army was an entirely unnecessary response to a situation that the civil authorities could easily have contained. Mr Sinha also concluded that there had been no large-scale threat to the Sikhs of Hoshangabad. The attack on the gurdwara, according to the findings, had been provoked by the Granthi after he objected to his daughter's relationship with a local Hindu youth and threatened to kill her and her lover. The youth and his friends had been trying to spirit the girl away so that she could elope with him when they were confronted by her father. A quarrel ensued in which the Granthi was killed. There was no explanation for the deaths of his wife and child.

Madho Singh, who lost all his sons and whose teenaged daughter was raped repeatedly by the mob, was arrested on charges of fomenting communal violence. According to the inquiry, it was his attacking a group of young men, peacefully mourning the loss of the prime minister, with swords that resulted in a small spontaneous riot in which his sons were killed. Charges of rape could not be substantiated. The other instances of Sikhs being attacked, such as the autorickshaw driver, were explained as a spontaneous expression of anguish and rage directed against the Sikh community by individuals, distraught at the murder of the beloved prime minister. There was absolutely no evidence, the report concluded, that there had been an organized effort to retaliate against the Sikhs of Hargobindpura.

In light of these findings, Mr Sinha opined that the ADC had not only disobeyed orders, but had also far exceeded his authority and shown extremely poor judgement by calling in the army, which directly led to the loss of five innocent lives. In light of my exemplary conduct thus far and my relative inexperience, it had been decided that I would not be dismissed from the IAS. I would be censured and sent on administrative leave for a month without pay, during which period I would receive my transfer orders. I learned later that it was Ramesh who had interceded on my behalf. I owed my continuing career as an IAS officer to him, but despite all my efforts, I was unable to see him before I left Hoshangabad.

As the train pulled closer to Saharanpur, a thousand conflicting thoughts swirled in my mind. I knew that the official report was a pack of lies. There had been a concerted effort to attack the Sikhs of Hoshangabad, which had been sanctioned by the highest levels of the government, with the district administration standing by idly and, in some instances, colluding with the attackers. There was no doubt in my mind that if I had not acted, there would have been a bloodbath in Hargobindpura, like the ones in Delhi, Kanpur and Bokaro. Yet I could not help feeling a deep sense of unease. My actions had resulted in the deaths of five people, four of whom were young lads who had probably got caught up in the events of the night. I feared that my career would never recover from the setback of the censure that would forever be a part of my official service record.

I was clear about one thing though. My mother, who had been the beacon of righteousness my entire life, would surely understand. She would be the Krishna to my Arjuna. She would comfort me, tell me that what I did was right, and righteous, for was it not my dharma to try and protect all the lives that I was responsible for? I felt my anxieties lifting as I got closer to our run-down neighbourhood and bounded out of the rickshaw eager for my mother's warm embrace.

That was when she slapped me.

The next three weeks were the most terrible of my life. Our little dining table was stacked with vernacular newspapers, all with lurid and incendiary headlines about how I had betrayed my own people. *Punjab Kesri*, in particular, accused me of trading the lives of innocent Hindus to protect Sikhs in the most irresponsible and cavalier manner. The article suggested that if my illustrious great-grandfather had been alive, he would have disowned me! I have to believe that my mother, worried sick about my future, would not have abandoned her precious and real commitment to righteousness had it not been for the rantings of the press. In three weeks, I had my new posting. A few days after that, I boarded a train for Dhanbad district in Bihar. My mother refused to accompany me to the railway station and, for the first time in my life, there was nobody to see me off at the Saharanpur station. As I stood forlornly at the doorway of the first-class carriage, waiting for the train to leave, I had hopes that someday she would forgive me and understand why I had been impelled to do what I did, but that was not to be. A month later, I got a telegram form my brother. My mother had lost her battle with cancer.

Her slap has stayed with me forever for it is a daily reminder of the hard choices that we have to make in our lives. Ironically, it was the most precious gift she gave me because rather than making me regret what I had done, its sting kept my conscience alive through the years of the soul-numbing mediocrity and corruption that I had to deal with at one dead-end posting after another. It kept me going for eighteen more years and I would like to believe that I served with honour and integrity and tried my best to make the lives of the people I was responsible for a little better.

In 2002, when once again the twin hands of politics and the civil service joined together in a violent act of bloodletting, this time in Godhra, Gujarat, I decided that I had had enough and quit the service to work with survivors of communal violence.

My mother was a strong woman who had great pride in her identity, her faith and her culture. I know that if she were alive, she would have recognized that her son was no traitor. She had drilled the words from the Bhagavad Gita into my head, which had taught me never to shy away from a righteous fight. I know in my heart that wherever she is, she recognizes that I was merely walking the path she put me on.

Night of the Restless Spirits

He lies with his face down in the dust, his white beard matted and the last few strands of hair sticky with blood. Flies buzz around the red blotches on his chest and belly. His once-proud turban is now a shapeless rag dyed a new colour. He can't feel the pain any more, just a dull throbbing sensation and the sticky wetness. He wishes that his last thoughts could be different; he would like to say the Sodar once again, but he can't collect his thoughts. Each time he tries to mouth the first verse, his thoughts disintegrate into visions of violence and anger and discord. His frail, old body gathers strength only to tremble in rage and lie still again.

What is left of Hukam Singh lies by him, between him and the marble wall richly adorned in red. Hukam Singh's hands are tied behind his back with his saffron *keski*. The last of the old-school, grand *ragi*s. He lives and breathes ragas and Gurbani. His voice is old and cracked, and it trembles, but every note is crystal clear and touches the basest of hearts. Hukam Singh's last performance is over and what a performance! His *joridar* who accompanies him on the tabla has fled, but the LMGs that the jawans carry sound like a perfectly tuned tabla. How sweetly the guns sound the *keherwa*: dhi na ka ti na ka dhi na dhi na ka . . . that fool of a joridar could never play the keherwa right. He should have been here to listen to the soldiers.

Hukam Singh's last performance is unusual. There is no *mangla charan* and no alap today. There is no time spent tuning the tanpuras and the tabla. And instead of sitting down and whispering in undertones, there is a deathly calm before he begins. The *sangat* is uncharacteristically quiet and calm. And their heads are bare. Such disrespect! Their hands are folded, tightly folded, but oddly behind their backs. They look scared. So scared! The perfectly timed keherwa begins on the guns and in an unbecoming and ungainly display the sangat twitches and jerkily dances to the beat. And then Hukam Singh's voice joins in joyous celebration of the rhythm. His voice soars to the sky in a wonderful new raga, rising and falling in ornate *gamak*-embellished *taan*s, effortlessly spanning tens of octaves, expanding until the gurdwara, then the village and then the entire Punjab echoes the sound of the furious melody crafted so carefully by the widow and her gleeful keherwa-pounding divisions. No longer a Sikh, but now a Sufi, dancing. Dancing in agony and unholy ecstasy, as each beat pierces his enormous body that is a magnet that sucks in their molten lead and the raga comes out stronger and louder through every new mouth.

It stops as suddenly as it begins. The last few notes bubble out of Hukam Singh's body and drip on to the old man's face. The sangat has stopped its undignified jerky dance and is sleeping, silent and sated. The widow's musicians have taken their music and left, searching for another audience. Baba Fateh Singh wipes the pool forming before his eyes, but there is still a haze before him, making him squint. He groans as he somehow manages to raise his head a few inches off the ground. Hukam Singh's lifeless face has a grimace frozen on it, as if he died in the middle of a particularly intricate movement in the raga.

All the three young *sevadar*s, who lie in a tangled heap, have an expression that is a mixture of fear and disbelief. The family from Udhampur, which makes a trip to Dukh Nivaran Sahib every year, has found a final resting place in one corner. The aged parents are worried no more about their unemployed son's future and the unemployed son doesn't care about their nagging either. Fateh Singh's head slips back to the cold marble floor and the satanic beat, lurking somewhere in the gurdwara, invades his head again.

The bolt-action rifles play a different tala. The tempo is slower and more deliberate. The heat in the lead bullets is the same, but the bullets are imported—'Made in England', not in the 100 per cent indigenous ordnance factory in Madhya Pradesh. '*Goli se chittar-bittar dega*' they have been announcing the past few days, but the crowd collects nevertheless, completely disregarding the deadly threat, mistaking it to be yet another bluff. The drummers have slit-like Mongolian eyes, broad, flat noses and smooth, hairless faces. Their khaki puttee-clad bow legs disappear into incongruously large regulation boots and they clip-clop like well-trained horses cantering in a show. The ustad has beautiful blonde hair, deep blue eyes and shining swords and stars on his shoulders. Fateh Singh's father yells '*Phokian! Phokian!*' when he hears the first loud crack, but the bullet that leaves a gaping hole in the back of his head declares that they do not fire blanks.

The drummers swoop down upon them without warning. It is a lazy summer night and the breeze pierces the heavy pall of the summer heat. He lies immobile on the *manji*, savouring each fleeting wisp of the wind that, like a flirting nymphet, disappears just as he begins to enjoy its coolness. The mountain of flesh on the cot next to him snores, but even his snores are musical, set perhaps to Maru Bihag or some other raga of the night. Through the open door he hears muted sounds as the family from Udhampur continues its endless quarrelling and nagging in an undertone, perhaps out of respect for its sacred surroundings. Dukh Nivaran Sahib is a shimmering vision in white marble, an infinite pool of blessings and fulfilled dreams, a magical sponge for the sufferings of the wretched who have no place left on earth to go to. They come here from all over Punjab and from Delhi and the Terai and Bidar and Gujarat and Shillong and Kathmandu and New York and Southall and Albuquerque and Botswana and Wollongong and everywhere else that Sikhs live. They come here flushed with the fever of their sufferings, and from the minute their burning foreheads touch the cool marble they begin to heal.

They come here to pray and unburden themselves of their fears and desires. They are enchanted by the power of old Hukam Singh's voice that melts the cold and hard lumps of lies, deceit and suffering that flow through their veins with their blood. They go back elated and purified, ready to face their lives again. The affluent Sikhs of Patiala come here too, the shop owners and the hoteliers and the businessmen and the farmers with their huge farms and tractors. Their daughters and daughters-in-law outdo each other in sweeping the floor and kneading dough and cooking chapattis, and they reverently hold each pair of dusty shoes that they receive in the cloakroom to their foreheads before cleaning them in a show of humility. They come in the mornings and evenings and the gurdwara buzzes with activity. After they have gone, everything is silent again and the only people left there are Hukam Singh, the sevadars, a few stray pilgrims and other old men and women like him who have no place else to go or cannot stomach the daily, petty humiliations they have to face in the households of their grown children.

Fateh Singh lies on his cot half-asleep, flirting with the faint breeze and listening to the sounds of the summer night and the musical snores. The rumble of heavy trucks is one of the sounds of the night as he continues to drift midway between the blood-soaked dreams of his boyhood and the bloodier realities of his beloved Punjab today. Even the whoosh of heavy hydraulic brakes does not sound any alarm bells in his head. They don't make any effort at stealth at all. The crunching of their loud metal-soled army boots on the gravel outside belies the administration's claims of a covert operation. They are not slit-eyed and bow-legged; they wear olive green fatigues. They quickly form a single file and enter the courtyard on the double, the Sten guns hanging from their shoulders marking time on the sides of their torsos as they slap back and forth. There is no hatred in their eyes, but no compassion either. They are dumb, mute automatons out to do their job. Hukam Singh swings off the cot with an oath, displaying the kind of agility that only extremely fat people have, and a rifle butt comes crashing down on the back of his unprotected head.

Fateh Singh is too old to fight and continues to lie on the cot until he is jerked roughly to his feet. The sevadars huddle together like Siamese twins mumbling incoherently out of fear, but their protests of innocence crumble before their eyes after bouncing off the inscrutable masks that are the soldiers' faces. Their lips are silent now, but their eyes dart around looking for a saviour or an escape route. Their keskis, which Hukam Singh insists every man, woman and child must wear at all times inside the gurdwara, are rudely snatched from their heads and used to tie their hands behind their backs. The old woman from Udhampur is lying prostrate on the ground, begging for her husband's, or at least her son's life, who cowers against the south wall with his hands tied behind his head with his turban.

Fateh Singh looks around and sees that there are at least twenty-five or thirty Sikhs in the courtyard. There are old men and women and little children. And there are young men with hard expressions and sullen faces who stare back proudly and fearlessly at death, clad in olive green and black shiny metal. There is Hukam Singh groaning with pain and muttering the foulest of curses, ones that would make truck drivers blush. The woman on the floor is wailing now and her mournful dirge is interrupted by gut-wrenching sobs that can see what is about to happen, even as her eyes cannot. The mouths of the Sten guns look as large as cannons as the white marble wall behind their backs begins to push them, slowly and relentlessly, towards the shiny black circles of death. Their eyes can only see row upon row of neat geometric circles getting larger and larger until they look as big as railway tunnels and blacker.

Fateh Singh forces himself to look away and then blinks and shakes his head before rubbing his eyes hard. He tries to jerk his feeble mind back to sanity, but the vision refuses to go away. Where there was just a small congregation of Sikhs seconds ago, he now sees a crowd getting thicker and thicker every second. His eyes, wide with disbelief, take in a scene not unlike one of the rustic cultural melas organized by the government, the ones in which villagers are asked to dress up in ethnic costumes and enthusiastically form a colourful melange in every kind of folk dress imaginable. There are noble Harappans dressed in solemn white robes, patiently awaiting their deaths at the hands of the conquering northern tribes. He sees the ancient people of Punjab who fell fighting Alexander's hordes. Their bodies are covered with sword wounds and there is terror in their eyes. He sees common people, traders and farmers lying helpless in the dust, lamenting the loss of their women to the pillaging Mongol armies. He sees the wailing women of Sayyidpur. He sees herdsmen and villagers groaning under the tyranny of Mughal rule. He sees the first martyrs with their bodies scalded by hot sand and boiling in cauldrons, and having their bodies chopped limb by limb by oppressors with ecstatic smiles on their faces. He sees two little children being bricked into the white marble wall. He sees thousands of peasants proudly wearing the symbols of their new faith, lying in heaps that reached the sky, laid waste by Ahmad Shah Abdali and his rampaging Afghans. Then he begins to see more familiar faces. His father—young, fearless and bold—and their neighbours and friends from his childhood in Amritsar. The crowd is growing every second, miraculously fitting into the tiny courtyard, squeezing in between the slowly creeping wall and the terrible hive of perfect circles.

The soldiers do not multiply like the crowd, but their faces are kaleidoscopes that change form and colour every second. One instant they are the jewel in the widow's helmeted head and the next they are Taimur's bloodthirsty soldiers. Suddenly, they become Greeks with plumed helmets and then they are the thin-lipped, cruel Pathans with beards but no moustaches. Now the widow's elite commandos have slit eyes and puttee-clad bow legs that disappear into incongruously large regulation boots and their modern Sten guns turn into bolt-action rifles. The strange multiracial crowd now has familiar faces as it fills the courtyard. He sees the important men of Amritsar as they rub shoulders with the ne'er-do-wells and the layabouts and the street urchins. All the local leaders are there, as are the boisterous college students who announced the meeting even before the dire pronouncement of 'Goli se chittar-bittar dega' had died down. The courtyard, by some act of sorcery, is now a walled-in maidan overrun with weeds, with a small platform at one end and a well on the other.

Fateh Singh clutches his father's hand, who strangely enough does not have a hole in his head. There is an air of festivity in the maidan, as if the crowd is there to celebrate a holiday. The ominous words of the lackeys of the British have had no effect on the crowd. They are all drunk, high on nationalism. It is a wonderful time that gives men opportunities to rise above the mean drudgeries of their daily lives and feel that they are doing something great and selfless. Passionate pleas for sacrifices mingle with passionate rhetoric as speaker upon speaker takes to the stage, raising the crowds to even higher peaks of nationalistic ecstasy. There is romance in this mad rebellion and the sensation borders on the sensuous as they find themselves inflamed and excited but not quite ready to die.

At that moment, the bow-legged, khaki-clad Gurkhas trot in with their bolt-action rifles and their blonde blue-eyed commander. The crowd sees visions of glorious arrest and canonizing incarceration, and trembles with joyous anticipation of the about-to-be-born epic tale, the about-to-be-sung ballad for the purpose of regaling the proud and free future generations of Indians, their children and their grandchildren. The crowd looks at them defiantly, almost mockingly, and the cries of 'Aa gaye, aa gaye' slowly die down. Like little clockwork figures, they train their rifles on the mob and a white-gloved hand comes down rapidly in a flash. The crowd hasn't lost its bravado as the first crack sounds.

Fateh Singh's father is the first one to loudly proclaim 'Phokian! Phokian!' until the hole in the back of his head settles the issue.

The little boy cowers under his lifeless father who even in his death protects him from the flying bullets and the stampeding, charging feet. A surreal vision unfolds before his eyes, a vision that he is to carry in his head through sixty-five years, sixty-five long years of dazzling peaks of deification and euphoria and the respect reserved only for the living martyrs of a proud new nation and sixty-five years of haunting nightmares and betrayal and disillusionment and bitterness. He cannot understand where the strange hordes that have suddenly descended on to Jallianwala Bagh have come from. They are screaming louder than the dying citizens of Amritsar as they receive their fair share of the thick hail of British bullets. They are oddly dressed and they shout in exotic languages, their words sound like gibberish but he cannot mistake the pain in their impotent laments. Later, many years later, when he recounts the strange vision, his mother and his uncles and even his wife do not believe him. You were a child, they say, and petrified, these are hallucinations, Fateh Singh. There are hundreds who survived the massacre; nobody else saw them; surely the violence and the anguish of your father's death must have turned your head.

They keep on firing until they run out of bullets and the crowd is dense no more. The white glove signals and like well-trained horses they clip-clop out just as they had come in, their faces inscrutable, their eyes unblinking, leaving behind them a Punjab riddled with bullets, bleeding, hurting, lying unattended among the weeds and the dust of Jallianwala Bagh. The well is choked with the cold corpses of those who jumped in to escape the bullets and drowned under the incessant crush above. The bare feet of the crowd as it stampeded, chappals and *juttis* and leather shoes discarded in their haste to find a way to escape, have claimed as many lives as the bullets, mostly little children. Fateh Singh's uncle loads his father's lifeless body in a cart and carries him home.

The drummers don't stop because they run out of bullets; there is nobody to shoot at any more, because unlike Fateh Singh they cannot see that the courtyard of the gurdwara is densely packed with the tormented lost souls of Punjab, who are summoned back each time tyranny returns and innocents are butchered. Again and again as the centuries pass they return, sick to their guts with anxiety trying to shield their children and their children's children from the pain that they have endured. Vainly they throw themselves in the paths of flashing swords, but the swords pass unchallenged through them and always unerringly find their marks and their ranks swell as they mournfully wait for the next act of violent oppression. Fateh Singh can see them as he lies on the ground as they, ever hopeful, form a dense ghostly wall around the groggy Hukam Singh. He sees their expressions of dismay as bullet after bullet passes through them and plunges into the massive frame until Hukam Singh too joins the ranks of the would-be protectors and makes ludicrous attempts at trying to save the young sevadars, kicking and pummelling the soldiers and weeping bitter tears of frustration, unable to stop the slaughter.

It is quiet and the soldiers have gone away. Hukam Singh and his motley congregation have left too; tonight is going to be a very busy night in Punjab. The spirits never rest, the fools. Centuries upon centuries of frustration haven't taught them better. Even as they lie down to rest for a moment, they are needed again and again, and they always heed the call hoping against hope that this time they might prevail.

So Baba Fateh Singh lies with his face down in the dust, his white beard matted and the last few strands of hair sticky with blood. As his life ebbs away, he is sad because he does not want to die, but he is glad that he understands what he saw sixty-five years ago, when he was lucky and the bullets of the Raj did not find his little body. He was right and his family was wrong. He wasn't hallucinating, he tells himself as he prepares for the restless existence ahead.

The Court Martial

He looked more like a professor rather than the General Officer Commanding (GOC) of Central Command, with his rimless spectacles and impeccably trimmed goatee. Lt General Bakshi, resplendent in his uniform, his chest covered with ribbons that spoke of his long and distinguished service in the Indian Army, looked at the officer standing ramrod stiff before him, his gaze fixed straight ahead. General Bakshi spoke in precise, clipped sentences, in the unmistakable dialect of India's public school–educated elite. 'Brigadier Cheramar, place your hand on the Bible and repeat after me.'

The young second lieutenant serving as a clerk to the General Court Martial (GCM) brought forth a well-worn copy of the Old Testament and held it flat for the officer who placed his left hand on the book and his right hand over his heart.

'I, Sylvan Cheramar, swear by Almighty God that I will to the best of my ability carry out the duties of presiding officer in accordance with the Army Act and the rules made thereunder, without partiality, favour or affection, and I do further swear that I will not on any account, at any time whatsoever, disclose or discover the vote or opinion on any matter of any particular member of the court martial, unless required to give evidence thereof by a court of justice or a court martial in due course of law.'

Brigadier Cheramar did not speak in the clipped manner of his GOC, nor was there anything patrician in his bearing. But despite his short stature, nondescript appearance and thick Malayali accent, which his brother officers who came from elite backgrounds secretly made fun of, he was widely respected and known to be one of the superstars on the GOC's staff. He had distinguished himself in the '71 war and was the kind of officer that men would follow off a cliff without question. His subordinate officers knew him to be tough and uncompromising but also scrupulously fair.

Four other officers had marched up to the GOC before the brigadier. Major Brar had been sworn in like the brigadier, but Major Modi, Captain Mukherjee and Captain Rizwan had been administered an oath of affirmation. The quaint rules governing a GCM, the military trial reserved for the gravest offences, had been handed down from the British, having been put in place after the Sepoy Mutiny of 1857, the First War of Independence.

As the brigadier took his place on the bench with his fellow officers, his thoughts drifted back to his conversation with the GOC three weeks earlier. The general had summoned him not to the command headquarters, but to his home one evening. After an excellent dinner had been served by the general's orderly, he was invited to the general's study for cognac and a cigar. Brigadier Cheramar, who came from a very humble background, sat comfortably in a leather armchair, nursing his cognac, and remembered his awkwardness and bemusement when he was first invited to the general's bungalow after his promotion. The general's very kind wife, Shelly, had sensed his awkwardness and had done her best to put him at ease. Now, three years later, he could puff his cigar like he had been born into this lifestyle.

'They're sending us the boys, Sylvan,' General Bakshi had said, his brow furrowed.

'But, Sir, I thought the courts martial were going to be handled by headquarters!'

'That was the original plan, Sylvan, but the top brass have decided that each command will deal with its own mutineers. The Ramgarh boys are our problem. Most of the lads who mutinied were raw recruits and their cases have been resolved through summary trials within their units. Most of them have served their twenty-eight days and been reassigned. The ringleaders, the instigators and some of the lads who committed the most egregious offences are being sent here. We have our work cut out for us, I'm afraid.'

Eight months had passed since Operation Blue Star and the mutinies that had broken out after the attack on the Golden Temple. The army had been shaken up like never before in independent India. For thirty-seven years, despite the rampant corruption that had become the hallmark of almost every public institution, the army had managed to stay untainted and effective. A mutiny in the Indian Army was unheard of, that too by Sikh soldiers who had formed its backbone for decades. It had seemed incomprehensible. And yet it had happened.

The mutinies had been quelled rapidly and press censorship in the wake of Operation Blue Star had ensured that they did not get too much attention. But they had to be dealt with, that too swiftly and discreetly. Several of the army generals had taken a hard line, no doubt feeling that the blot the mutiny would leave on the army's reputation could only be erased by making an example of the mutineers. The defence ministry, on the other hand, preferred a softer approach as inquiries conducted after the mutiny had shown that the actions of most of the soldiers had not been premeditated but an emotional response to the attack on the Golden Temple. The ministry also believed that the army chain of command shared a good portion of the blame for its very poor communication to the Sikh rank and file, both during and after Operation Blue Star.

There were practical considerations as well. In 1959, a battalion from the Assam Regiment, posted in Kashmir, had mutinied. Most of the soldiers, who were predominantly Mizos, were court-martialled and sacked. The former soldiers, unemployed and disgruntled, had ended up joining the Mizo National Army, a rebel force that had launched an armed insurrection several years later. Letting a large band of angry and disgruntled Sikh soldiers loose in post–Blue Star Punjab definitely did not seem to be a wise move.

It was completely understandable why General Bakshi was not keen on presiding over the courts martial of the Ramgarh rebels.

The general went on to explain why Brigadier Cheramar had been summoned to his bungalow. The courts martial were to be held at various regimental centres in Jabalpur. The most important one was to be at the Grinder Club at the Grenadiers' Regimental Centre. On trial would be Subedar Sumedh Singh, one of the Junior Commissioned Officers (JCOs) from the 9th Battalion of the Sikh Regiment that had mutinied in Ramgarh. Two other JCOs and two jawans, or privates, would be tried with him. Interest in Sumedh Singh's trial ran all the way up the chain of command to the defence minister himself, as he had been flagged by numerous eyewitnesses as one of the ringleaders of the mutiny.

Brigadier Cheramar was to lead the bench at the General Court Martial of Subedar Sumedh Singh. 'Your job, Sylvan, is to throw the book at the subedar, but you will need to be scrupulously fair. The ministry and the top brass have their eyes upon us,' General Bakshi had said with an uncharacteristic sigh of resignation.

The brigadier, who had arrived early at the Grinder Club on the morning of the court martial, was greeted by a large sign outside the entrance that solemnly announced: 'Silence, GCM in progress'. The mood in the club, usually steeped in bonhomie and the site of many a rambunctious gathering, was sombre. Missing were the young officers who were usually the last to show up for breakfast and the impeccably dressed bearers who scurried to serve them. The large dance floor had been turned into a makeshift courtroom, its centre occupied by an impressive-looking mahogany table, behind which were six dining chairs.

Adjacent to the large table, on either side, were two smaller tables facing each other and separated by almost twenty feet, three

chairs behind each. Smack in the middle of the two tables was a
metal chair that looked singularly uncomfortable. It faced the large
mahogany table. Several feet behind the solitary metal chair sat
five more identical chairs, and further behind them was a row of
comfortable-looking club chairs.

The brigadier paced the makeshift courtroom, absently
straightening the rows of chairs that were already aligned with
military precision, as he thought about the task that lay ahead. There
had been a few unexpected developments in the days leading up to
the court martial. Since the five accused soldiers who were to appear
before the court were either JCOs or enlisted men, it had been
General Bakshi's expectation that a defending officer be assigned.
The accused would almost certainly not have the wherewithal to
engage private attorneys. Since it was important that the GCM be
perceived as being fair, General Bakshi had authorized the hiring
of a local Jabalpur lawyer, Hira Singh Chauhan, on a per diem
payment of Rs 250 to supplement the defence. However, a week
before the GCM, Rajinder Singh Sodhi, a well-known Supreme
Court lawyer from Delhi, visited Jabalpur and retained the best and
most expensive lawyers in the city to defend the accused soldiers.
The defence team was headed by R.K. Bhatt who was well known
in Jabalpur legal circles as a sharp and tough attorney.

The appearance of a crack defence team was a mixed blessing.
On one hand, it would bolster the argument that the GCM was
fair. However, Lieutenant Colonel (Lt Col) Bhardwaj, one of the
superstars in the office of the judge advocate general (JAG), who
had been appointed the prosecuting officer, would now have his
work cut out for him.

The Grinder Club was slowly filling up. The brigadier's
adjutant, Lt Pande, scurried around, showing the new arrivals to
their seats. In a few minutes, almost every seat in the courtroom,
with the exception of the six metal chairs, was full. General Bakshi
arrived a couple of minutes before the official start time of the
GCM and took a seat at the very back of the courtroom.

Brigadier Cheramar sat at the centre of the large table, while his fellow officers on the bench surveyed the room. To his right sat R.K. Bhatt, with two junior attorneys. Opposite the defence team, to the left of the bench, sat Lt Col Bhardwaj and his assistant. The third seat at that table was taken by a major from the office of the judge advocate general. As none of the officers on the bench, including the brigadier, were legal experts, his role was to serve as their adviser on all legal matters.

Brigadier Cheramar called the GCM to order. The first order of business was the swearing-in of all the officers on the bench and the judge advocate general. Once the formalities were complete and the bench was seated, Lt Pande strode out of the room and barked an order. A couple of minutes later, seven men marched past him in a single file, the first and last in crisply starched uniforms and carrying gleaming bayoneted rifles. The five in the middle were Sikhs. Four of them were young, not one of them older than twenty-one or twenty-two. The last Sikh, who seemed to be in his early forties, had a bushy salt-and-pepper beard and wore a crumpled white kurta-pyjama in contrast to the four young men who wore wrinkled uniforms and ammunition boots. The two guards smartly marched the men on trial into the courtroom and retreated after an about-turn, leading the men to the five metal chairs, facing the bench.

Lt Col Bhardwaj was the first to address the bench.

'The Sikh Regiment is the most decorated in the Indian Army. Fourteen Victoria Crosses, twenty-one Order of Merits, two Param Vir Chakras, two Ashoka Chakras, fourteen Maha Vir Chakras and numerous other honours from the time of its inception to the present day. The first battalion of this regiment was raised in 1846, just before the fall of the Sikh empire, and since then it has been one of the most storied in, first, the British Indian Army and, later, the Indian Army after Independence. In June 1984, the actions of a few irresponsible men put a blot on the escutcheon of this venerable regiment. Today, it is my duty to try and erase this blot by bringing to justice some of the men who bear the greatest responsibility for this shameful episode, which has dishonoured not just the Sikh Regiment but the entire Indian Army.

'Eyewitness testimony will prove to the bench that the five defendants who are being tried by the General Court Martial today wilfully instigated their comrades to mutiny, seize the armoury at the Ramgarh Cantonment, attacked their superiors, committed murder, misappropriated government and private property, terrorized the civilian population and fired upon their brothers of the Indian Army. It will be further established that these men were motivated by intolerance and religious bigotry that followed their systematic radicalization by forces external to the army. Once I am able to establish their guilt, I intend to ask the bench to impose the harshest of sentences on these men. The Indian Army is known to be one of the most disciplined in the world and the word "mutiny" has never been associated with it ever before. Unless an example is made of these men, the honour of the Indian Army cannot be restored. I do not exaggerate, gentlemen! Nothing less than the honour of the institution that we so proudly serve is at stake in this General Court Martial today.'

R.K. Bhatt's opening statement was brief.

'The prosecuting officer would have the bench believe that my clients were the instigators of the mutiny in Ramgarh Cantonment, which followed the army's attack on the Golden Temple. He would have you believe that these men were conspirators and that they hatched a plot that was designed to damage the Indian Army. I will prove to the bench that there was no such plot. We Indians are all attached to our faiths, no matter which religion we follow, as is our right guaranteed by the Constitution. There is no denying that the Sikh Regiment mutinied. However, it is disingenuous to cast a spontaneous response to a traumatic event as a premeditated conspiracy. The evidence will show that the mutiny and the tragic events that followed were a direct consequence of the ill-considered attack on the Golden Temple, and the abject failure of the Sikh Regiment's chain of command to assuage the fears of their soldiers through clear and timely communication. I will ask the bench to be extremely lenient once the mitigating circumstances have been clearly understood.'

The bench listened carefully, taking notes as the charge sheet was read.

'The accused (1) No. 3368610 Subedar Sumedh Singh, (2) No. 3381849 Lance Naik Balraj Singh, (3) No. 3382130 Lance Naik Gurmeet Singh, (4) No. 3381905 Sepoy Hakam Singh, (5) No. 3381982 Sepoy Gurnam Singh, all of the Sikh Regimental Centre charged with:

'First charge: Army Act, Section 37(C) against all accused persons—BEING PRESENT AT A MUTINY IN THE MILITARY FORCES OF INDIA, NOT USING THEIR UTMOST ENDEAVOURS TO SUPPRESS THE SAME—in that they together at Ramgarh, on 10 June 1984, while on guard duty at the training battalion *kote* [armoury] of the Sikh Regimental Centre, and when soldiers of the said centre advanced towards the training battalion armoury in a mutinous spirit to loot the said kote, failed to use their utmost endeavours to suppress the said mutiny.

'Second charge: Army Act, Section 37(E) against accused 1 only—ENDEAVOURS TO SEDUCE ANY PERSON IN THE MILITARY FORCES OF INDIA FROM HIS DUTY OR ALLEGIANCE TO THE UNION—in that at Ramgarh, between 4 June 1984 and 10 June 1984, the accused addressed several JCOs and sepoys with inflammatory religious rhetoric and urged them to retaliate against the Indian Union by mutinying, looting the kote and attacking their senior officer. Further, the accused was one of the principal architects of the plan to commandeer army and civilian vehicles to rush to Amritsar to avenge the attack on the Golden Temple.

'Third charge: Army Act, Section 63 against accused 2 and 3 only—AN OMISSION PREJUDICIAL TO GOOD ORDER AND MILITARY DISCIPLINE—in that they together at Ramgarh, on 10 June 1984, while on guard duty at the training battalion armoury of the Sikh Regimental Centre improperly omitted to protect the said battalion kote, which resulted in the loss of following arms:

(a)   Rifles 7.62 mm AI - 1330
(b)   Carbine Machine 9 mm - 111
(c)   Gun machine 7.62 mm 1B - 96
(d)   Gun machine 7.62 mm IC - 06

'Fourth charge: Army Act, Section 38(1) against all accused persons—DESERTING THE SERVICE—in that they, at Ramgarh on 10 June 1984, absented themselves from the Sikh Regimental Centre until apprehended by personnel of 4 Para on National Highway 31 on 11 June 1984.

'Fifth charge: Army Act, Section 53(B) against accused 4 and 5 only—WITHOUT PROPER AUTHORITY EXTRACTS FROM ANY PERSON MONEY, PROVISIONS OR SERVICE—in that on National Highway 2 on 10 June 1984, the accused consumed food from one Lucky Dhaba and refused to pay for the same before exiting the premises.'

Brigadier Cheramar looked at the five soldiers on trial as the charge sheet was read out in Punjabi. Subedar Sumedh Singh sat ramrod straight, completely impassive, his face betraying no trace of emotion, looking somewhat incongruous in his rumpled kurta-pyjama. The lance naiks, Balraj Singh and Gurmeet Singh, looked extremely worried, visibly wincing as the charge sheet was read. Hakam Singh and Gurnam Singh, both of them under nineteen, looked unperturbed, the gravity of the situation beyond their comprehension. Both of them grinned and briefly looked at one another when the last charge was read, as if at the memory of a sophomoric adventure.

The first witness for the prosecution was Captain Saxena, one of the training officers at Ramgarh, who had been an eyewitness to the looting of the armoury.

'Around 11:30 a.m. on 10 June, I was at my company, going over the training plans for an upcoming exercise, when I was interrupted by one of the JCOs responsible for guarding the kote. He was quite breathless as he had run all the way from the kote, which is quite a distance from my company. He informed me that a large body of armed soldiers was advancing towards the kote. I quickly informed my CO, Lt Col K.K. Varma, and both of us ran towards the kote with the JCO behind us. As we turned around a bend and the kote became visible, we heard the roar of gunfire. The kote was under attack and from a distance we could see some of the guards, heavily outnumbered, trying to return fire. Lt Col Varma and I ducked into an unmanned sentry post and took cover. Before us we saw fifty men take up the lying-down position, some forty yards from the front of the kote, and firing in unison. The guards, finally realizing how heavily outnumbered they were, started to flee.

'I raised my weapon to fire at the mutineers, but Lt Col Varma stopped me saying that if I fired one shot, forty rifles would turn towards us within seconds. He got to his feet and tried to reason with the men, but despite his pleas they continued to fire. When the return fire from the kote had completely died down, the mutineers surrounded our sentry post. "Murder them all," a voice shouted in Punjabi and several of the soldiers laughed. A JCO, who seemed to be in command, stepped forward and briskly saluted us both. "Please return to your company, Sir," he said very calmly. "We will do what we need to do and nobody will stop us today." They then relieved us of our weapons and sent us away unmolested. Later, we learned that they ransacked the kote and left with hundreds of rifles, machine guns and ammunition.'

R.K. Bhatt's cross-examination of Captain Saxena was brief but effective. When asked if he could identify any of the accused as having been among the men who ransacked the kote, Captain Saxena merely said that he could not be certain because all Sikh soldiers looked alike!

Lt Col Bhardwaj entered into evidence reports filed by the army units that had eventually stopped and arrested the mutineers. The reports clearly stated that every mutineer who had been apprehended had been armed. While all the five accused had denied storming the kote, they had clearly armed themselves with weapons looted from there. That, he said, made them accessories and he asked for the severest penalties that the charge warranted.

Lt Col K.K. Varma was the next witness called by the prosecution. The second charge, against Subedar Sumedh Singh, was of the greatest interest to the top brass and Brigadier Cheramar had been advised of the sensitivity by General Bakshi before the GCM. Lt Col Varma, whose encounter with the mutineers had already been described by Captain Saxena, was visibly agitated as he delivered his testimony.

'I had foreseen the trouble,' he said. 'Several months before the mutiny, several of the men stopped trimming their beards and started showing up for physical drills wearing kirpans, daggers that orthodox Sikhs always carry on their person. I had also been informed that many soldiers had been turning down their ration of rum. It was obvious to me that they had been indoctrinated. I had heard rumblings that cassette tapes with speeches of Bhindranwale were being circulated. One of my officers actually brought me a tape, and I listened. To my shock, I discovered that he been exhorting Sikhs to give up all drugs and alcohol, grow their beards long, go through the initiation ceremony called *amrit sanchar* and start wearing kirpans! The boys' heads were being filled with religious nonsense. Small wonder then that they mutinied!

'I confronted the JCOs, including Subedar Sumedh Singh who had also grown his beard out by then and was himself wearing a kirpan while leading the drill that day. He informed me that many of the Sikhs had joined the Amritdharis, which to the best of my knowledge is a very dangerous sect inimical to the integrity of the Union of India. This, by the way, was also mentioned in the army journal *Guftagoo*. Furthermore, he displayed a piece of paper with a rule dating back to British times, which permitted Sikh soldiers to carry kirpans. It felt like borderline insubordination to me. There were other troubling signs of the religious bigotry that had been creeping in. There is a regimental gurdwara at Ramgarh, where a full Sikh service is conducted every Sunday. After the service, *karah* prasad, a consecrated sweet, is distributed. For many years Dalda, or hydrogenated vegetable oil, was used to prepare the karah prasad. Subedar Sumedh Singh started agitating that desi ghee be used instead! Of course, we did not tolerate such nonsense! It is my opinion that while Operation Blue Star may have indeed been the flashpoint of the mutiny, the groundwork had been laid much before through the actions of Subedar Sumedh Singh and several other JCOs who had been similarly radicalized. His openly expressed disgruntlement and insubordinate demeanour made it impossible to come to any other conclusion.' Clearly, Lt Col Varma had no doubt that Sumedh Singh was one of the main instigators of the mutiny.

R.K. Bhatt, who had been looking bemusedly at Lt Col Varma as he delivered his testimony, stood up to cross-examine, holding a stack of books and pamphlets against his chest. He walked up to the Lt Col and very deliberately handed him a book from his little stack. 'Lt Col Varma, can you please read the title of this book and the names of the authors for us?'

'*The Sikhs: Their Religious Beliefs and Practices*. The authors are W. Owen Cole and Piara Singh Sambhi.'

'And would you mind reading the capsule biography of Mr Cole?'

'Dr W. Owen Cole is a pioneering educationist staunchly committed to the transformation of religious education from instruction primarily in Christianity to a subject that would develop an understanding and appreciation of world faiths. His role, nationally and internationally, in furthering an informed understanding of Sikh tradition is incalculable.'

'Would you say that he seems like a credible source on the beliefs of the Sikhs?'

'It seems so from the bio!'

'Please open the book and go to the page indicated by the bookmark, and read the section about Amritdhari Sikhs.'

'Amritdhari: One who has been initiated into the Khalsa order created by Guru Gobind Singh in 1699, in accordance with the rules and rites laid down in the Rahit Maryada, the Sikh code of conduct, and who lives in obedience to the vows taken at the ceremony known as amrit sanchar. Amrit sanchar, the initiation into the Khalsa, starts with a period of initiation in which the initiate grows his hair and beard long and abstains from prohibited actions such as consuming tobacco and alcohol. This is followed by a formal ceremony that recreates the original initiation in 1699. After the initiation, the Amritdhari is required to wear on his person the five symbols of the Khalsa order, including the kirpan, and never cut his hair.'

R.K. Bhatt allowed Lt Col Varma to finish reading the description of an Amritdhari Sikh and then deliberately said nothing for almost a minute, letting the import of the words sink in, before turning to the bench.

'I would like to draw the attention of the bench to the following. First of all, Amritdharis have existed for almost three hundred years and certainly predate Bhindranwale. The order was started by none other than Guru Gobind Singh, the tenth Sikh guru, who is a national hero and well known for his valiant battles and sacrifices in the quest for justice. Now, I will ask Lt Col Varma to read two more short paragraphs.'

R.K. Bhatt handed Lt Col Varma a thin pamphlet and asked him to read the title, followed by a marked passage.

'The Constitution of India, Article 25: All persons are equally entitled to freedom of conscience and the right freely to profess, practise and propagate religion.'

After another dramatic pause, R.K. Bhatt handed Lt Col Varma a second pamphlet, which the Lt Col, now understanding where the argument was headed, began to read somewhat sullenly.

'The Universal Declaration of Human Rights, Article 18: Everyone has the right to freedom of thought, conscience and religion. This right includes freedom to change his religion or belief, and freedom, either alone or in community with others and in public or private, to manifest his religion or belief in teaching, practice, worship and observance.'

Once again, R.K. Bhatt addressed the bench.

'The Universal Declaration of Human Rights was adopted by the United Nations in 1948 and our great nation is a signatory to the document. Lt Col Varma would have the bench believe that the accused, Subedar Sumedh Singh, as well as several of the other soldiers in the Sikh Regiment, displayed signs of radicalization before the mutiny. However, what we have just heard contradicts that argument completely. What Lt Col Varma observed was simply a group of men trying to live according to their faith, which as Indian citizens, they have the inalienable right to do. Unfortunately, this ignorance of the fundamental religious beliefs of the Sikhs seems to be widespread in the Indian Army.

'I will now read two excerpts from *Guftagoo*, the Indian Army bulletin, which is circulated throughout the force. These excerpts are from serial number 153 published in June 1984:

'Some of our innocent countrymen were administered oath in the name of religion to support extremists and actively participate in the act of terrorism. These people wear a miniature kirpan around their neck and are called Amritdharis.

Although majority of the terrorists have been dealt with and a bulk of arms and ammunitions recovered, yet a large number of them are still at large. They have to be subdued to achieve the final aim of restoring peace in the country. Any knowledge of the Amritdharis, who are dangerous people and pledged to commit murder, arson and acts of terrorism, should be immediately brought to the notice of the authorities. These people may appear harmless from outside, but they are basically committed to terrorism. In the interest of us all, their identity and whereabouts must always be disclosed.'

R.K. Bhatt looked at the panel. With the exception of Major Brar, who looked completely impassive, the rest of the panel, including Brigadier Cheramar, looked somewhat nonplussed. R.K. Bhatt, betraying no emotion, swooped in for the kill.

'The Indian Army is celebrated for being incorruptible and secular. Ever since the dawn of Independence, our brave Sikh soldiers have played a disproportionate role in keeping our nation safe and have exhibited great gallantry during every war that we have had to fight. This is a well-known fact and I do not need to present evidence of this to the panel. In great part, the legendary military prowess of the Sikhs can be traced back to that fateful day in 1699, when Guru Gobind Singh transformed an entire community through the first amrit sanchar, infusing them with a martial spirit that has endured to this day.

'It is then a matter of deep shame that an institution known for fairness and balance would wilfully try to paint an entire community as terrorists. The excerpt that I read from *Guftagoo* is reprehensible, as is Lt Col Varma's suggestion that his men were prone to mutiny because they chose to exercise the freedom to practise the faith of their forefathers, a freedom that is guaranteed by the Constitution of India. It is ironic that the British understood the connection between the valour of their Sikh soldiers and their faith much better than the Indian Army does today! The British never interfered with their faith in any way and gave them full freedom to practise it.

'The charge against Subedar Sumedh Singh is absurd because it rests on the assumption that he must have been radicalized and he must have been an instigator of the mutiny because he is an Amritdhari Sikh. Based on the evidence presented, I urge the bench to throw this charge out. To further establish the absurdity of the charge, I would like to call upon a witness.'

The energy in the room changed palpably as Subedar Sumedh Singh was sworn in as a witness. Until that point in the court martial, none of the accused had been called to testify. It seemed to be a risky strategy. While Sumedh Singh was one of the most respected JCOs in his regiment, known to be a very calm person, he was a simple rustic who risked being destroyed during cross-examination by Lt Col Bhardwaj, reputed to be one of the army's most brilliant lawyers.

R.K. Bhatt looked at his client and asked in a barely audible voice. 'Subedar Sumedh Singh, why are you not in your uniform?'

Sumedh Singh spoke in Punjabi, in a low but firm voice. One of the Punjabi-speaking officers had been instructed to translate as he spoke. Brigadier Cheramar listened intently. 'For six generations, the army has been the mother and father of my family. It has been our livelihood and it has been our honour. Six generations of my family have proudly worn this uniform in times of war and peace. But, Sirji, I cannot wear it any more.'

'Can you tell the bench why, Subedar Sumedh Singh?'

'Sirji, my family has been serving in the Sikh Regiment for one hundred and thirty-eight years, but we have been serving in the Khalsa army of Guru Gobind Singhji for twice as long. My ancestors were at Anandpur Sahib on the day that Guru Gobind Singhji created the Khalsa. They too were initiated with the amrit that the guru prepared. Since that day, our lives have been dedicated to the guru. Yes, we are soldiers, but we are Khalsas first. We fought at Saragarhi and we fought in Belgium and France and Egypt and Iran. We fought in El-Alamein and we fought in the Philippines and Burma. We fought in Kashmir and we fought in Bangladesh. Every time we fought, no matter whether it was in Punjab or Europe or Africa or China, we fought proudly as the Khalsas. We always carried the Guru Granth Sahib into battle with full honours. The British sarkar knew this and the Bharat sarkar seemed to know this is well. But, Sirji, everything changed last year when the Brahmani attacked Darbar Sahib.'

Lt Col Bhardwaj objected to the late prime minister Indira Gandhi being pejoratively referred to as 'the Brahmin woman' and the bench instructed Sumedh Singh to keep his tone respectful as he continued.

'Sirji, in India, when there is trouble that the police or the politicians cannot handle, the army is called in. The army gives everyone confidence because it is not corrupt or political. But all that changed after the attack on Darbar Sahib. The Brahmani used the army for her political ends and ordered it to attack Darbar Sahib. How can anyone have confidence in the army again? When I saw that the army had lost its honour, I decided to take off my uniform and never put it back on.'

R.K. Bhatt looked at Subedar Sumedh Singh sympathetically and said, 'Lt Col Varma has claimed that you and the other men were radicalized by Bhindranwale and encouraged to become Amritdharis. Is this true? Did you encourage the jawans under you to become Amritdharis as well?'

Sumedh Singh looked straight at Lt Col Varma as he responded. 'Sirji, I am forty-five years old. I took amrit and became a Khalsa when I was thirteen years old! The jawans look up to me and respect me. Over the years, many of them have come to me for guidance on all kinds of matters—family issues, marriage, promotions and disputes, everything you can imagine. And yes, since I was an Amritdhari, they asked me about that as well. I always told them that it was a wonderful thing to do, but they had to be completely committed to the disciplined life of an Amritdhari. No more rum. No more whoring. They would have to grow their beards and not trim them any more. They would have to adopt the symbols of the Khalsa, including the kirpan. They would have to commit to morning and evening prayers each day. Many would change their minds after hearing about the requirements and the restrictions, but some would request that they go through amrit sanchar.'

'Was any of this influenced by Bhindranwale?'

'Sirji, Santji was a great soul, but the Amritdharis have existed before him and will continue to exist after him.'

Lt Col Bhardwaj spoke. 'I would like to draw the bench's attention to the fact that the accused just referred to the deceased terrorist Bhindranwale as a great soul.'

R.K. Bhatt now turned in a rather unexpected direction, as he questioned his witness further. 'Subedar Sumedh Singh, you are a highly decorated soldier with a long and distinguished career, and an unblemished record. Yet you are being charged with mutinying and inciting other soldiers to mutiny. Can you explain this to the bench?'

Every eye in the courtroom was on Sumedh Singh as he began to speak reflectively. 'Sirji, mutiny is a dirty word. A mutiny is a dishonourable act by a coward who has no character. What happened in Ramgarh on 10 June 1984 was no mutiny. I have been a soldier my entire life. I know how to take orders and follow them. The discipline of the army has ruled my life since I was seventeen years old.

'Right after the attack on Darbar Sahib started, rumours began to fly. There was no news, of course, but some of the civilians who worked in the cantonment started getting phone calls from Punjab. It was clear that something terrible was happening, but nobody knew exactly what. On 7 July, word started to get around that the Akal Takht had been attacked with tanks and demolished. I refused to believe it. How could the Indian Army ever attack Darbar Sahib! That too with tanks! I tried to calm the jawans down and told them not to believe in rumours. I even went up to my CO and asked him to address the men and tell them that the rumours were false. At that time, I could not understand why my CO got so angry with me. But, of course, now I understand. My CO is a man of honour. He could not tell the jawans that the rumours were false, because they weren't!

'On the morning of 9 June, I got a phone call from my father-in-law who lives in Amritsar. It was then that I learned that the impossible had happened. Darbar Sahib had been attacked. The Akal Takht had been reduced to rubble and thousands had died. I was shocked. It felt like the earth had vanished from under my feet. Many other jawans and JCOs got phone calls from Punjab as well. Since there was a news blackout and travel was severely restricted, nobody seemed to know exactly what was going on. There were rumours that villages were being attacked and young men were being rounded up and shot, that women were being dishonoured. By the evening of the 9th, the mood of the jawans had started to turn uglier and uglier. Many JCOs went to their officers to tell them that the men were restless. Someone in a position of authority needed to talk to them, tell them what was going on, reassure them that civilians in Punjab were safe. But the top brass said nothing. Instead, they got angry at the JCOs and told them to do their duty and control the boys.

'I spent the night at the regimental gurdwara, in prayer. I truly did not know what to do. That night, it felt like even the Guru had turned his back on me. The regimental Granthi had started an *akhand path*, an uninterrupted reading of the Guru Granth Sahib, earlier that day. The kind, old man could think of no other way to respond to the terrifying news and rumours that were flying around the regiment. I stayed at the gurdwara and read the Guru Granth Sahib all night but got no relief. The gurdwara, which would usually be deserted at night, saw a steady stream of jawans and JCOs who came to pay their respects all through the night. Several were weeping unabashedly. They would bow their heads, make an offering and sit for a few minutes, listening to the recitation of the Guru Granth Sahib. Then they would leave and more would trickle in.

'By dawn, I was exhausted and lay down in the Granthi's room to rest. It was mid-morning when one of the jawans shook me awake and told me that the kote had been taken. The soldiers had taken matters into their own hands and more than a thousand men were ready to leave the cantonment. They could take it no more. Their anxiety had reached fever pitch and they were going to Punjab to see what had happened with their own eyes.

'I did not hesitate for even a minute. It was as if all my doubts had suddenly vanished and my path lay clear and illuminated before me. I looked at the crumpled uniform I had slept in. Let me tell you, there is nothing on earth that I am prouder of than my service in the army. I have discharged every duty with honour and dedication, and I never besmirched the uniform I wore so proudly my entire life. I went back to my quarters and took off my uniform for the last time. I wish I had had enough time to wash it, starch it and iron it. But I didn't. I folded it very respectfully, laid it on my bed and saluted it. I knew that there would be no coming back and that I would never don my uniform again. Then I put on civilian clothes and ran to where the jawans and JCOs bound for Punjab had gathered.'

There was pin-drop silence in the room. R.K. Bhatt looked at Lt Col Bhardwaj and spoke quietly. 'Your witness.' The prosecuting officer turned to the bench and, to everyone's surprise, declined to cross-examine Sumedh Singh, noting that the accused had effectively confessed to taking off his uniform and joining the mutiny willingly.

Lunch had been arranged for the bench at the nearby Cobra Officers' Mess. Brigadier Cheramar had invited General Bakshi to join them as well. The bench had been instructed not to discuss the case with anyone until a verdict had been reached, but they had barely started eating when Major Modi, who had spent his teen years in England, declared that it was a rum business. Brigadier Cheramar listened quietly as Captain Bhardwaj and Captain Rizwan weighed in as well, mostly agreeing that the whole Amritdhari business had definitely left some egg on the army's face.

'Clever chap, that civilian lawyer,' said Major Modi with grudging admiration. 'He is running circles around Lt Col Bhardwaj.' Major Brar, however, maintained a studied silence, appearing to eat his mutton chops with great concentration. General Bakshi, ever a stickler for rules, refrained from commenting on the proceedings, instead reiterating how important it was that an example be made of the men on trial, while being scrupulously fair.

Lt Col Bhardwaj rose to address the third charge after the recess. Lt Col Varma was called to the stand again to provide an inventory of the arsenal that had been looted from the kote. The bench looked grave as the loss of more than fifteen hundred guns, including more than two hundred automatic weapons, was detailed. The inventory was admitted into evidence without any objection from the defence team, as the looting of the kote was beyond dispute. R.K. Bhatt did, however, make the observation that while Lance Naik Balraj Singh and Lance Naik Gurmeet Singh had been on guard duty at the kote, they had been completely caught unawares by the attack by a large force of their fellow soldiers. He argued that the guards were heavily outnumbered and had no inkling of the attackers' intentions, and that it was completely understandable that they did not fire at them. Lt Col Bhardwaj, however, responded by emphasizing that the NCOs had a specific responsibility to protect army property, weaponry and ordnance, which they had clearly neglected to discharge by not intervening when the kote was being looted. Further, it was beyond dispute that the two accused NCOs had joined the mutiny after the attack, as they had been among the armed men who had been apprehended the following day. Lt Col Bhardwaj also entered into evidence the testimony of a jawan who had alerted the guards of the kote about the impending attack, at least half an hour before it began. The accused had not requested that additional ammunition be issued. The accused had not informed their superior officer. This, according to the prosecuting officer, clearly indicated that the accused were colluding with the attackers. Further, no resistance whatsoever was offered, neither was a shot fired nor was there a single casualty on either side! Both NCOs looked on ashen-faced as Lt Col Bhardwaj's arguments were translated, and R.K. Bhatt chose not to ask them to testify, instead reiterating the argument that the events of 10 June were so out of the ordinary that the accused could not be faulted for not engaging with the attackers. He also reminded the bench that Lt Col Varma and Captain Saxena too had looked on during the attack and not intervened.

As the GCM turned to the fourth charge, Lt Col Bhardwaj brought in Subedar Maghar Singh as a witness. After being sworn in, the subedar was asked to tell the bench what happened after the kote was looted.

'My name is Maghar Singh; my rank is subedar and I serve in the 9th battalion of the Sikh Regiment.' Subedar Maghar Singh cut a fine figure as he stood ramrod straight and delivered his testimony. Tall and lean, his uniform impeccably starched and ironed, and his boots polished to a high gloss, the JCO looked younger than his fifty-plus years. On his head sat a perfectly wound khaki turban and his salt-and-pepper beard was neatly contained in a hairnet that he wore on his cheeks and under his chin. His moustache was neatly waxed into impressive-looking handlebars.

Lt Col Bhardwaj slowly walked up to the JCO, looking almost jubilant as he presented his star witness. 'Subedar Maghar Singh. Will you tell the bench what happened on 10 July after the kote was looted?'

Subedar Maghar Singh, who had been looking at Sumedh Singh, complex emotions playing on his face, turned his eyes somewhat guiltily towards Lt Col Bhardwaj and cleared his throat.

'I was inspecting the motor pool, which was my responsibility, when I heard a barrage of gunfire. I was quite startled because I was unaware of any firing drills on that day. As I stepped out of the motor shed, I could see many of the younger jawans running around in a most undisciplined manner. Some were in uniform and some were not. They seemed to be heading in the general direction of the parade ground, which was not visible from the motor pool. Sensing that something was amiss, I started to follow them. As I got closer to the parade ground, I could hear the hubbub of voices.

Every few seconds, I heard shots that were definitely coming from the direction of the parade ground.

'As I turned around the last set of barracks that stood between me and the parade ground, I saw a sight that I will never forget. There were hundreds of jawans, NCOs and JCOs at the parade ground. Not part of a drill but milling about in a most unruly manner. Every man was armed. Most of the jawans had rifles and several of the NCOs had LMGs. Every now and then, a jawan would discharge his weapon into the air, drawing raucous cheers from the mob, and then the others would follow. As I tried to make sense of the madness, I started paying attention to the snatches of conversation.

'I was shocked to learn that the CO had been shot dead and the kote had been looted. In my thirty-two years in the army, I had never imagined that something like this could ever happen. The jawans were excitedly talking about going back home. For several days, they had been getting phone calls from home and everyone knew that something terrible had happened in Amritsar. Like the other JCOs, I had asked my officers for information on what was happening, but we were told nothing. I was very apprehensive that the chaos I was witnessing would lead to some kind of disaster. Despite my anger at what I was seeing, I made my way to the centre of the parade ground where some kind of command structure seemed to have formed.

'Ringed by almost a couple of hundred jawans, five JCOs and NCOs sat cross-legged in a circle. They were all Amritdhari Sikhs, as I am. Each of them was personally known to me and I had respect for each of them, knowing them to be outstanding soldiers and the kind of leaders the jawans would follow anywhere. However, at least two of them were known to me as hotheads, which worried me. As I approached them, I learned that they had been nominated the "Panj Pyare", or the five beloved ones, who would lead the jawans from that point on.

'One of the Panj Pyares saw me approach and greeted me, and then muttered something to the others. In a second, five pairs of eyes were looking at me. "Subedarji," one of them asked softly. "How many trucks do we have in the motor pool?" I replied that we had twelve Shaktimans and ten Nissans, and then asked them why they wanted to know. That was when I first learned of the purpose of the jawans. To return to Punjab!

'I was powerless to do anything, when the five commanded that the keys to the motor pool be handed over to them. I could have resisted but I could see that bloodshed would follow, for the jawans were in a frenzy and would not be dissuaded from at least making an attempt to return home. All twenty-two trucks were then driven up to the parade ground, the Panj Pyare maintaining perfect order, as if they were organizing a sanctioned mission. When it became clear that there weren't enough trucks to accommodate all the men, one of the leaders sent for two Jongas and filled them with armed jawans. They called for volunteers who could drive a truck and a sea of hands went up. Twenty jawans who could drive were ordered to get into a Nissan and the little convoy set out for the town of Ramgarh, leaving behind a cloud of dust. In less than an hour, they returned with sixteen Tata trucks in tow, each bearing the sign of a different transport company.

'By the time another hour passed, more than a thousand armed soldiers had gathered at the parade ground, lined up in groups of twenty to thirty, each man with a knapsack or a small suitcase, as if they were going home on leave. I was watching all this in bemused silence when I saw a knot of men coming towards the parade ground from the direction of the regimental gurdwara. Even from a distance I could see that at the head marched a soldier carrying the Nishan Sahib, the saffron-coloured flag that flew proudly at the gurdwara. As they came closer, I could hear them chanting. "*Soora so pahchaniye, jo lade deen ke het; purza-purza kat mare, kabhu na chadde khet.*"'

When Lt Col Bhardwaj addressed the bench, asking that the words be translated, Lt Pande returned with a thick book.

'Valiant ye know him to be who fights for the poor and weak;
Chopped will be from limb to limb, of running will never speak.'

Subedar Maghar Singh continued. 'As they came closer, I could
see that they were all barefoot. Behind the Nishan Sahib marched
the Panj Pyare, each carrying a drawn sword. They had shed their
uniforms and were wearing blue turbans and saffron robes. Behind
them walked the regimental Granthi, solemnly bearing the Guru
Granth Sahib on his head. A dozen jawans followed, all singing
with great gusto, one of them holding a yak-tail whisk that he
reverently waved over the scripture.

'The little procession went past me, towards the Shaktiman
truck that was to be at the head of the convoy. As a couple of
jawans clambered into the back with a large bundle, several others
jury-rigged the Nishan Sahib to the front of the truck. The lads at
the back untied the knots on the bundle and swiftly covered the
back of the truck with white sheets. A silken canopy was rigged
inside the truck and, with great fanfare, the Guru Granth Sahib
was installed under it. As all the jawans stood reverently around
the truck with folded hands, many barefoot after having kicked
their combat boots off, the Granthi led the *ardas*, or prayer, and
then opened the Guru Granth Sahib at random to read a *shabad*,
or hymn. The conclusion of the reading was marked by five lusty
*jakara*s, or shouts, of "*Jo bole so nihal*" by the Panj Pyare. The
thunderous calls of "*Sat Sri Akal*" in response resonated all over
the cantonment.'

Maghar Singh, never one to display emotions, paused as he
looked at the panel, his face somewhat flushed as he addressed
Brigadier Cheramar. 'That was the moment, Sir, I decided to get
into one of those trucks. Until that point, everything I had seen
had made me uncomfortable, and my plan had been to quietly
return to my quarters. But something changed then. I cannot
explain exactly what, but it did. Mutiny is a dirty word and the
most dishonourable thing a soldier can ever do, but as I got into a
truck, I did not feel like a mutineer in the least. I was also worried

about the jawans. They were all so young and certainly did not understand the significance of what they were about to do.'

Lt Col Bhardwaj pursed his lips, visibly unhappy with Maghar Singh's reverie. 'Move on, Subedar,' he said brusquely. 'Tell us what happened next.'

Maghar Singh immediately snapped to attention, acknowledging the rebuke. 'Sir, one of the Panj Pyare climbed into the cabin of the first truck, while the other four fanned out to different parts of the convoy. In twenty minutes, all the soldiers were in the trucks with their baggage. After another hearty chant of 'Bole so nihal' from the truck in front, the convoy rolled out of the cantonment. I was in the fourth truck, sitting in the cabin. My driver was Harnam Singh, one of the jawans from the motor pool. Harnam Singh, in his mid-twenties, was one of my master mechanics. He had grown up in a farm close to Amritsar and had been tinkering with tractors since he was a child. He was a bright young man with a cheerful disposition, and I remember how excited he was to be going home. His wife had delivered a baby boy just a month earlier and he had applied for leave. I had persuaded him to wait for a few weeks because we had three new boys in the motor pool who he had been training. There were thirty jawans in the back of our Shaktiman and we could hear their excited chatter. Each of them was armed but neither Harnam Singh nor I had a weapon.

'Ramgarh is roughly seventeen hundred kilometres from Amritsar. The Panj Pyare had planned to cover the distance in about forty hours, with a short break every four hours or so. Six of the trucks were towing tanker trailers, which would be sufficient to refuel the convoy once, which we planned to do when we were close to Agra. When Harnam Singh asked me what the plan was, I had no answer. I had been wondering about that myself. We were definitely headed to Punjab, but what we would do once we got there was anybody's guess. I had asked one of the Panj Pyares the same question before climbing into my truck. The answer I got was: "It is in Waheguru's hands."

'As we rolled through the neighbourhoods surrounding the cantonment, crowds of onlookers started to gather. We must have been quite a sight! A large convoy, teeming with armed soldiers, some in open civilian trucks, with the leading truck flying a saffron flag. Oblivious of our intent, the onlookers cheered each time the rambunctious jawans thundered jakaras and raised their fists to the sky. Soon our convoy was on National Highway 2, making good time as it rolled north-west.

'Of course, within an hour some of the jawans in my truck started grumbling that they were hungry. When I shouted back that we would not halt for another three hours or so, they grudgingly brought out some of their dry ration, which I am sure did not last very long. After we had been driving for almost four hours, we halted at a popular truck stop, just off the highway after crossing Madanpur. The stop had eight dhabas scattered on either side of the highway, which in minutes were swarmed by the hungry jawans. Despite all attempts by the Panj Pyare to hurry things along, it was a full two hours before the convoy was fed. It was night by the time the convoy got back on the road.

'When we had left Ramgarh and got on to National Highway 2, it had been as busy as ever. There had been a steady stream of traffic in the opposite direction and every petrol pump we passed and every cluster of roadside dhabas had been teeming with people. As we got closer to Varanasi, I noticed something odd. There was almost no traffic on the highway other than our convoy and, strangely, all the petrol pumps and dhabas were shuttered. Anyone who has travelled on this highway, also called Grand Trunk Road, knows that there is usually a steady flow of trucks throughout the night, and the petrol pumps and dhabas always stay open. I have fought in three wars and at times I feel that I have developed a sixth sense for danger. The deserted highway and the darkened dhabas were starting to make me very nervous. Clearly, I was not the only one because on the outskirts of Varanasi the leading truck pulled over and came to a halt. As the convoy stopped, the leaders got into an animated conversation at the helm of the convoy. I stayed in my truck and could not hear them, but I could see that it was a vigorous discussion.

'Their conference concluded, the leaders, grim-faced, visited each truck to talk to the men. Until then, the jawans had been riding a wave of euphoria, excited about going home. The mood changed palpably at the prospect of the inevitable firefight ahead. Most of the jawans were young recruits who had barely begun weapons training. I could see that several men at the back of my truck looked ashen. I said a silent prayer. "Oh Waheguru! I do not know why you have sent me on this insane journey but now that I am here, please let me somehow protect these children." For they were children.

'The plan had changed. The convoy was split and the fuel reserves divided equally. I was to follow the first truck in the convoy, the one flying the Nishan Sahib with the Guru Granth Sahib at the back. We were to leave Grand Trunk Road and strike out towards Lucknow, via Jaunpur. Twenty-two trucks swung out of the convoy and followed us. The rest were to continue on Grand Trunk Road towards Allahabad.

'Harnam could see the worry on my face and, true to his nature, tried to cheer me up. "Don't worry, Sirji," he said. "Nothing will happen. Our brothers will never open fire on us and we will never fire back. What is the worst that can happen? We might be stopped. Or we might be sent back. We might be disciplined too, but it is okay. At least our honour will be intact." I nodded silently, but my unease did not diminish. The smaller highway we were on was as deserted as Grand Trunk Road. If anything, my sense of foreboding had become more pronounced. I was very relieved when the leaders called for a night halt, which had not been in the original plan. They had decided that it would be safer to continue at daybreak.'

Every eye in the room was on Maghar Singh. While the bench and the officers attending the GCM were aware of how the mutiny had ended, they had never heard or read a detailed eyewitness account. Brigadier Cheramar looked at Maghar Singh with empathy, moved by the emotions that he was clearly struggling with, and nodded slightly, encouraging him to continue.

'The villages that ring the highway had begun to stir when we resumed our journey. The jawans were tired, hungry and subdued. While we could see the smoke of cooking fires as we drove through little settlements, every roadside dhaba was shuttered. Later, we learned that the army had shut down every petrol pump and dhaba in our path and suspended traffic on six highways. We had fuel and water, but the dry rations had mostly run out and the young men were ravenous, having eaten nothing since our stop at Madanpur.

The highway curved past a tiny village, a few kilometres from Jaunpur; its name I cannot remember. I do, however, remember that it was completely deserted. Usually at that time the shops would be opening and all the tea shops and dhabas would be doing brisk business. There would be local buses with the conductors singing the names of their destinations as they clamoured for customers. There would be tongas and the odd scooter rickshaw waiting for fares. But on that day, nothing. I remember my heart sinking as we swept through the eerily empty village and then, once we were clear of the settlement, I saw the barricade.

'The road ahead went straight up a small hill, at the top of which was a pile of sandbags, blocking it completely. There were almost identical two-storeyed brick buildings on either side. Beyond them I could see boulders surrounded by thick undershrub. Even from a distance, I could see the morning sunlight glinting on the barrels of the machine guns behind the sandbags. Once the firing began, I could tell that they were equipped with Sterling LMGs that have a range of two hundred metres and can fire more than five hundred rounds a minute.

'The leading truck halted a good three hundred metres from the barricade. In a couple of minutes, a small huddle formed behind it. The animated discussion that started was quickly interrupted by the boom of a loudspeaker. The voice spoke in Punjabi. Not the Punjabi that I and the jawans speak, but the Punjabi of educated city dwellers.

"'The 9th Division will lay down its arms and return to its cantonment immediately! You have shamed yourself and the Indian Army, and there will be consequences. But if you surrender peacefully, nobody will get hurt. My men do not want to open fire on their brother jawans, but if you do not surrender, I promise you they will. You have fifteen minutes to put down your arms. Every man shall lie flat on the ground next to his truck."

'I got out of my truck and joined the huddle. I could see terror in some eyes, but most of the leaders looked impossibly calm. The discussion was animated but respectful. When one of the Panj Pyares suggested that the only reasonable thing to do would be to surrender, he was offered the option to leave, which he declined. The leader who had volunteered to parley quickly fashioned a makeshift white flag from a tree branch and a ragged cleaning cloth stained with motor oil. Dressed in his flowing robes, he slowly started to walk uphill towards the wall of LMGs.

"'Halt!" the loudspeaker boomed when he was about fifty metres from the barricade. We could clearly hear what the officer on the loudspeaker was saying, but our envoy was too far away and we could only guess what he might have said. Soon enough, it was clear that the negotiation was not going well. The voice on the loudspeaker got louder and angrier. "How dare you refuse to surrender! Do you think this is a game? How can we let you go to Punjab? You have mutinied. You have shot and killed your superior officer. You have looted your armoury and seized weapons. You have stolen army property . . . What? Your Guru is more important to you than your honour? You behenchods are all bloody Bhindranwale's men. How dare you fly the flag of Khalistan on an army truck? Do you think I am stupid, behenchod? You can call it your Nishan Sahib or anything you want, but I know that is the flag of Khalistan. We have been briefed by Intelligence.

Do you think we are all *chootiya*s who will believe your nonsense! Behenchod Sardar terrorists. If you want to die, I am ready to mow all of you down."

'As I listened with dismay, I saw our envoy slowly turn and walk back towards us. And then a single shot rang out. Sirji, that was the loudest shot I have ever heard in my life. I do not know who fired it. I do not know if it hit anything. But it was so loud. And then there was silence for a few seconds. Our envoy kept walking, not quickening his pace one bit until he seemed to fly as the silence was shattered by the sound of hundreds of LMGs firing in unison.

"'They are firing!" said Harnam Singh in shock, as our windscreen turned into a thousand shards of glass. Miraculously, I was not hit and managed to drop to the floor. When the firing stopped, I raised my head and saw Harnam Singh slumped over the wheel, his olive green turban soaked in blood. I crawled out of the cab and went to the back of my truck. I found the lads cowering on the floor, ashen-faced, their weapons discarded. On my hands and knees, I crawled under the undercarriage of my truck and made my way slowly to the lead truck, which had borne the brunt of the fusillade. The Nishan Sahib, which had so offended the officer on the loudspeaker, hung forlornly in tatters. Every man inside the truck was dead. The Granthi lay slumped at the back, sprawled over the holy book, his blood staining its pages. The white sheets were all splattered red.

'The pin-drop silence was interrupted by the stentorian voice on the loudspeaker. "There is no escape. Surrender now, jawans, and return to your cantonment. I promise you will be treated fairly. But time is running out. If you don't surrender in fifteen minutes, I will be forced to take further action." Taking cover behind the trucks that followed mine, I made my way to the middle of the convoy where a war council had been hastily convened. One of the Panj Pyares had been killed and he was replaced by an Amritdhari JCO. A heated discussion was going on when I got there. I told them of the heavy casualties we had taken and advised them to surrender. We were ill-equipped and outgunned and the barricade looked impregnable. I was quickly shouted down. One of the younger leaders insulted me and called me a coward, but I ignored him. My concern was solely for the jawans.

'I was then asked to leave as the council deliberated. I slowly made my way back to my truck, Harnam Singh's fate weighing heavily on my mind. I had barely climbed into the back of the truck to offer encouragement and comfort to the distressed young recruits, when I heard the rumble of trucks behind me. Three Shaktimans had pulled out of the convoy and were rumbling towards the front. As they passed the shattered shell of the leading truck, they all three lined up on the highway until they were abreast and then accelerated towards the barricade. Later, I was to learn that each driver had thrown an ammunition box filled with sand on the accelerator.

'Crouching behind the rear wheel of my truck, I felt like I was watching everything in slow motion. The trucks were met with a hail of machine-gun fire, but they kept accelerating until they smashed into the barrier and came to a halt, taking fire from three sides as carefully positioned snipers in the buildings by the side of the highway joined the massacre. All three drivers, of course, were killed. A handful of armed men, bravely and foolishly shouting "Jo bole so nihal", emerged from behind the trucks. They had barely managed to fire a few rounds before they were down on the ground.

'When silence returned, I found myself surrounded by a handful of JCOs from the rear of the convoy. I was the ranking JCO and knew what I had to do. I threw my hands up into the air and started walking towards the smouldering wreckage. Within fifteen minutes, all the jawans had surrendered their weapons. In an hour or so, the remnants of our convoy were heading back to Ramgarh under armed guards.'

The men under trial seemed to be in deep thought as they relived the events of the day after the mutiny. Lt Col Bhardwaj broke the silence as he walked up to Maghar Singh. 'Thank you for your testimony, Subedar, and thank you for your role in ending the mutiny. Your actions that day prevented further loss of life and limb and you deserve our thanks for that.'

R.K. Bhatt's cross-examination was brief and to the point. Taking care to never be disrespectful, he had Maghar Singh confirm that he had received a full pardon, despite having joined the mutinous convoy. Maghar Singh flushed a bit and looked at Sumedh Singh, who stared straight ahead stoically, as he nodded his assent. 'Was Subedar Sumedh Singh one of the leaders of the convoy?' asked Bhatt.

'Not to my knowledge, Sir,' was the curt reply. 'I did see him before we left Ramgarh, but I did not witness anything that might suggest that he was. As I have indicated, all the leaders were killed when they launched the attack on the barricade.'

'Were Lance Naik Balraj Singh and Lance Naik Gurmeet Singh directing the men during the mutiny to the best of your knowledge?'

'No, Sir. It was a large contingent and I do not even remember seeing them either at the parade ground or during the surrender.'

'What about Sepoy Hakam Singh and Sepoy Gurnam Singh? Can you tell us about the role that they played in the mutiny?'

Maghar Singh looked at the two lads somewhat fondly and his stern face softened into a smile. 'These two I know well. They were in my truck and were complaining the loudest because they were hungry. The older men gave them most of their dry rations. After all, they are just children.'

'Did they play an active role in the mutiny?'

'No, Sir. They were terrified when the firing started and never lifted their weapons.' The two lads looked down shamefaced, not comprehending that the JCO's testimony was actually helping them.

R.K. Bhatt then summarized by pointing out that the facts about what had happened during the mutiny, particularly the stand-off at Jaunpur, were not disputed. It was clear that while all the accused had left Ramgarh Cantt and joined the mutiny, they did not play a leadership role in any way. Subedar Maghar Singh's testimony had helped establish that they were no guiltier than he was! Bhatt implored the bench that the accused be dealt with no more severely than Maghar Singh in the interest of fairness.

All the members of the bench had been listening intently and taking notes during Maghar Singh's testimony, as well as Bhatt's cross-examination. Lt Col Bhardwaj looked worried because from the bench's body language, particularly their frequent head nods, it seemed that Bhatt's arguments were starting to have an impact. He kicked himself for not prepping Maghar Singh more thoroughly. The JCO's testimony had been far more nuanced than he had expected and it seemed that he had succeeded in humanizing the mutineers, which could only be detrimental to the prosecution's case. When Brigadier Cheramar called a short recess, Lt Col Bhardwaj could be seen mopping his brow with a large white handkerchief.

One more charge remained to be prosecuted. When the GCM resumed, Lt Pande escorted a cheerful-looking man, probably in his mid-thirties, dressed in a stained and ill-fitting safari suit that his prosperous paunch strained against, into the courtroom. 'Myself Luckky Sharma,' he announced grandly, as he was sworn in as a witness.

Lt Col Bhardwaj, looking at Luckky Sharma with ill-concealed distaste, asked him to state what he did for a living. 'Sirji, I am having top-class dhaba on G.T. Road, Luckky Tope-Class Hotel.'

'Can you tell us what happened on 10 June at your establishment?'

'Sirji, I had finished cooking for dinner, but traffic was very light. I had chicken curry, saag-paneer and dal makhani ready, but traffic was very light. Then suddenly many trucks came. Some were *miltri* and others were civil. I said "jai Mata di" because after the trucks stopped, more than a hundred Sardar jawans came to my hotel. They finished everything I had cooked,' Luckky Sharma said, beaming. 'Best khana, Sirji, in Madanpur.'

Lt Col Bhardwaj nodded curtly and walked over to where the five accused sat. 'Mr Sharma, do you recognize any of these men?' Luckky Sharma looked intently at the five Sikhs seated in the courtroom and broke into a smile as he recognized Hakam Singh and Gurnam Singh.

'Ji, Sirji. I recognize two of them,' he said, stifling a little giggle.

'Well, then point out the men you know and tell the court how you know them.'

Luckky Sharma nodded and clearly pointed at the two young soldiers. 'I would like to draw the bench's attention to the fact that Luckky Sharma has clearly identified accused Sepoy Gurnam Singh and Sepoy Hakam Singh,' said Lt Col Bhardwaj, before turning his attention back to his witness. 'Go on, Mr Sharma. Tell us what happened.'

'Sirji, these two boys came to me after the rest of the soldiers had eaten. They said they were very hungry, but my pots were empty. They asked me if I could give them anything to eat. Sirji, it is my duty to serve our brave jawans. Nothing was cooked, but I had two dozen eggs. I told them I would make egg parathas, and I did. Sirji, they were very hungry because they ate it all. I made twelve big egg parathas and they polished them all off,' said the giggling Luckky Sharma, looking at the lads who smiled back a bit shyly and nervously.

'What happened next, Mr Sharma?'

'Sirji. They did not have money. They told me they were new *rangroots* and had not started getting their salary yet. At the cantonment, they had no need for money. When they left, their pockets were completely empty.'

'Mr Sharma, are you saying that they consumed food at your establishment and refused to pay?'

'Sirji, it was more like they were unable to pay.'

'Let it be noted then that Sepoy Hakam Singh and Sepoy Gurnam, in violation of Section 53(B) of the Army Act, extracted provisions and services from Mr Sharma with no authority to do so. Your witness.'

R.K. Bhatt, who had been rolling his eyes a bit at Lt Col Bhardwaj's officious tone, got up and approached the witness.

'Sharmaji, how many jawans ate at your dhaba on 10 June?'

'About one hundred, Sirji, or maybe one hundred and twenty-five.'

'I see! And did anyone else refuse to pay you for the food you served them?'

'*Nahi*, nahi, Sirji! Every man paid what they were asked.'

'Did you earn good money that day?'

'Ji, Sirji. By the Mata's grace, everything in my dhaba was sold out. It was a good day.'

'And yet you filed a complaint against these two boys?'

'Nahi, nahi, Sirji. What complaint? It is my duty to feed our jawans. So what if they could not pay!'

Bhatt looked at the witness reflectively. 'Then why are they being charged and why are you here?'

'Sirji, the miltri police came for investigation and asked many questions. It was at that time that it slipped out that two jawans did not pay for the food they ate.'

'There were more than a hundred jawans in your dhaba that day, Sharmaji. How was the Military Police able to identify these two lads?'

'Sirji, they were very ashamed that they could not pay. *Ekdum pani-pani*. Water-water only. They promised to come back and pay when they were back at their cantonment after returning from Punjab. I told them no, no, that there was no need. But they said their mothers would beat them with brooms if they found out they ate without paying. They wrote their names and addresses in my notebook, Sirji. That is how the miltri police found them.'

R.K. Bhatt addressed the bench solemnly. 'If the lives and careers of these young jawans were not at stake, this would be funny. Two hungry boys ate at a dhaba. They did not threaten or coerce the proprietor. He fed them willingly. They were so embarrassed that they could not pay that they left their real names and home addresses in the proprietor's notebook with a promise to come back and pay him. The proprietor filed no complaint. And here we are, charging them under Section 53(B), which is used to prosecute gross misconduct and corruption! This charge cannot be taken seriously and must be dismissed.'

The GCM was adjourned for the day. Deliberations were to start the following morning, as all witness testimony had been completed.

Dinner that evening was a sombre affair. Brigadier Cheramar could tell that every officer on the bench was reflecting on the testimony they had heard during the day. The impending decisions should have been easy and clear-cut, but clearly the situation during the mutiny had been more nuanced than the brigadier had comprehended before the start of the court martial.

The following morning, the courtroom had been cleared for the bench's deliberations. Apart from Brigadier Cheramar, Major Brar, Major Modi, Captain Mukherjee and Captain Rizwan, only the court stenographer was present. The major from the office of the judge advocate general was outside, on call in case he was required to provide a legal opinion during the deliberations.

The brigadier, who was reflectively pacing as the other four officers sat, was the first to speak.

'We have an important task ahead of us, gentlemen, and there are many things at stake. I have been reflecting deeply on the testimony we have heard and while we have learned a lot about that happened, if anything, our task has become even more difficult. The primary purpose of these proceedings is to bring the mutineers to justice. Let there be no doubt about that! The Indian Army's reputation has been sullied by the unthinkable and what we do here today will be a step towards fixing it. We must be unyielding in our commitment to this and yet the outcome must be fair. We will not be doing our duty if we don't consider the extenuating circumstances fully. While we must deliver a clear message to the mutineers, we have sworn to be fair and we need to make sure that our deliberations are informed by a desire to deliver real justice.'

Major Modi, Captain Mukherjee and Captain Rizwan nodded vigorously, but the brigadier noticed that Major Brar sat impassive and poker-faced, his face betraying no emotion whatsoever.

'We will consider the charges one by one, and it will be my preference to come to a unanimous verdict on each. If we are unable to come to a unanimous verdict, we will vote, though I am very hopeful it will not come to that. We will address sentencing after we have reached a verdict on all the charges. The first charge against all five is that they were present at a mutiny and that none of them made an effort to stop it. Your thoughts, gentlemen?'

Major Modi suggested that this one was rather cut and dried. Even the defence counsel had not disputed that the accused had mutinied. A guilty verdict would be the only fair outcome. All the officers nodded and the verdict was recorded.

'The second charge is only against Subedar Sumedh Singh, who is accused of inducing other personnel to revolt.' The brigadier looked at the other members of the panel. 'This one is a bit of a sticky wicket. I would like to hear from each of you. Please remember that we are not trying Sumedh Singh for his religious beliefs!'

Major Modi, always willing to take the lead, was of the opinion that Sumedh Singh was guilty of the charge. 'He is a self-confessed Amritdhari Sikh and I will place my faith in the *Guftagoo* circular rather than the fancy words of his defence counsel. It is clear that he was radicalized and that he was encouraging jawans to become Amritdhari Sikhs as well. Men like Sumedh Singh were directly responsible for the loss of life and the loss of face that the army has suffered. Not holding him accountable would send the wrong message.'

Brigadier Cheramar looked very uncomfortable as Major Modi was speaking and looked ready to interrupt him multiple times, but he let him finish. Captain Rizwan disagreed with Major Modi. 'There is no direct testimony or evidence that proves that Sumedh Singh was one of the instigators. If we pronounce him guilty, we will be penalizing him for following his religion. How can we possibly do that? The army is a secular institution where each jawan is encouraged to follow his faith because it gives him strength. Why should Sumedh Singh be an exception?'

Captain Mukherjee jumped into the fray, taking issue with Captain Rizwan's arguments. 'Practising his religion would not be an issue under normal circumstances, but it cannot be ignored that all the mutineers were Sikhs. It cannot be ignored that Sumedh Singh was one of the authority figures among the jawans. It cannot be ignored that the basis of the mutiny was the irrational level of pride that some of the jawans had in their faith. Of course, their faith is important, but is the nation not more important than anyone's faith? Sumedh Singh in his testimony clearly put his faith above the nation and the army. To me, that makes him guilty.'

Major Brar was his usual reticent self. He just observed that Sumedh Singh had referred to the late prime minister in a disparaging manner and that he had expressed admiration for Bhindranwale, daring to openly call him a saint. That was clear proof that Sumedh Singh had been radicalized and that he was filled with anger. It would be unreasonable to assume that his anger had not induced him to mutiny. He was angry and the jawans had looked to him for guidance. To Major Brar, all that pointed unequivocally to Sumedh Singh's guilt.

The discussion continued for almost three hours with Major Modi and Captain Rizwan doing most of the talking. When it was clear that a unanimous decision would not be reached, the brigadier put it to a vote. Major Modi, Captain Mukherjee and

Major Brar would not budge from a guilty verdict. Showing clear signs of unease, the brigadier signed off on the decision.

The brigadier then went on to the matter of Lance Naik Balraj Singh and Lance Naik Gurmeet Singh who had been charged with failing to protect the kote while on guard duty. 'Gentlemen, the dereliction of duty is not in question. It is clear that the two soldiers failed to take proper and timely action, but we must consider the mitigating circumstances. Nobody could ever have imagined that the kote would be attacked and ransacked. What could have the accused done after all? Opened fire on their comrades? That would only have escalated the situation and led to loss of life. I would like to hear from all of you.'

Major Brar had been looking at the brigadier as he had been speaking. 'Sir, the bedrock of the institution we serve is the sanctity of duty. If a soldier or an officer fails to discharge his duty, he suffers the consequences. All of us are held to these standards. Why should we relax our standards in this instance? Yes, the situation was tough, but there is no escaping the fact that Lance Naik Balraj Singh and Lance Naik Gurmeet Singh had a duty to protect the kote, and they failed miserably. How can we consider any verdict other than guilty?'

The head nods from all the other officers told the brigadier that further discussion would be unnecessary. A guilty verdict was recorded.

'The next charge is also rather cut and dried. All the accused are charged with desertion, which is not in doubt at all. Can I assume that we will return a unanimous verdict on this charge?' Every head nodded and the verdict was recorded.

'The charge against Sepoy Hakam Singh and Sepoy Gurnam Singh is extracting money, provisions or services without proper authorization. Gentlemen, I feel that we are guilty of being overzealous! We have returned guilty verdicts on all the charges thus far. Do we need to waste further time on this? If you will allow me, I would like to throw this one out and move on to the sentencing.'

Major Modi, Captain Mukherjee and Captain Rizwan quickly nodded in assent, but Major Brar looked back at the brigadier. 'Sir, is it not unseemly for men in uniform to plunder a restaurant without paying? The army is known for its discipline. Dismissing the charge is tacit endorsement of this shameful behaviour! And looting a civilian establishment! No, Sir! I will not sign off on dismissing this charge. I hope my fellow officers will reconsider their positions.'

'I would like to reconsider my position,' Major Modi chimed in. 'Major Brar definitely has a point. While this is not a serious crime, letting it go unpunished will send the wrong message. I am with Major Brar on this, Sir.' Captain Mukherjee raised his hand too and the verdict was recorded as guilty with a 3–2 vote.

The brigadier spoke. 'I would like to do things a little differently in the sentencing phase, gentlemen. I think we should cover the common charges of mutiny and desertion, which apply to all the accused, and then separately consider the individual charges if we need to. Is that acceptable? Very well then! I would like to hear each of you on how these men should be punished for mutiny and desertion. Once again, it is important to exercise judgement in the interest of fairness and mitigating circumstances must be considered. As a starting point, I would like to suggest that the subedar and the lance naiks must receive a dishonourable discharge. Are we all in agreement? Wonderful! Now your thoughts on the actual sentences, please.'

Major Modi suggested that two years' rigorous imprisonment was warranted in the very least for the JCO and the NCOs, and that twenty-eight days would suffice for the two jawans. The brigadier thought it was fair, given the seriousness of the offences the men had been found guilty of. As there was no argument from the rest of the bench, the sentences were recorded against charges 1 and 4.

'And now we must consider the individual charges. The most serious one, of course, is against Subedar Sumedh Singh, and we have found him guilty of leading the mutiny and instigating subordinate jawans and NCOs to desert. Do we need to add to his sentence, given the guilty verdict on Charge 2? I will give you my take first. Sumedh Singh has a long history of service and a spotless track record. Yes, he was wrong to mutiny, but the testimony clearly showed that there were substantive mitigating factors that we must take into account. For a career soldier like Sumedh Singh, who comes from a military family that has been serving for generations, a dishonourable discharge and two years' rigorous imprisonment will be devastating enough. I feel that we should add a token thirty days' additional imprisonment to his sentence to acknowledge his conviction on Charge 2 and leave it at that. Thoughts, gentlemen?'

Major Modi and Captain Mukherjee looked extremely uncomfortable, but did not say anything as Captain Rizwan nodded in agreement with the brigadier. It was left to Major Brar to speak again. 'Of all the five accused, Subedar Sumedh Singh bears the greatest responsibility. He was a JCO. A highly respected leader. And what did he do? He defiantly took off his uniform and set a terrible example for the jawans who looked up to him. A token sentence when he has been found guilty of this most serious charge is unacceptable, Sir. We must not let compassion weaken our resolve! We must remember that a mutiny like this one has never happened before. As much as we are responsible for dispensing justice, we are also responsible for sending a strong message that the army will never tolerate such behaviour. There must be consequences and they must be substantive!'

'What would you recommend then, Major Brar?'

'Sir, I would recommend an additional eight years' rigorous imprisonment and loss of pension.'

The brigadier turned to the rest of the bench. 'But surely this is too harsh! Ten years! And the man has earned his pension by serving in an exemplary manner for decades. How can this ever be considered a just outcome?'

Once again there was a long discussion, but Major Brar, with Major Modi and Captain Mukherjee squarely in his corner, would not budge. Finally, the matter was put to vote and the outcome was exactly the same as the vote on Sumedh Singh's guilt.

Brigadier Cheramar's suggestion that Lance Naik Balraj Singh and Lance Naik Gurmeet Singh be treated with some leniency was similarly shot down, this time with Major Modi taking the lead. It was resolved that an additional year be added to each man's sentence for failing to take adequate measures to defend the kote.

Wearily, the brigadier moved on to the sentencing of Sepoy Hakam Singh and Sepoy Gurnam Singh.

'We have already sentenced these two boys to twenty-eight days' rigorous imprisonment. Surely there is no need to punish them further,' he asked almost belligerently, as if daring the other officers to challenge him. Once again, it was Major Brar who spoke.

'The army is an institution the general public believes in. We are trusted, and this is based on a history of honourable actions. While I would agree that Hakam Singh and Gurnam Singh committed a fairly minor offence, it was nevertheless a huge betrayal of trust. To me, the notion of a soldier of the Indian Army walking into a civilian establishment and extorting the owner is deeply repugnant. Once again, a message needs to be sent. The purpose of this sentence is not just to punish the accused. It is to let the world know that such behaviour will never be tolerated. There is no need to add additional jail time to the sentence of Hakam Singh and Gurnam Singh. However, they have no place in the army. They, too, must receive a dishonourable discharge.'

The brigadier looked around wearily and nodded. He did not expect to sleep well that night.

The GCM was in session again. The bench was seated, as were the defence and prosecution teams. Attendance had been severely restricted. Lt General Bakshi was present with a handful of officers from his staff. A balding, heavyset man in civilian clothes was a new addition. The GOC had informed Brigadier Cheramar that an observer from the ministry of defence was expected to arrive by the time the verdict would be announced. There had been heavy press interest too. Journalists from *The Hindu*, *Times of India*, *Indian Express* and *Hindustan Times* had all applied for passes, but their applications had been summarily rejected. It was clear that the top brass intended to keep a tight lid on the verdict.

Lt Pande briskly marched the accused in, under guard, and escorted them to their seats. Subedar Sumedh Singh was perfectly calm, but the two lance naiks looked like they hadn't slept a wink. The two young sepoys, who had polished off a substantial breakfast, looked very pleased with themselves and didn't seem anxious at all.

Brigadier Cheramar instructed the defence team and the five accused to rise as he solemnly produced a typewritten page and put on his reading glasses.

'The bench has heard the evidence and concluded its deliberations. The verdict shall now be read.

'On the charge of being present at a mutiny in the military forces of India and not using their utmost endeavours to suppress the same, we find Subedar Sumedh Singh, Lance Naik Balraj Singh, Lance Naik Gurmeet Singh, Sepoy Hakam Singh and Sepoy Gurnam Singh guilty.

'On the charge of endeavouring to seduce any person in the military forces of India from doing his duty or allegiance to the Union, we find Subedar Sumedh Singh guilty.

'On the charge of an omission prejudicial to good order and military discipline, we find Lance Naik Balraj Singh and Lance Naik Gurmeet Singh guilty.

'On the charge of deserting service, we find Subedar Sumedh Singh, Lance Naik Balraj Singh, Lance Naik Gurmeet Singh, Sepoy Hakam Singh and Sepoy Gurnam Singh guilty.

'On the charge of without proper authority extracting from any person money, provisions or services, we find Sepoy Hakam Singh and Sepoy Gurnam Singh guilty.'

Sumedh Singh continued to stare ahead impassively, not betraying any emotion, but his fellow defendants now looked uniformly fearful, as if the true import of the court martial was just sinking in. R.K. Bhatt looked visibly shaken, his face ashen. The defence counsel had been incisive and his cross-examination of the witnesses had gone very well. It had appeared that his arguments were making an impression on the bench. The guilty verdict on all counts was certainly unexpected.

Brigadier Cheramar solemnly directed Subedar Sumedh Singh and R.K. Bhatt to stand. 'I shall now deliver the verdict to each of the accused.'

'Subedar Sumedh Singh. You have been found guilty on the charge of being present at a mutiny in the military forces of India. Guilty on the charge of endeavouring to seduce any person in the military forces of India from doing his duty or allegiance to the Union. And guilty on the charge of deserting the service. You are sentenced to ten years' rigorous imprisonment. Upon the completion of your sentence, you shall receive a dishonourable discharge without pension.

'Lance Naik Balraj Singh. You have been found guilty on the charge of being present at a mutiny in the military forces of India. Guilty on the charge of an omission prejudicial to good order and military discipline, and guilty on the charge of deserting the service. You are sentenced to three years' rigorous imprisonment. Upon the completion of your sentence, you shall receive a dishonourable discharge.

'Lance Naik Gurmeet Singh. You have been found guilty on the charge of being present at a mutiny in the military forces of India. Guilty on the charge of an omission prejudicial to good order and military discipline, and guilty on the charge of deserting the service. You are sentenced to three years' rigorous imprisonment. Upon the completion of your sentence, you shall receive a dishonourable discharge.

'Sepoy Hakam Singh. You have been found guilty on the charge of being present at a mutiny in the military forces of India. Guilty on the charge of deserting the service, and guilty on the charge of without proper authority extracting from any person money, provisions or service. You are sentenced to twenty-eight days rigorous' imprisonment. Upon the completion of your sentence, you shall receive a dishonourable discharge.'

Hakam Singh looked at the brigadier in disbelief as he broke down. 'Sirji, please do not dismiss me from the army. My father will die of shame.' As the lad sobbed, the brigadier gestured to Lt Pande who had a guard escort him from the courtroom.

'Sepoy Gurnam Singh. You have been found guilty on the charge of being present at a mutiny in the military forces of India. Guilty on the charge of deserting the service, and guilty on the charge of without proper authority extracting from any person, money, provisions or service. You are sentenced to twenty-eight days' rigorous imprisonment. Upon the completion of your sentence, you shall receive a dishonourable discharge.'

Balraj Singh, Gurmeet Singh and Gurnam Singh looked devastated as they stood in shocked silence.

Subedar Sumedh Singh, completely unruffled even after hearing the sentences, looked boldly at the bench and thundered, 'Jo bole so nihal.' The call was loud and robust, but there was no response. The only 'Sat Sri Akal' that was heard came from the subedar's own lips. Lt General Bakshi's face darkened at the subedar's defiance and he looked at the brigadier, as if prompting him to respond in some manner. The brigadier caught the glance but looked away.

The GOC arranged a lavish dinner for Brigadier Cheramar and the rest of the bench at one of the regimental messes. Scotch had been served from the GOC's personal stock. Everyone except Major Brar was smoking a cigar and the GOC was holding forth on the virtues of single malt. The general was flying to Delhi the following morning, where he would be debriefed by the defence minister, and decided to call it a night. Major Modi, Captain Rizwan and Captain Mukherjee, who had all enthusiastically and somewhat immoderately imbibed the general's Scotch, decided to make their way to their quarters as well, leaving only Major

Brar and Brigadier Cheramar at the table as the bearers started to clear it.

Major Brar had hardly said anything during the meal and had sat quietly nursing his glass. The brigadier too had been quiet, barely acknowledging the general's praise of the manner in which he had conducted the court martial. After he had been sitting with the major for a few minutes, he looked at him a few times, as if about to say something, but then checked himself at the last moment and stared into his drink.

Finally, Brigadier Cheramar decided to speak.

'Major Brar! If you will indulge me, I was curious about something and wanted to ask you a question.' The major looked a bit startled but nodded.

'We followed the guidelines we had been given and the process that the JAG had laid out faithfully, and I know that the top brass is quite pleased with the outcome. However, I can't help feeling that you personally tipped the scales significantly, both on the verdicts and the sentences. On the one hand, I admire your loyalty to the army! After all, you are a Sikh yourself and more than the rest of the bench, you had to have a good understanding of the mutineers' state of mind. The circumstances were extraordinary and it is clear that the decision to mutiny was an emotional one. I would have expected you to be much more lenient, but you were the one who took the toughest stand. I am very curious about why you did what you did.'

The major's face darkened as he regarded the brigadier balefully, taking almost a minute to respond. 'I am a career soldier, Brigadier, and come from a proud military family. Of course, you don't know this, but my family has been serving since 1846. I have fought in multiple wars. I have been decorated many times. And yet when you look at me, all you see is another Sikh who wears a turban and has a beard, just like the bastards we killed during Operation Blue Star.'

'I don't understand,' the brigadier stammered, taken aback by the vehemence of the major's response.

'There weren't five men on trial during the court martial, Brigadier. There were six!'

'What do you mean, Major Brar?'

'Every fucking Sikh officer is on trial after the mutiny, Brigadier!' Major Brar said bitterly. 'I will tell you my story, Brigadier, but I will trust you to be discreet.

'As you know, Brigadier, I serve in the 46th Armoured Regiment and command a squadron of tanks. What you probably don't know is that my squadron was deployed during Operation Blue Star.'

'I see! But how does that have any connection with the court martial? And I still don't understand what you meant about being on trial.'

'I have been on trial since Operation Blue Star, Brigadier, and will continue to be until I retire from the army. On 6 June 1984, I was charged with supervising the cremation of bodies that were being pulled out of the Golden Temple complex. There is a cremation ground right next to Gurdwara Shaheedan. I had four jawans with me and a handful of municipal workers. A Sikh Granthi had been provided to perform the last rites of each person being cremated by chanting the ardas. We had disposed of about sixty bodies when a police truck pulled up with three more corpses. Much to my surprise, they were the bodies of Bhindranwale, Bhai Amrik Sikh, leader of the All-India Sikh Students' Federation, and another Sikh named Bhai Thada Singh. I noticed that Bhindranwale's leg was dangling at an unnatural angle and, out of curiosity, I lifted it and saw that his shin had been shattered by three bullets. The three were then cremated like the rest. The next day, two Intelligence officers came for me, accompanied by a RAW agent. I was interrogated for six hours! One of the jawans had reported that Major Brar had touched Bhindranwale's feet before he was cremated!

'Can you believe that, Brigadier? I was accused of touching that bastard's feet in obeisance! Me! An Indian Army officer! What did I have to do with those religious fanatics? For years, I had been aghast at what had been happening in Punjab. I had volunteered for Operation Blue Star. My tank squadron, I am proud to say, played a huge role in our decisive victory. I was proud to be a part of the operation that ended the severest threat to our country's unity and integrity after Independence! And here I was, being charged of secretly supporting Bhindranwale! I was shocked beyond belief. And it only got worse. It had also been reported that when the Granthi performed the *antim* ardas for Bhindranwale, I bowed my head, prayed with him and folded my hands. Brigadier, all Sikhs participate in ardas thousands of times during their lifetime. When we are children, we are taught the etiquette to be followed during prayer. It becomes second nature to fold your hands during ardas. I do not even know if I folded my hands! I may well have because it is in my muscle memory and that of every Sikh's. When we hear the words of the ardas, we bow our heads and listen with folded hands.

'Well, they had been investigating me. Two days before that, I had been sent to Chiwinda Devi village close to Amritsar to disperse an angry mob of Sikhs. The local magistrate had been fearful that the Sikh mob would attack the Hindu residents and had requested the army's help. I had my men draw their guns and take their positions. Just the sight of my soldiers was enough to make the crowd disperse. But do you know what the RAW agent said? He asked me why I hadn't ordered my men to open fire? Was it because I was secretly a terrorist sympathizer? Should I not have been lauded for defusing the situation without loss of life instead?

'I was subjected to a formal inquiry. Thankfully my CO, who has known me since I was commissioned, supported me fully. He knew that there was absolutely no possibility of my being a terrorist sympathizer. He said that emphatically and repeatedly during the inquiry. My name was formally cleared, but do you think the shadow has lifted? No, Brigadier, it has not! My brother officers whisper around me. This is on my record and will never go away.

It will affect my future. My career. Everything. I will always be under a magnifying glass as long as I serve in the army.

Brigadier Cheramar looked at the major with an expression that was one part sympathy and three parts horror.

'When my CO learned that Sikh officers were being sought to serve during the courts martial of the Ramgarh mutineers, he volunteered my name. You see, Brigadier. It was an opportunity to redeem myself.'

The Martyr

His smiling face looks out of the *Tribune*'s front page. Black headlines loudly declare the news of his death. 'Prominent young editor gunned down by militants', they read. His face is handsome: a shock of thick, unruly hair and a handlebar moustache, but his lips are thin, almost thin enough to appear cruel. There's a hint of a sneer in his smile, as if he's laughing at the sudden attention being paid to him on his death.

The main story on the front page describes his execution in the minutest detail. The registration plate of his motorcycle and its colour are mentioned. A reporter, who would probably do well writing potboilers, gleefully documents the size and location of each bullet hole and the vital organs that each pierced. He paints vividly in print the patterns that his blood made on his white kurta. He speculates endlessly about the assassins' military precision, about how they must have planned this weeks in advance and how an insider had to be involved.

On page nine is a lengthy eulogy that praises Monty's fearless writing and his unflinching stand against the militants that finally led to his assassination. It talks about the uncompromising integrity that distinguished Monty, which he had inherited from his uncle, Ranbir Singh, the much-respected writer and journalist. It traces the history of Ranbir Singh's publication *Nava Din*, which Monty began to run after the death of his uncle.

I too want to pay my respects to this great soul who fell to an assassin's bullets for fearlessly defending his ideals.

I board a bus from the main depot in the city for Samaalsar, a small town near Doomchheri. My neighbour in the next seat hasn't heard of Monty's death; he does know Doomchheri though and tells me scary tales of ghosts who haunt the once-magnificent-but-now-deserted *bhoot* bungalows of the village.

I get off the bus at Samaalsar and look for a tonga to take me to Doomchheri. The sky, dull and overcast since the news of Monty's death, suddenly splits open and the heavens too begin to weep, moved by the tragic death of the innocent martyr. How appropriate, I think as I scurry for shelter. The thought of this celestial tribute is moving and at the same time ennobling.

I pick up today's paper lying on a table in the tea shop. There is a picture of Monty's bereaved widow on the front page. Her eyes and face look swollen and she seems to be shattered by the tragedy. The potboiler-writing reporter is in his element again. There is a story with excruciating details of Monty and Rupa's romantic affair, when they were students at St Stephen's in Delhi. He gushes over their passionate love affair and their eloping despite their parents' objections. His heart-rending portrait of the traumatized Rupa brings bitter tears to my eyes. From the depths of my soul, I curse the human vultures who have done this to her.

I rebuke myself for my hesitation to visit Doomchheri. My reluctance on account of the bad weather and uncomfortable journey seems so cheap and trivial in retrospect. Slowly, my visit is turning into a pilgrimage and I feel that I have changed. I too want to live my life by Monty's standards. Once upon a time, several years ago, I was idealistic too. I even had talent—my writing meant something. I should have had the courage to keep trying, but I didn't. I do make a comfortable living writing film reviews and covering sports. I have a scooter and send my son to Little Flower, but there has to be more to life than that. Perhaps if I had not given up I could have been like Monty today. I am ashamed at the depths to which I had sunk—I didn't even subscribe to *Nava Din*; I never even read what Monty had to say. I make a silent resolve. All of this has to change. Monty's death is more than a tragedy. It is a sign for me, a challenge to make something out of the joke that my life has become.

The rain is now a drizzle and I leave the tea shop. The tonga-wallah asks for fifteen rupees because I'm the only passenger, but I don't care. I can't wait any longer. There is a strange force, one that keeps getting stronger by the minute, that is pulling me. There is a strange feeling of exhilaration mixed with my sorrow. This is the final phase of my journey.

My head is too small to contain my thoughts. I need to express my gratitude to Monty, who in death has almost given me new life. I ask the tonga-wallah if he knew Monty. He wants to know if I am referring to the boy from the *vaddi* haveli who was shot a week ago. I am a little displeased at the way he speaks of Monty, but I shrug it off thinking that he is after all a rough peasant with a crude manner.

He winks at me and asks if I am going to vaddi haveli. He warns me that it is empty now and that all the boys have gone to Chandigarh—they're too scared to stay here any more. And he says that the good times are over. I ask him what he means, but he winks at me again.

I dismiss the man as an imbecile and get off at the Doomchheri bus stop. I ask a little boy standing by the tailor's shop if he will take me to the big haveli. He says that he is afraid of the dogs and won't go, but he points out the way to me. I ask the tailor if there is anyone at the haveli, but he doesn't look me in the eye and seems to swear under his breath, mumbling that they are big people and that he knows nothing about the affairs of big people.

I am a little taken aback. Surely Monty with his impeccable credentials must have been a man of the people. Did he, after all, not die for a popular cause? The tailor's boorish behaviour is odd. Perhaps he holds some grudge against the family.

I take the dirt road that winds its way through empty, desolate flat fields. It seems that I am no longer in Punjab. Everything is so quiet, so barren, so lonely. The vaddi haveli is a crumbling bungalow with its gates shut. The surrounding wall has several openings in it, and I gingerly step over a pile of fallen bricks.

There is a big brass padlock on the main door. Most of the windowpanes are broken and I can see makeshift curtains made using a motley collection of bed sheets and gunny bags. I turn with a start to see a very old man, dressed in just a long shirt, squinting at me through a pair of cracked eyeglasses. '*Koi nahi hai! Koi nahi hai!*' he says and waves his stick at me. 'Where is Rupa Bibi?' I shout into his ear. 'Koi nahi hai,' he says and points his stick at the hole in the wall.

A barefoot young woman, wearing a tattered salwar-kameez, takes the old man by the arm and leads him away. I follow them to the little shack at the back of the house. She asks me who I am and what I want. My enthusiasm has dampened a little, but I express my admiration for Monty, his selfless fight against terror and his heroic end. She stares at her bare feet as I say all this, steals a quick look at my face and then looks away. I ask her where Rupa is. She looks at me, surprised, and begins to speak, but the old man gets extremely agitated again, his stick raised as he wheezes 'Koi nahi hai' and points to the door. I leave the house perturbed.

The fading sign over the locked door says 'Nava Din'. I can hear someone singing in the little room by the office building and I knock. A tall, thin form lolling on a charpoy waves me in. A little girl sits in a corner of the dingy room, singing tunelessly to a rag doll. The chowkidar asks me what I want and I tentatively say that I came to see the office where Monty worked. He looks at me, seeming surprised, and asks me to sit down. I ask him to open the office and, helped along by a ten-rupee bill, he escorts me in. Inside I see piles of paper, books, a lot of dust and stacks of back issues of *Nava Din*.

I greedily pounce on one of the stacks and begin to leaf through the magazines. I turn pages upon pages, but I don't find any articles written by him. I ask the chowkidar if he used another name. He laughs, this time nervously. I pick up more issues, but I still can't find his name. I find poems and short stories and recipes and platitudes, but I don't find a single article that has anything to do with militants, either against them or in support.

I am thoroughly confused. I look at the watchman and ask why they killed him. He looks down and says Monty was a great editor. 'He was very brave,' he mumbles. I am totally perplexed now and have to get to the bottom of this.

It is getting dark. If I don't get to Samaalsar soon, I'll miss the last bus back to the city. But I am consumed with curiosity and unease. I walk into the Doomchheri police station. The SHO is a friendly young fellow who orders tea for me. When I tell him that I write film reviews, he gets excited and asks me about the latest films. He has to take his wife to the city for a film and doesn't want to waste money on one that doesn't have good songs and dances. His manner changes abruptly when I ask him about Monty.

'*Arre*, Sahib, just another random death,' he says. 'Who knows why they shot him. Maybe it was a mistake, maybe someone held a grudge against him. Maybe he bumped into one of the "boys" in Samaalsar. Who can tell! Maybe he twisted his moustache in front of one of the "boys" who got offended and shot him, or maybe they just wanted to rob him . . . This has always been a violent area, Sirji. In my father's time we had Naxalites. Then we had smugglers. Please excuse my language, Sirji, but now every idle behenchod has picked up an AK-47 and become a "boy". There are so many *jathe*. All of them wear round turbans and have beards that reach their bellies, but who knows what they really believe in! Sometimes they fight each other. Sometimes they settle old scores. The police are outgunned and we can do nothing. I don't want my son to be an orphan! So I go home on time and don't come out again until late morning. The night belongs to the "boys" and they do what they want.'

'But why are the papers making such a fuss about him and his bravery?'

'Sirji, his uncle was a big man, and his father-in-law is a big politician in Delhi with the ruling party. Now they will get a huge sum in compensation from the government. His wife will get a ticket to contest the next election and she will win. The magazine will get government advertisements and government subscriptions.

'It's all a tamasha, Sahib.'

'But how did he die, and why did they kill him?'

'Late one evening, last week, he was going to Samaalsar, to buy some rum. You see, there was a party at the vaddi haveli. On that day, the "boys" had announced a curfew and he didn't know. He was on his way to Samaalsar on a motorcycle with his brother, Channi. Since Monty had his hair cut, he did not look like a Sikh. They were stopped near Samaalsar by two "boys". They asked Channi where he was taking the *bahman*. He pleaded with them, begged that he was his real brother, took off his turban and put it on Monty's head to show them the resemblance, fell at their feet, but they didn't listen. They shot him. Why? Nobody will ever know.'

I stagger in through my front door in a daze. My wife asks me where I have been. She says that Ramavtar, the peon, had come from the office while I was gone, with two tickets for the new movie at Minerva Talkies.

She has sent our son to Biji's house, so we can enjoy the movie and I can write my review.

The Survivor

Rani puts her arms around him and says it's all right. It's only a bad dream and everything is going to be fine. Her regular heartbeat against his cheek comforts him and he goes back to sleep. She shuts her eyes but can't sleep; his demons invade her mind too and she is on edge. She clutches him, tighter, runs her hand through his long hair as if soothing him would somehow calm her down too. She looks at Lali's face, softened by the light of the full moon that creeps in through a crack in the curtains. Such an innocent, tender face, and so serene with no hint of the terrible memories and the anguish. Her eyes brim; in a rush Lali's pain flows through her mind, almost in a motion picture–like series of frames. She shudders. She can't shut out the memories. Once again, she asks herself the question that nobody has an answer for: 'Why?'

She gasps at the sight of the ragged bloody forms lying unattended on the floor of the second-class waiting room at New Delhi Railway Station. The Central Reserve Police Force (CRPF) lance naik vaguely points to one section of the room and mumbles, 'Tinsukhia Mail.' Seven years of reporting for the *Indian Express* have not prepared her for this. There is a strange stale and nauseating smell in the room. She staggers retching into the ladies' washroom.

Rani rubs her sleepy eyes to see Lali dressing before the large mirror. His beard has grown to its full length now and he slaps on a liberal dose of Fixo before brushing. He ties on his *thatha* and begins to wrap his turban around his head. Once, he had confided in her that he had often thought of cutting his hair off in the past. Now he would never do it. He wears the sign of his faith proudly, as a badge of honour, a challenge to the world. Neat fold rests upon another fold and soon enough he is done, a regal saffron turban adorns his head. He gives his moustache a jaunty twist. Rani is slow and lazy in the morning. She chose not to become a Sikh when they got married, and she can't bring herself to wake up at five in the morning and go to Bangla Sahib to listen to the Asa Di Var.

A thrill of pride runs through her as she looks at her handsome husband. He is a regal figure in his saffron turban and his flowing robes, or *bana*. She thinks of the respect he commands in the Delhi Sikh community and feels a warm glow. He leaves the room quietly as she drifts off into her dreams again. She dreams of a large, low, white bungalow on Ashoka Road. She is supervising the gardener as a white Ambassador drives up to the porch. A uniformed man opens the door and Lali, dressed not in his usual bana, but in white khadi, steps out. An aide with a black file folder follows him in as the security man salutes. She wakes up with a start. She has overslept again. She remembers a 10 a.m. appointment with her editor and rushes to get dressed.

'Are you okay, Madam?' She swims back to consciousness and can feel a painful bump at the back of her head. She is lying in a pool of her vomit and the *jamadarni* helps her up. She looks at an ashen, ghostly face in the mirror and tries to clean herself. She steels herself and enters the waiting room. The smell hits her again, the smell of blood and infection and burnt flesh and naked fear. She winces but gathers courage and looks around. Women and young children huddle in a corner, terror in their eyes. A cordon of CRPF jawans separates them from two neat rows covered with white bed sheets.

She gets up from her desk and opens her filing cabinet. 'SIKHS MASSACRED ON TINSUKHIA MAIL', the headlines scream.

Terrified children stare at her from the newspaper clipping and the white sheeted rows bear silent testimony to the orgy of violence that swept through the ill-fated train. Rani's words, unsoftened by journalistic niceties, spell out the story in graphic, gruesome, anguished detail. The single adult male Sikh to survive the massacre looks completely stupefied. His beard is burnt on one side and his hair, untidily chopped, hangs down in dirty, tangled locks.

'They're all dead,' Lali sobs. 'They killed them all: my brothers, my bhabhis, the children, Biji. Why didn't they kill me too! His left eye is shut, caked with blood, and his arm dangles limply. His beard and his eyebrows, both singed, are a dirty brown. Rani looks closely at him. Under the mask of blood and burnt hair, she sees a handsome, if slightly fleshy, face. His forehead is high and he has a fine nose, but his mouth appears to be a little weak. There is a childlike innocence about him, and her heart goes out to him instantly. She wants the whole world to know what has happened to him. She wants the nation to be ashamed, she wants to make sure that such a thing never happens again.

'Have you gone mad, Rani?' Kumar asks. 'If I publish this article and these photographs, they'll have my head and yours too. This is India, you know, not the United States of America. Have you ever seen such pictures in a newspaper before? Young children will see them. What kind of an effect will they have on them? Besides the situation is already very tense. God knows what will happen if this story is published. The Sikhs are quiet now, and numb, but who knows how things will be tomorrow. Do you know what kind of violence a story like this may provoke in Punjab?'

Rani is adamant. She doesn't care if she loses her job. She wants the country to know Samsher Singh's story. She threatens to take her story somewhere else and that gets Kumar to agree. Lali's first-person account is the lead story in *Indian Express*.

'My name is Samsher Singh. I am called Lali by my family and friends. I am twenty-four years old and a graduate of North Point College in Darjeeling. My family runs a small construction business in Guwahati, which was started by my father five years ago, after he retired from the army. Every year in October-November, our family visits Kot Issa Khan, a small village near Patiala, where Sant Fauja Singhji conducts a *samagam*. This year too, on 30 October, we left Guwahati for Delhi on the Tinsukhia Mail. There were eleven of us travelling by second class: Biji, Channi Veerji and Manju Bhabhiji with their two children, Jeeta Veerji and Guddi Bhabhiji with their two sons, my sister Babli and myself. Biji, my bhabhis, Babli and the children were all in the ladies' compartment, which has a door that can be locked.'

Rani shuts the file and puts it back on the table. It has been three years, but she knows the story by heart. She wrote it with Lali. She sits down and wonders how the mere thought of the massacre can unsettle her even after so much time has passed. Poor Lali! He saw it all happen before his eyes, and his own dear ones, and God, the children! So many sleepless nights filled with anguished nightmares. Lali, in his dreams, howls like an animal in agony. How bravely he tries to cope with the tragedy. Anybody else would have probably gone mad, but not Lali. He has selflessly spent the last three years working for the relief and rehabilitation of the widows and orphans of the Delhi riots. He is not a human being, but a saint. A true Sikh who has truly understood the spirit of Bhai Kanhaiya, the compassionate Sikh disciple of the tenth Guru. When other hotheads talk of revenge and punishing the guilty, he talks of healing and forgiving the foolish. In the last three years, he has become a man, a pillar of strength. Each day of his life is devoted to seeking out the victims and helping them get on with their lives.

Lali refuses to be taken to a hospital. He is terrified that the mobs will return. Rani asks a colleague, Bishan, whose wife is a good friend of hers, to take him in until he recovers. She is the only one Lali trusts, and each day she spends hours soothing him, gently drawing out the story of the carnage. Lali, traumatized, does not want to talk about it. Each word he utters is accompanied by terrible contractions of pain and memories that refuse to dull or fade. She dreads her task because she knows how much pain it causes him, but she has to do it. The world has to know and perhaps it will heal him too. She can't understand his guilt, his terrible death wish, his insistence that he has somehow betrayed his loved ones by surviving.

'My name is Samsher Singh. I am called Lali by my family and friends. I am twenty-four years old and a graduate of North Point College in Darjeeling. They're all dead,' says Lali, sobbing. 'They killed them all: my brothers, my bhabhis, the children, Biji; why didn't they kill me too! There were eleven of us travelling by second class: Biji, Channi Veerji and Manju Bhabhiji with their two children, Jeeta Veerji and Guddi Bhabhiji with their two sons, my sister, Babli and myself. *Sab chale gaye.*' He won't say more, but she begs and pleads, asking him to speak in the name of justice. He opens his mouth, but all that emerges is an intense howl of agony in the language that nightmares are written in.

Rani reaches home to find Kohli, secretary to the minister of parliamentary affairs, waiting for Singh Sahib. The Party is observing Sadbhavna Divas in memory of the victims of the 1984 riots to foster communal harmony in the capital. The Leader himself will be there and the ceremony will start with a havan, a namaaz, shabad kirtan, a Catholic service and chants by Tibetan lamas. Several speeches will be made and the government will announce new loan packages for 1984 widows. Lali has been asked to make a speech too. After all, the only male survivor of the Tinsukhia Mail carnage is a living model of communal harmony. One who has suffered so much and has filled his heart with compassion. He will also be involved in the loan scheme and will be the liaison between the loan office and the applicants. The pot-bellied Kohli, who has a pockmarked face and wears dark glasses like his master, delivers the invitation and leaves.

Rani wants to leave Tinsukhia Mail behind so that she and Lali can get on with their lives, but the ghosts of the train will not leave them alone. Whenever they go to a party, the conversation invariably turns to the massacre and Lali now doesn't hesitate at all in talking about it. It irks her sometimes that his story is always a little different; sometimes graphic and sometimes a little restrained, as if the gory details, in their nakedness, might injure the sensibilities of their sensitive friends. She remembers everything, Lali's first hesitant telling of his story, in bits and in pieces, emerging slowly like a grotesquely deformed baby that a mother knows is hers but does not want to acknowledge.

'My name is Samsher Singh. I am called Lali by my family and friends. Every year in October–November, our family visits Kot Issa Khan, a small village near Patiala, where Sant Fauja Singhji conducts a samagam. This year too, on 30 October, we leave Guwahati for Delhi on the Tinsukhia Mail. Biji, my bhabhis, Babli and the children are all in the ladies' compartment, which has a door that can be locked. The train is running very late and we reach Patna in the afternoon. There we hear that Indiraji has been hit by bullets. Guddi Bhabhi is glad, but Biji is very angry and rebukes her. Phapaji had been decorated in the Bangladesh war and had received his medal from the hands of Indiraji herself. Biji loves and admires her tremendously. Guddi Bhabhi is very angry due to Blue Star, but we don't care much. Punjab is another country, we have never lived there, we are busy with our business. The *lala* sitting in our compartment with his family tells Veerji, "Sardarji, I have heard that it was done by three Sardars. Everybody in our bogie is talking about the shooting." As I get off to get some water, the Bengali family sitting near the door looks at me strangely. The babu says something to his wife in an undertone and she silently nods. I get a strange feeling as I stroll about on the platform; everybody seems to be staring at me. Having lived in Guwahati and Darjeeling, I am used to people staring at my pagri, but today the stares are different. It almost seems as if people are suddenly afraid of me. Our train pulls into Danapur. The lala comes back with news that Indiraji is dead. The babu's wife quietly weeps in

the corner of her compartment. The lala solemnly says that this is a
bad thing the Sikhs have done and Channi Veerji agrees. It's almost
as if we are in a passenger train instead of Tinsukhia Mail. We stop
at almost every station and the train gets even more delayed. We
reach Mughalsarai very late at night, where our diesel engine is
switched to an electric engine. Everybody in the coach is awake,
unsettled by the tumultuous news from Delhi. The night-time tea
sellers on the Mughalsarai station do good business.

'Jeeta Veerji and I get down to buy tea and puris. Perhaps it is
my imagination, but I think that the stares are no longer fearful but
hostile. We go into the ladies' compartment and all of us eat puris
and drink chai. There is another Sikh family of five in our coach.
Harnam Singh and his wife, Bibi Bachhan Kaur, are travelling to
Ludhiana with their three grandchildren. Harnam Singh comes to
the compartment looking very worried; he has heard disturbing
news from the guard. Since yesterday evening there has been
rioting in Delhi. Several Sikhs have been killed in the *danga*s. There
are rumours that mobs of armed men are roaming the streets of
Delhi, pulling Sikhs out of their houses and killing them. All hell
has broken loose in Punjab too. The Howrah Mail has come back
from Punjab laden with Hindu corpses and Sikhs have poisoned
the drinking-water supply in Delhi. Channi Veerji tries to comfort
the old man and tells him that in times such as these rumours are
sure to fly. Nothing like this can ever happen in Delhi. At worst
there must have been a few clashes, trains will be running late
and we will probably be delayed a few hours in Delhi, but there
is nothing to worry about. Harnam Singh goes back, not entirely
convinced, and we see a frown of worry on Biji's forehead.

'We are awakened by a loud banging on the bogie door.
I look out of the window. We are at some small station that
is not even a junction. Nervously, the lala gets up to open the
door. A uniformed havildar of the Railway Police climbs into
our coach. "Are there any Sardars here?" he asks. He sees me
and Jeeta Veerji and sits down on my berth. He has come to

warn us. "The violence has spread to many cities in the north. There has been a terrible bloodbath in Delhi. In Bokaro, several Sikhs have been burnt alive. The news of the trainload of corpses from Punjab has spread everywhere. In every city, Sikhs are being pulled out of buses and trains. They are being beaten, even killed. The railway authorities have stopped the train outside Kanpur so that all the Sikhs inside can be warned to hide and not show their faces before the train reaches Delhi." Channi Veerji says, "Havildarji, why are you scaring people unnecessarily. Who has given you this news? Is it official or is it just a rumour?" The havildar says that he is warning us for our own good and it is up to us to believe him or not.

'Harnam Singh is terrified. He begs Biji to let his wife and grandchildren into the ladies' compartment, because at least it has a door. Biji thinks that the old man is paranoid but takes pity on him and lets his family in. It's already crowded inside with four adults and four children, and now it gets worse. Harnam Singh sits down on my berth, closes his eyes and begins to pray. Jeeta Veerji nudges Channi Veerji. We look at the frightened old man and all of us smile. The lala looks worried too and rebukes us, saying, "Sardarji, this is not a joke. Anything can happen. There are ladies with you and small children, do not take this lightly." Jeeta Veerji replies saying, "Lalaji, we have Hindu–Muslim riots, even Sikh–Muslim riots, but have you ever heard of Hindu–Sikh riots?" The lala gets up and walks around the coach. Most of the steel shutters are already down and he shuts any windows that are not. He finds that only one family is getting down at Kanpur. He asks them to sit by the door and tells them that they must get off as soon as the train reaches Kanpur. He goes to each compartment and tells everyone what the havildar had said, and warns them not to get down at Kanpur. He adds that whatever happens, they should not open the door.

'Channi and Jeeta Veerji are extremely amused at the lala's warlike preparations. "Phapaji should have been here," Jeeta Veerji

says. "He and Lalaji could have planned the defence together."
I am a little afraid too, but I smile and laugh at their jokes. The
entire coach is awake now and I can hear a buzz of conversation.
Indiraji, *katal*, Sardar, *dangey-phasad* are the words I hear over and
over again. I too feel that nothing will happen, but I have never
been as brave as my brothers, I am afraid.

'It is quite bright outside by now. Our shutters are all down, but
some light comes in through the chinks. Somebody has switched
on All India Radio. "Vande Mataram" has just finished and some
shastriya singer is singing a slow alap in some raga. Our train is
slowing down—we must be nearing a station. The train slows to
a halt and my ears prick up for the telltale sounds of a railway
station, but there is complete silence. The lala opens his window
a crack, pads barefoot to the door and swiftly escorts the family
that is getting down out. He quickly shuts and locks the door and
returns to his seat. It is seven in the morning, but Kanpur station
is unnaturally silent. There are no shouts from people selling tea
or puris or magazines or beedis. There are no coolies lining the
platform, and there are no passengers.

'Several minutes have passed. There is the same eerie silence and
the train does not move. We are restless as the coach is turning into
an oven with the shutters down. We begin to hear footsteps on the
platform and faint murmurs. It is too hot and stuffy. The fans have
stopped and slowly, in defiance of the lala's orders, windows start
opening. Kanpur is a ghost station today. There are a few railway
officials in their blue uniforms and a few jawans of the Provincial
Armed Constabulary (PAC). The babu shouts to a passing TTE
[travelling ticket examiner], "Sahib, why is the train not moving?"

'"There is trouble ahead. We have orders to halt here until the
line is cleared." The TTE says there has been violence in Kanpur
too. Several buses have been burnt and shops have been looted.
There is a curfew and that's why the station is deserted.

'We are all hungry and hot and sweaty and irritated. We want
to go to the platform and buy some chai and some breakfast, but

the lala won't let us. Jeeta Veerji says that we will surely miss our connecting train in Delhi. Biji says that it is just as well and we can stay the night at Sis Ganj Sahib. The dull, lazy morning somehow makes me lose my fear. My palms are no longer sweaty and my mouth is dry no more. I feel that familiar impotent irritation that one feels while standing in never-moving queues, or when your bus gets stuck in traffic. I had never wanted to go on this stupid trip anyway . . . but Biji never listens.

'Suddenly we hear a strange sound in the distance, getting closer, made louder still by the tomb-like silence of Kanpur station. The sound, clearer now, is a babel of voices not sharp or high-pitched but modulated, not unlike the humming of an angry horde of bees. The sound is even louder now and very near. It invades our ears and mutes our tongues, as we all strain to discover its source. It's still a hum but horribly loud. It enters the coach through every door window and crack. It is now heavy and gelatinous, and it settles in our coach like quicksand, completely paralysing us all. All my eyes can see now is its mucous-like consistency as it shudders and vibrates. It enters my nose and my lungs when I breathe and it invades every pore in my body. I am terrified. I want to scream, but it chokes me. Through the translucent haze of the hellish noise, I see a ragged band floating into the station through every entrance. The sound is a fast river now and it sweeps mostly men, but a few women too, on to the platform.

'They cling together in sullen knots and begin a bizarre dance. The knots expand and shrink, and from their mouths raised to the sky flow swift streams that joyfully flow into the sound. They are all tall, hellishly tall with thin, skinny legs. Their faces are long with bloodshot eyes and snarling lips. The streams that gush from their mouths are blood red. They flow back into their heads and come out again, stronger and bloodier. The sound gets even louder and now the platform is packed with dancers. They have a conductor now, a dark khadi-clad man with a scar above his left eye. He signals and the dance changes. The dancers have wolflike faces now and they are on their hands and knees, sniffing, searching looking. Suddenly, a wolf, almost comical in a full PAC uniform, points his lathi towards our coach. The wolves turn and raise their heads to the sky. The sound is no longer a vibrating hum but a terrible bloodthirsty howl. A drum begins to beat and with slow and deliberate steps they creep towards us.

'The sound is momentarily shadowed by horribly loud pounding and thumping, but as the coach door is opened it surges back in, even louder than before. It sweeps everything, including the poor lala, from its path. Harnam Singh's pagri is washed off his head by the sound. The wolves have changed into a motley collection of raging beasts and men. Harnam Singh is thrown into the air and not a shred of his tattered flesh reaches the ground. The beasts have tasted blood and want more. Channi Veerji's kirpan flies from his hand. It buzzes around him, as if possessed, and finally finds a resting place in his belly. All three of us are dragged by our hair, out of the coach, and are taken to a courthouse on the platform. The conductor sits in a high-backed judge's chair with a powdered wig on his head. He is flanked by two wolves who are his bailiffs. Merciless justice is swiftly handed out. One swipe of a butcher's knife takes off our *jooda*s and Jeeta Veerji's scalp and everything is bright red. The packed courthouse galleries scream for more and Channi Veerji is garlanded with a rubber tyre. He is adorned in festive red too, lying motionless on the platform with his entrails hanging out, but when the tyre bursts into flames he gets up and dances like a dervish, singing out loud, but he slips on himself and falls and gets up again and dances until he is red no more but black.

'It is my turn. They dance around me in a circle and wave their lathis in the air. Each time the drum beats, the lathis trace sensuous, curvy paths and come crashing down. The dance goes on until eternity, and I am made of jelly. There is no pain, only anticipation. Suddenly it stops and I feel a cool, cool wetness on my face. I open my dry mouth to drink, but it is bitter and

I choke. Far, far away, a torch is lit, but suddenly I am alone.
The axe thuds against the door, again and again and again until
it gives. High-pitched wails and screams and the baying of
human hounds. The courthouse is a butcher's shop. Six lambs
with human faces writhe on meathooks hung high up on the
bloodstained walls. There is a sea of the hungry, fighting and
jostling for the best cuts. The conductor squats before a giant
cutting board with an enormous cleaver. His bailiffs are by his
side with a pair of scales and weights. His cleaver flies possessed.
His assistants, like clockwork, sort out little fingers and toes
and tongues and weigh them for the ravenous mob. I watch
fascinated, forgotten. Warm blood drips down the sides of their
mouths as they feast.'

She wakes up drenched in her own sweat. She picks up the
file, which has fallen to the floor, and shuts it. She switches off her
reading light and tries to go back to sleep. It is 11 p.m. and Lali
hasn't returned yet. The Sadbhavna Divas organizing committee
meeting must be going on longer than expected. She wishes that
he was home.

Sadbhavna Divas begins on a cool, crisp Delhi October morning.
Kohli arrives promptly at 9 a.m. to pick them up. The Sunday
morning traffic is light and they quickly reach Chanakyapuri. They
pick up the Party MP from Sikkim, a personal friend and admirer
of Lali's, from Sikkim House and go towards Boat Club. The
grand spectacle of Rashtrapati Bhawan towers on their left and
down Rajpath she can see the bold outline of India Gate. This is
her favourite part of Delhi. Ever since she was a young reporter
covering each cliché-ridden Boat Club political rally, she could
not help but feel uplifted while driving past Rashtrapati Bhavan.
Their car pulls into the makeshift VIP parking lot and the Leader's
chief aide comes forward to greet them. "Good, you are on time,"
he says, "but Kohliji is with you, how could you be late!" Most
of the ministers and MPs have already arrived, and several of them
are already sitting on their throne-like red velvet seats on the dais,

with enormous flowers made of blue and red satin ribbons pinned
on the lapels of their khadi jackets.

In the maidan below the stage, the crowd is swelling. Three
hundred truckloads of farmers have been specially brought from UP
for the rally. The previous rally had very few people and the press
did not let the Party hear the last of that for months. Sadbhavna
Divas is important and the Leader wants to make sure that the last
fiasco is not repeated. A separate enclosure has been reserved for the
1984 widows and orphans. The press is busy clicking photographs
of hundreds of bored-looking women in salwar-kameezes and little
boys wearing colourful patkas. Seva Dal volunteers, in crisp khadi,
patrol the maidan, carrying lathis and controlling the crowd. There
is heavy police and CRPF bandobast and hundreds of jawans in
riot gear wait at a discreet distance.

The Leader arrives in a wail of sirens and flashing lights. A
single file of Black Cat commandos quickly climbs up to the dais
and takes positions around the bulletproof shield surrounding
the speaker's podium. The Leader, with his sumptuously dressed
wooden wife in tow, slowly walks to the dais, surrounded by
more Black Cats. He ignores the velvet sofa at the centre of the
stage and humbly squats on the floor, at the feet of the strange
melange of holy men sitting in one corner. An excruciatingly long
multireligious service begins with each priest performing with great
gusto. The Leader seems to be equally moved by each segment.
He bows with folded hands to each contingent and finally takes
the podium. The afternoon is rent with cries of 'Long live our
great leader'. He is quite brilliant today. He begins by launching
a scathing attack on the Opposition, which is fanning communal
fires around the country for political gains. He then solemnly
describes the threat to the Unity and Integrity of the Country
from the Forces of Destabilization and The Foreign Hand. Tears
stream down his face as he remembers the terrible riots of 1984
which took so many lives. He deplores communal violence and
beseeches the Opposition to give up its nefarious designs in the

National Interest. He announces a massive loan package for the 1984 widows and orphans to resounding cheers and more cries of 'Long live our great leader' from the crowd.

The lone Sikh minister in the Cabinet then strongly attacks militancy in Punjab and reiterates how Sikhs are a part of the mainstream and shall always remain so. He condemns violence unequivocally and pleads that militant groups lay down their arms and come to the negotiating table. He then introduces Lali to the crowd, who grimly recounts his story. Lali is in devastating form. His earnest forehead glistening with sweat, regal in saffron and white, he downplays his own ordeal and focuses on relief efforts for the 1984 widows and orphans. Exhausted, Rani is quite glad when it is all over.

The strike at the textile factory is big news again. A senior manager was beaten up last night and Centre of Indian Trade Unions (CITU) workers are being blamed. Today's paper has a report on Sadbhavna Divas. The Leader's photograph is on the front page and his speech is faithfully reported. Lali is not even mentioned. She marvels at the fickleness of the public. She can remember the yet-unhealed Lali being hounded at every step by reporters hoping to extract a gory detail that had been missed. Today, Tinsukhia Mail and 1984 are only part of dusty files that come out of the cabinets every now and then, pushed by painful memories or expectations of political gains.

The telephone rings, it is Suresh, the trainee reporter she had hired a few months ago. He is on an assignment in Kanpur, covering the sale of a minor girl into prostitution. He is excited, undeniably excited, and jubilant but hesitant at the same time. He wants her to come to Kanpur immediately. She asks him if he has gone crazy. He says that she has to come in person, immediately, and that it is about the Tinsukhia Mail massacre. She catches the afternoon flight to Lucknow and drives to Kanpur.

'My name is Mangat Ram, son of Bagicha Ram. I am also known as Mangtu Kaka. Three years ago, I retired from the railways. I served as head peon in the stationmaster's office at Kanpur railway station for twenty-seven years. I was on duty on 1 November 1984. We got news of Indira Mai's death and by evening there were riots in Kanpur. The city was under curfew. I was unable to go home that evening. Since the railway station is always a safe place whenever there are communal riots, I slept on the platform. Because of the curfew, the station was deserted. All the coolies and vendors had gone home and we could not get any tea. It was very cold at night and the PAC jawans, who were on duty at the station, broke some crates and started a fire. We sat around the fire the whole night and the havildar had three bottles of rum. Since I was sitting there too, they gave me two pegs and I went to sleep.

'All the passenger trains had been cancelled, and the express and mail trains too were running very late. Only two trains passed through the station the whole night. There might have been one or two more, but I was asleep. When I got up in the morning, Tinsukhia Mail, headed for Delhi, was standing at the platform. Dharam Pal told me that it had already been standing there for more than an hour, waiting for clearance. It was quite bright, but strangely most of the windows were shuttered. The platform was quite empty. There were a few jawans and TTEs walking about, and a few people had got down from the train and were standing on the platform, smoking beedis and cigarettes. A young PAC jawan was talking to a Bengali babu, sitting in the coach in front of me, through his open window. I could hear a few words of their conversation. They were talking about Indira Mai's death and of the wretched Sikhs who had killed her.

'Around 9 a.m., some people started coming to the platform. They were mostly young men from the city, who seemed to be loitering around, looking inside coaches and aimlessly wandering on the platform. Slowly more and more people started coming and soon I could hear a buzz of voices as they started collecting in groups on the platform and talking. At about 10 o'clock, different

kinds of people started coming into the station. I could see several
city badmashes and 420s in the crowd and many of them were
carrying lathis and short iron rods. The conversation had by now
turned into a roar, there must have been at least seven hundred
people on the platform by now. It was then that Ghanshyamdas,
the ex-Party MLA, came to the station. The crowd cheered for
him and he began to give a speech.

'He started talking about Indira Mai's tragic death and how
her ungrateful Sikh bodyguards had riddled her frail, old body with
three hundred bullets. Tears streamed down his face as he told the
story. His eyes were blazing with anger. He said that the Sikhs
had to be taught a lesson. Too long they had held the country
to ransom with their headstrong ways. This time they had gone
too far and had to be punished. He told the crowd about how
patriots in Delhi had taught Sikhs, who were celebrating Indira
Mai's death, a lesson. He wept again, horrified that the Sikhs in
Punjab had retaliated by massacring Hindus and sending trainloads of
corpses to Delhi. He asked the mob what a more fitting reply there
could be than killing every Sikh who dared to show his face outside
Punjab and sending his corpse home. The crowd cheered wildly,
enthusiastically, and his followers brandished their lathis and rods.

'The crowd was in a sullen and angry mood, but not yet angry
enough to do anything. Ghanshyamdas took the PAC havildar
aside and they conferred for several minutes, after which he called
all the PAC jawans and talked to them. In the meantime, some of
Ghanshyamdas's henchmen entered the station building and began
searching the rooms. The babu on duty at the ticket window was
Ujjagar Singh who had spent all his life working at the Kanpur
station. They brought him to the platform, kicking him as they
dragged him along and shouting abuses at him. A big crowd
gathered around him and started to beat him up. It was as if all
of them had gone mad. They beat the old man so mercilessly that
his skull cracked. Fortunately, he did not die, though he was in
hospital for many months.

'They were all shouting "*Khoon ka badla khoon*" and "*Maro, maro*" as they turned their attention to the train. They entered whatever coaches were unlocked and started dragging out anyone who was a Sikh or who they thought was a Sikh. They did not spare anyone with a long beard. I prayed to Ram to stop this sight, but it only got worse. They dragged the men out and beat them without mercy till they were covered with blood. Suddenly the young PAC jawan, who had been talking to the babu, pointed with his stick to the coach in front of me and said something to the goondas. They immediately rushed to the door and started banging on it. For a few minutes nothing happened, but when they threatened to pour petrol on the coach and burn everyone inside, a terrified passenger opened the door. What happened after that I cannot forget for the rest of my life.

'Screaming like hungry animals, they charged into the coach in which they knew some Sikhs were hiding. I could hear horrible sounds from inside and fearsome screams. Later, I heard that they found an old Sikh man who they literally tore from limb to limb with their bare hands. There were also some young Sikhs inside who tried to resist, but they were overpowered quickly and dragged to the platform. With my own eyes, I saw three young men being dragged out by their hair. They were all bleeding and had been beaten badly. One of them was totally covered with blood and had a long knife sticking out of his stomach. It was the most horrible sight I had ever seen in my life, but I could not look away. "Khoon ka badla khoon! Maro, maro!" they screamed. One of them pulled out a long knife and I thought that they were going to be killed there and then. But they used the knife to chop off their long hair. One of the young men was lucky and died almost instantly when the knife cut into his head instead of his hair.

'Animals! They were animals! They brought a tyre and put it around the head of the one who had tried to fight. They poured petrol on the tyre and set it on fire. Even now I have not been able to rid my nose of the horrible smell of rubber, hair and flesh.

The poor man writhed and screamed in agony, but this only drove the crowd crazier. After he was dead, they turned their attention to the third one. Oh God! How they beat the poor boy. He was surrounded by savages with lathis and they rained blow upon blow on his head and body. It is a wonder that he did not die. When they got tired of beating him, they poured petrol on him to burn him too, but he begged them not to kill him. He grabbed at their feet, but they kicked him, he tried to clasp his hands together, but his arms were broken. Somebody lit a match and he screamed, loudly. I was surprised. I did not think that he had any life left in him.

'Sahib, I lost my faith in Ram that day. I could not blame the poor boy. He was in pain after all, and suffering so much, he was only human. Later, I found out that the women and children that he sent them after to save his own life were his own mother, sister, sisters-in-law, little nieces and nephews. He was a frightened child, but he could have saved them all. The passengers in the coach did not betray them, he did. But I do not blame him, I blame Bhagwan for robbing men of their reason and committing acts that beasts would be ashamed of. He must have loved his mother and the little children and his sisters, like we all love our mothers and children and sisters. Perhaps if we are faced with what he faced . . . martyrs live only in history books, Sahib. I am an old man and considered wise in my family, but that day I learned of the true nature of human beings. You see, he was in pain . . . terrible, unimaginable pain.

'Hey Ram! How can I forget! Somebody brought a huge axe and they broke down the door of the ladies' compartment. There were two old women who they set on fire there and then in front of the children. The children, my God, the children! They were terrified, screaming. They could not understand what was happening. One by one, they were snatched from the women who clung to them, desperately. They tore off every shred of clothing from the women's bodies. I looked down in shame, prayed to God to stop this somehow, but he was not listening. They fought with each other, the animals and the strongest ones carried the women away, high above their heads, like shining trophies. What became of the poor women nobody knows until today. The children, one by one, were hacked to pieces on the platform. What kind of butchers were these! Their lust for blood was not sated. I learned that they had killed every male Sikh on the train and loaded their corpses back on before it left Kanpur. I could never go back to work at the station after that.'

Rani put down Mangat Ram's statement and looked at Suresh. Her brow was furrowed.

The Express Diwali party was a great success. It was yet another feather in the cap of Suresh, the rising young head of the urban-news desk. Rani gracefully accepted everyone's congratulations on behalf of her protégé. In a corner, a wide-eyed audience listened to Lali's story . . .

Kultar's Mime[*]

1

He's a little Sikh boy, his name's Kultar
Lives in a place they call 'Jamuna Paar'
Smiling cherubic face, he looks so cute
You can hardly tell he's deaf and mute
Just your average child from a poor home
Is on first glance I am wont to say
I see him busy with his friends at play
When the streets of Tilakvihar I roam
What is it here that I hope to find
In these dusty alleys, forbidding, unkind.

2

Little Billoo, an elfin nine-year-old,
Plays hide-and-seek with our hero young
She's full of life boisterous and bold
But sensitive too, quick to be stung
Angad is older than both of them

---

[*] 'Kultar's Mime' first appeared in *Kultar's Mime: Stories of Sikh Children Who Survived the 1984 Delhi Massacre* by Sarbpreet Singh and J. Mehr Kaur, CreateSpace, 2016.

A street urchin now (he was a gem)
Been two years since he went school
He's into petty theft and plays the fool
Wants to grow up tough be a macho man
Does boast one day people near and far
Will know of Angad Singh of Tilakvihar
Under bluster and bravado, hide he can
But those of you who've heard his screams
Do know for sure of his fearful dreams.

3

Sweet Rano, so fair, is a demure nineteen
Lucky; she lives in her uncle's house
There was a time she was calm and serene
Now she's jumpier than a little mouse
She's a lovely little lady; a trifle sad
(Rumour has it that she might even be mad)
She's always lost in her private thoughts
She winds her way through the rickety cots
Of the local hospital's mental wards
She was finally able to find some work
Soothing chasing demons that lurk
In infant minds ripped into shards
Her body is young, eyes are old and wise
Sudden sound makes them widen in surprise.

4

You may well ask, what's all this about
What's so unique 'bout this motley bunch
The deaf, mute boy, little girl, young lout
By now, my friends, you must have a hunch
A story I have to tell; indeed it's true
Tilakvihar! Now you have [a] clue
Clusters of houses, little shanty town
In dull shades of grey and dirty brown

Blister in the face of that cruel land
Like many others of its colour and kind
Destitution, poverty and the daily grind
Rub faces and dreams deep into the sand
Oh and what a story do I have to tell
Burning passion, blind hate and sanity's knell.

5

But let my thoughts not wander too far
For our story now has just barely begun
Our hero has more friends in Tilakvihar
'bout whom we have to learn more; anon
Bishan Singh too was a hardy young lad
Was good at times, sometimes he was bad
You could see him running from his room
His mother chasing him with a broom
Walked with a jump and a skip and a hop
As he swaggered down the narrow street,
As dear friends [and] strangers he would greet
And to chat and joke with all he'd stop
But fate's been too cruel, chance unkind
The once-gregarious lad is blind.

6

And young Sukhi, another precocious child,
Thrived in the warm glow of love and care
Affectionate, obliging, sweet-tempered, mild
Lovely smile would hardest heart ensnare
Father's darling, Mother's pet, the lucky one,
At work and at play like a star she shone
What? Is that the same girl? It cannot be!
Wicked illusion, what do my eyes see?
Withered shell, pale cheeks, sunken eyes
No signs of the old spark or even life
What caused all this? What kind of strife?

What changed laughter to heaving sighs
We begin to see that all is not well
Each child in the town has a tale to tell.

7

And Kultar plays on in the heat and dust
Unaware of the peeping, prying eyes
That want to pierce his innocent crust
And the ears that strain to hear his sighs
Kultar and Billoo are now playing house
Billoo is feeding her famished spouse
Who's had a very long and tiring day
Chopping wood or maybe stacking hay
An amused Angad lolling in the chair
In the shade of [a] filthy corner tea shop
Laps tea from a saucer to the last drop
Towards each passer-by shifts his stare
Summer afternoon, lazy, languorous, long
Tea-shop waiter sings an off-colour song.

8

Look down the street; what do we see
Dhoti-clad man trudges his way home
His back is hunched, he's bent of knee
Sweat glistens on his balding dome
On his back he carries a box of soap
From his shoulder falls a heavy rope
Busy with dinner, Kultar doesn't look up
He and his wife just play and sup
Sudden movement makes our hero start
And look at the stranger's bent back
The sinuous, sinister serpent black
Face pales, fear clutches at his heart
Emotions confused play on his face
The little boy in a trance-like daze.

9

Gets excited, painful memories stream
His palms tighten on his deaf ears
His lips do part in a soundless scream
His face, it mirrors his darkest fears
The sight of the fibrous, twisted snake
Makes him tremble uncontrollably, shake
His head explodes, he goes back in time
A deathly dance in grotesque mime
He grabs Billoo by the hand and they run
Away from their homes towards the square
Where in times forgotten happier, fair
The children would gather; have some fun
And laugh and play in the cooling shade
Of the towering banyan's natural arcade.

10

Turns to the tree, his shoulders heave
He looks like he's jumping up and down
Each fibre of his body seems to grieve
On his face you can see a puzzled frown
He drags to the tree a most heavy load
Stops at every step to prod it and goad
When it tries to fight him and to resist
He pounds on it with his feet and fist
Stretches his hand for an imagined rope
And fashions from it a hangman's noose
Peers at it closely, checks if it's loose
Calls mates imaginary to help him cope
With his struggling father as he slips
The noose around his neck and trips.

11

Kultar becomes his own father then
His eyes roll around and legs do twitch

His agony, my friends, beyond our ken
Lifeless body falls into the ditch
Eyes do bulge, tongue does protrude
Legs leaden as from granite hewed
And thus does the little boy reprise
His father's violent, tragic demise
Angad is here; trembling body lifts
And carries him into the tea shop
Gently lets him in a corner drop
Sprinkled with water; up he sits
Eyes shut tight, keep out the fears
Cheeks are wet with salty tears.

12

If only he could also shut his mind
Exorcize his demons once and for all
Erase the memories harsh and unkind
That ravage his mind tender and small
How can he forget that fateful day
His head in his mother's lap he lay
Like a thunderclap the news did break
Tears in their eyes hearts did ache
They heard the Widow'd been shot dead
Grey-haired Widow with streak of black
Imperious immortal, no fear of attack
Her body was cold to the death she bled
Violence she sowed, violence she reaped
Thousands like Kultar's parents grieved.

13

To them she was dear; Mother they said
The only one who'd ever cared for them
Their goddess fierce, proud nation's head
The only one who the rot could stem

They cared not about the web she'd spun
With the help of her urbane and 'clean' son
She'd done them good was all they knew
Blind loyalty did their reason skew
She always got their faithful support
Although without the sign of a qualm
She did decree their brethren's harm
And still she got their precious vote
To her they felt they owed a debt
And so they beat their breasts and wept.

14

Meanwhile in a different part of town
Far from the slums of Tilakvihar
Flock in homage to the fallen crown
Mourners and idlers from near and far
Canards do fly and rumours are rife
About the bloody end to the Widow's life
The crowds get thicker, the mobs do swell
Louder and louder sounds her knell
Politicians abound every colour and hue
Like vultures drawn to a rotting corpse
The hypocrites pull out the stops
Burst into wrenching sobs anew
Like a virus vile this show of grief
Rages unchecked throughout her fief.

15

In Tilakvihar the mourners weep
Scared, confused, dumbfounded, dazed
Much like a frightened herd of sheep
That mills without its shepherd fazed
Know not but of the gathering clouds
That cover the sun like silent shrouds

The storm of vengeance about to burst
With an all-consuming bloody thirst
How can they guess what is to pass
For are they not the faithful ones
Have they not and their wives and sons
Stood by the throne steadfast en masse
The mother's dead, what's done is done
They look with hope to her only son.

16

Somewhere in the city in a darkened room
The plotters gather and make their plans
They seek to spread mayhem and doom
To begin a surreal murderous dance
Deep, piercing eyes; thick tuft on chin
Lyricist of gruesome song of sin
Pot-bellied, thin hair and glasses dark
Face mottled with spots and many a mark
Trade union leader, minister-to-be
Once rabble-rouser, political leader now
Before him all the petty criminals bow
Is the last one of the notorious three
From 'up above' their orders have come
To 'teach a lesson' to the arrogant scum.

17

Who dared defy and shake a fist
At the power of the glorious crown
They must be made to recant desist
Their heads so proud; they must hang down
What better chance could there ever be
Of a brilliant dazzling victory
The nation's shocked now, silent still
Plunder and kill till you've had your fill

Seek out the ones with beards and long hair
Loot their houses and rape their wives
Violate their daughters and take their lives
Cast them all into depths of despair
Teach them the price of raising their head
Pile the streets high with the maimed and dead.

18

The plans are ready and the trio of doom
With its bloody blueprint in its sights
Emerges in haste from the darkened room
And summons the Party's lesser lights
City councillors and some local thugs
Their favourite troublemaking lugs
The Party's goons, its salaried sods
Are the leaders of the killer squads
All's ready; groundwork has been done
The leaders are led to a meeting place
Excitement writ on each leering face
Waiting's over, the massacre's begun
It's a golden chance, a proving ground
For later favours are sure to abound.

19

The city's been divided in several parts
And each one is to a leader assigned
Each group towards its 'borough' starts
To carry out its mission, inhuman, unkind
Chain of lorries, each group has a fleet
Inside there are stacks and piles so neat
Of iron rods, sticks knives and spears
Crude weapons of death; tridents fierce
Gasoline-filled there are piles of cans
That will soon set the whole city alight

Yes, it is an awesome and terrible sight
As out towards its goal each convoy fans
But wait, everything is not quite set
Foot soldiers are to be recruited yet.

20

Columns of death slowly make their way
To the outskirts of the new city slum
Where the Party holds unrivalled sway
On the city's idle felons and scum
Promises are made: plunder, rape, loot
Reprisals they know will be quite moot
Over their heads sits the Party's Hand
Who can touch them throughout the land
Others move to the little shanty towns
'Twere built by the Widow's younger son
Thousands of willing recruits are won
For bloody juggernaut ready to pounce
Of murderous hoodlums there is a slew
Ever eager to join the macabre crew.

21

The Party meanwhile is hard at work
Feeding more grist to the rumour mill
Stories are spread of Sikhs who smirk
Distribute sweets and dance their fill
Rejoice openly at the Widow's death
Even as the nation holds its breath
Cunning merchants of death and doom
How cleverly they did fire the loom
Wove a net of falsehood, lies and deceit
Apathetic eyes are to misery blind
And are made by canard much more unkind
So the common citizen, man in the street,

Is ready to stand by and just look on
As the Party displays its crushing brawn.

22

Did it happen? I'm tempted to ask
Did men become such brutal beasts?
A look at Kultar's face, grey death mask
Brings visions back of devilish feasts
The Party's hordes that are let loose
Unleash terror, death, mayhem and abuse
The column's dust can be seen from afar
As it thunders down on Tilakvihar
'Blood for blood' maddened mobs shout
As from their trucks screaming emerge
And begin their devastating purge
Like a herd of cattle people mill about
As they try to escape the avenging wrath
Of fallen Widow's posthumous bloodbath.

23

Door splinters, breaks, there is a crash
A crowd of men with blood in their eyes
With sticks and swinging clubs do smash
Waste everything that in their path lies
Kultar knows not if he's awake or dreams
Opens his mouth and screams and screams
What a blessing his silent vocal chords
That hide him from the flashing swords
They take his father by his long hair
Beat and kick him as they drag him out
Hurl filthy abuse, 'revenge' they shout
Neighbours dazed just stand and stare
His father fights, tries to break free
As they drag him to the banyan tree.

24

Kultar shakes his head, opens his eyes
Looks at Angad's anxious and grim look
Looks at little Billoo as she too cries
As she hugs herself; in her little nook
'It's all right now,' he hears Angad say
Snap out of it, chase those dreams away
How can those memories fade or dim
Young eyes do again begin to brim
Once more he sees the hangman's noose
It's slipped around his father's neck
A neighbour at the ringleader's beck
Takes Kultar's father's dusty shoes
The rope is tossed up into the tree
A mighty heave and his feet are free.

25

Death doesn't come easy to the old man
He twists and twitches, his body shakes
The vile ones yank as hard as they can
They hear a loud snap, his neck breaks
Kultar writhes too on the dirty floor
Soul's in a noose, he can't take more
His mind's a wild animal in a cage
His little body has become a stage
Each and every day the drama of death
Is staged here for the world to see
Come one, come all, it's all for free
Do not stop now to catch your breath
For it's not over by far; there's more
So many tales, it's hard to keep score.

26

All over the city they loot and burn
Plunder, pillage, rape, torture, kill

The innocents have nowhere to turn
The mobs haven't yet had their fill
Tilakvihar is just one of the names
The rest of the city too is in flames
Proud community, courage was its fame
Hangs down its head and weeps in shame
The keepers of the law have run amok
Aid the mobs in their dastardly deed
Turn their backs on those who plead
Arrogantly they taunt and mock
You said you were fighters most brave
As they send them to the smoking grave.

27

When I walk the streets of Delhi today
I still see blood mixed with the dust
Each silent stone does seem to say
Scream out aloud you must, you must
Relive those terrible days of fear
Faces in the crowd seem to leer
Blood-soaked earth it speaks to me
Are you so blind you cannot see!
Brothers and sisters, I hear you
Don't ever think that we'll forget
Sweet martyrs; we are in your debt
Millions more; they can hear you too
Look in our eyes, tears pungent brine
Your resting place to us is a shrine.

28

Not warriors, not heroes were you
Just common folk from common stock
You did not ask for the martyrs' brew
That made you different from the flock
You were meek, you sought not to lead

You had no wish to suffer or bleed
Was it destiny or a quirk of fate?
Exalted you to this hallowed state
To the halls of martyrs did you send
Nameless victims of turbulent times
What did you do, commit what crimes
To merit such a violent, inhuman end
Whose visions cause my blood to chill
Make even relentless time stand still.

29

Yells and the chants are heard afar
Mingled with painful, agonized screams
As the pogrom continues in Tilakvihar
Brutality beyond our wildest dreams
Breath in gasps eyes reflect her fears
Down her cheeks stream desperate tears
Four times already the mob has come
Can't shut out its ugly, sinister hum
Four times her father and brothers two
Rushed brandishing their shining swords
Four times repulsed the angry hordes
But then more came and the mob grew
To hope for mercy they cannot dare
Their eyes are shut in silent prayer.

30

Even louder now is the terrible hum
Once again they pick up their swords
An urgent beat sounds on Death's drum
The river of reason the mob now fords
Launches its final, murderous attack
Each man to the wall now has his back
They try to protect the ones they love

What courage, what valour, but God above
Even He looks away or has shut His eyes
There are just too many; they do prevail
To pieces is hacked each and every male
The women mute, shocked, cower like mice
Their peril so urgent, acute and so real
Of satanic laughter they can hear a peal.

31

She's never been so afraid in her life
She's too young and innocent to comprehend
As they come to her waving stick and knife
She thinks they'll kill her; this is the end
Sweet Rano, don't bother to hold your breath
Pray harder yet, but for the boon of death
Don't fear the knife, embrace it you must
It's all that lies 'tween you and their lust
You're young and you cannot even think
These are not men but lust-crazed beasts
Tonight you're one of their carnal feasts
There are depths where they're yet to sink
They circle around like beasts of prey
Her beautiful face is pallid, ashen grey.

32

All she can see is a huge circle of hands
Fingers that flex, squirm in lecherous glee
Big hands, small hands, dark hands, pale hands
On all of them spots of blood she can see
The lascivious hands and their lewd dance
Realization comes to her in a single glance
She begins to tremble and frightfully shake
As a firm hold on her body the hands take
Her body is lifted up high up in the air

By the hands and carried to the next room
Oh desperate day of pain, death and doom
She struggles, kicks, weeps, tears at her hair
They toss her roughly on a rickety bed
A resounding blow she feels on her head.

33

The hands get to work, do their cruel deed
Her innocent body shrinks in utter disgust
The maddened hands pick up terrible speed
To maul the object of their bestial lust
Fearsome feeding frenzy; without a hitch
They tear into shreds each and every stitch
She feels a most violent, searing pain
And again and again and again and again
By ravenous mouths the hands are joined
They bite and spit out her flesh and blood
Young, innocent body pure and tender bud
Violated and wasted her honour purloined
Sated, spent the beasts about her drool
Of raw bubbling flesh her body a pool.

34

The women strike up a mournful dirge
As more and more are put to death
Unabated continues the unholy purge
Don't even stop to catch their breath
In the midst of the mob Sukhi sees a face
Familiar from another time and place
For a friendly hand the child does grope
On her face appears a dim ray of hope
She says, 'Uncle, you're my father's friend,
Please save him for he will die for sure

You know him well, you shared food and more
How can you cast him off; let his life end'
For her trouble she gets a slap on her face
Sends her to the ground in a painful daze.

35

Her father lies in the dust supine
They set on him with blows and kicks
His friend shouts loudest kill the swine
And they beat him once more with sticks
The sobbing Sukhi crawls through the band
And takes her father's bloody hand
Looks around and sees a scene from hell
But wait! What is this horrible smell!
Her father's clothes are suddenly wet
Stream of liquid is poured from a can
A deluge of gasoline covers the man
The terrified child, her father's pet
Sobs turn to screams pitched even higher
As they light a match, set him on fire.

36

The child still dazed from the hard blow
Refuses to let go of her father's hand
Pain and grief dull her mind, she's slow
She gazes blankly, fails to understand
'Pull the child away, she must be mad
We don't kill babies, we're not that bad'
Hands grasp her and so hard they try
But they cannot infant fingers pry
Father and daughter their bodies merge
They scream in unison, writhe in concert
Heart-rending sounds of pain and hurt

They kick her, scream, cajole her, urge
But with a grip firm deadlier than death
She hangs on till his very last breath.

37

Her little hand the flames did char
Her eyebrows and her hair are burnt
Her face is the colour of coal tar
The crowd's silent; a lesson's learnt
Their heads do now hang down in shame
They thought it was some kind of game
You callous cowards angels of doom
In you too for shame is there room
Smoke from his body will become a ghoul
And haunt you all to the day you die
To corners of the earth you may fly
You can't escape this stench so foul
Her pain will grow thousandfold
In your hearts like cancer take hold.

38

May you never have any happy dreams
May you never sleep the peaceful sleep
May you ever wake to sound of screams
May rotting guilt in your souls seep
May the fires keep burning in your mind
May you never see joy or one act kind
May your souls burn forever in hell
May your only music be the knell
May your dreams be scattered to the wind
May your hopes be ground into the dust
May you for forgiveness forever lust
May you lie helpless, unmoving pinned

Under the weight of your terrible crimes
Gruesome unrivalled even in these times.

39

The trio triumphant roams the streets
Gloating at its successful plan
They marvel applaud the deadly feats
Encourage the mobs whenever they can
The murderers line up to get their fees
A bottle of liquor and a hundred rupees
The union leader like a general proud
Jubilant smiles mingles with the crowd
Few voices of reason are heard to plead
They carry lurid tales of violence seen
To the lackeys of the proud fallen queen
Help them they beg, to death they bleed
Her haughty son does the statement make
When a great tree falls earth does shake.

40

Proud inheritor of your mother's throne
Don't forget that we're all mortal men
The seeds of violence that have been sown
Will sprout in each desert, hill and glen
They'll flower and when fruit they bear
Cloaks of lies they'll to shreds tear
You don't know what evil you've done
You are the inheritor, fortunate son
The tears and sighs of the wounded ones
Will come together in a terrible curse
Will goad you and yours indeed do worse
The widowed wives and the orphaned sons
Each and every day and night they'll pray
A measure of their pain you feel some day.

41

Bishan is terrified, fears for his life
He cowers in his Hindu neighbour's house
Lajo, the neighbour's kindly old wife,
Hides him where they keep their cows
The boy peers out through a tiny crack
From there he can see his own home's back
The street is quiet, weird deathly calm
But he's heard stories of horror and harm
His father's fled, mother's all alone
The brave old lady who knows no fear
They won't touch me; I will stay here
So she's left behind to guard the home
They'll keep me safe my hairs so grey
You don't know them, oh please go away.

42

He hears a low, most unnatural sound
Its dark he's almost gone to sleep
He jumps to the crack with a bound
Rubs his weary eyes, bends to peep
By the field in which they played games
He can see the towers of mounting flames
By the flickering light what does he see?
A crowd of men, a thousand there must be
Danny the Gurkha is in the lead
His kukri raised high above his head
He hacks at a shape; is it alive or dead
Mob advances at a slow, menacing speed
A man with a list in no obvious haste
Points out homes to be laid to waste.

43

His eyes are shut, he begins to pray
As the mob continues its ominous march

He prays for a miracle, let it go away
But on it comes, it's now by the arch
To the floor in despair does Bishan drop
Behind his house the mob comes to a stop
Despite his fright he has to see more
He raises himself up from the floor
Their little shack has been set alight
It can't be true; he continues to stare
As they drag his old mother by her hair
His heart lurches at her terrible plight
He knows that if he goes out he is dead
Frustrated on the wall he bangs his head.

44

Like a bird that's by a snake entranced
He looks again with fear and much dread
His heart is by a burning stake lanced
On her ageing body there isn't a shred
His soul is racked by shame and pain
On his conscience is a permanent stain
Wants to turn away but is forced to watch
They violate the naked old body, debauch
Till a merciful soul executioner kind
Dagger swoops whistling a mournful note
Rush of blood, slits the woman's throat
A terrible peace falls upon his mind
At her death he grieves but is also glad
They can do no more, her tormentors mad.

45

Stupefied, dumbfounded he lies on the floor
Soul writhes in agony, he weeps and weeps
A part of him cringes, afraid there's more
Through his being a terrible emotion sweeps
Slowly, fearfully the boy opens his eyes

Terrible sight, in anguish out he cries
For as hard he tries with all his might
He can't shut out that terrible sight
Whichever way he turns his head and looks
He sees his mother's ravaged body again
In his eyes he feels a most burning pain
Cruel memory, in him deep has its hooks
The pain in his eyes grows more intense
Of time and place he loses all sense.

46

Like the maddened king Oedipus of yore
When he happens to chance upon the truth
The boy's eyes too refuse to see more
Anything to shut out that vision uncouth
His hands rise towards each burning moon
Falls collapses, in a numb dazed swoon
When peace returns Lajo finds him thus
Lying in a pool of his blood and pus
She screams out loud as she sees his face
For where once burned two shining coals
All she can see is a pair of black holes
She shakes the boy right out of his daze
Bishan gets up, smiles a smile of peace
The vision has gone, the memory flees.

47

Yes, these are the children of Tilakvihar
These are their stories of blood and gore
In the corners of Delhi near and far
Go and ask, you're sure to hear many more
Each of these children is a living shell
Each day each lives in his private hell
The ones that did all of this roam free

Live under the leafy shade of the tree
That was planted deep by the Party's Hand
How can they touch their faithful dogs
The Party machine's most valuable cogs
Whose writ does run throughout the land
You may plead for justice till you die
There's none to heed your desperate cry.

48

Your wounds are your own, will never heal
Don't look to them for a soothing balm
They do not, cannot, feel what we feel
No demons in their heads, they're calm
My brothers come here from places far
Lay roses at the shrines of Tilakvihar
Each day remember this gruesome deed
I pray forever may our hearts bleed
Your agony for us is a burning cross
We will gladly bear it upon our back
Our memory will never loosen or slack
You'll shine always in history's dross
We'll never forget your terrible pain
Your suffering will not be in vain.

Acknowledgements

It was while I was a busy executive in the tech industry that I was introduced to T. Sher Singh, the editor of web magazine *Sikhchic*, whose encouragement and nuanced feedback influenced my work when I started writing a column for the magazine. He has been a terrific mentor over the years and I will always be grateful to him. My wife, Ritu, and my children, Mehr and Amandeep, have been my biggest cheerleaders and been very supportive during my journey as a writer. My editor at Penguin Random House, Anushree Kaushal, has been a joy to work with; the manner in which she embraced this work will be a source of encouragement for me in my future endeavours. I am also grateful to Anuj Bahri of Red Ink Literary Agency for finding a brilliant home for this work.